25 Oc...

think INSIDE the box

JAMIE CLARKE

LIVE
OUT
THERE

Everest to Arabia

The Making of an Adventuresome Life

Jamie Clarke

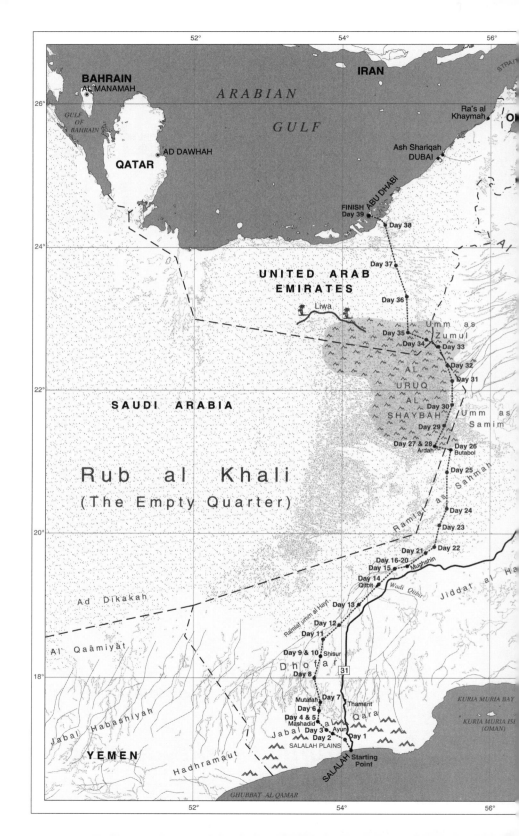

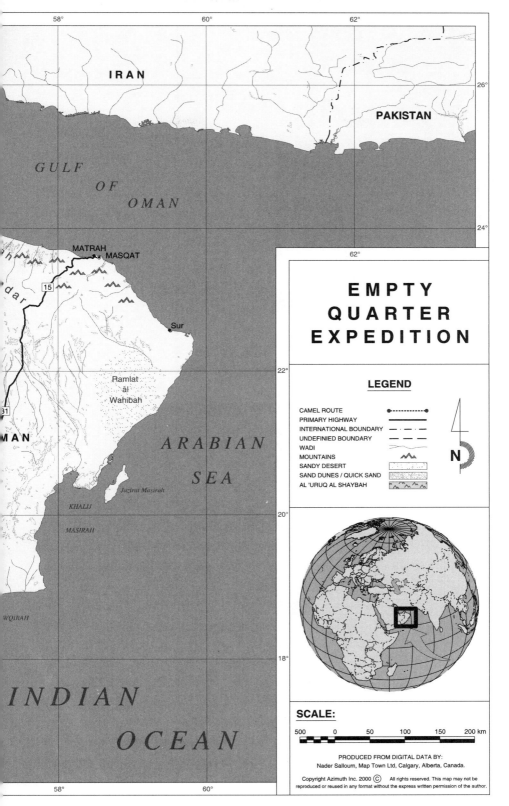

IRAN

PAKISTAN

58°   60°   62°

26°

24°

GULF

OF

OMAN

MATRAH
MASQAT

15

dar

31

Sur

OMAN

Ramlat
āl
Wahibah

ARABIAN

SEA

KHALIJ

MASIRAH

Jazirat Masirah

WQIRAH

INDIAN

OCEAN

62°

EMPTY
QUARTER
EXPEDITION

LEGEND

CAMEL ROUTE	•----------•
PRIMARY HIGHWAY	———————
INTERNATIONAL BOUNDARY	— · — · —
UNDEFINIED BOUNDARY	— — —
WADI	
MOUNTAINS	⌃⌃⌃
SANDY DESERT	
SAND DUNES / QUICK SAND	
AL 'URUQ AL SHAYBAH	

N

22°

20°

18°

SCALE:

500   0   50   100   150   200 km

PRODUCED FROM DIGITAL DATA BY:
Nader Salloum, Map Town Ltd, Calgary, Alberta, Canada.

Jamie Clarke's narrative, of his adventures across the
Arabian Desert, is well written and from time to time drew
me back to Everest. His sensitive and caring manner with
local people and his insights into both cultures—Bedu and
Sherpa—is well chronicled. The experiences of his
Everest Climb and the Arabian Desert Crossing
proves a good read from an interesting adventurer.

Edmund Hillary
Fall 2000

Among my most memorable journeys were those I undertook in the deserts of Arabia and the mountains of western Asia. In Arabia, the Bedu with whom I traveled gave me companionship and unfailing loyalty. The purity and silence of the desert I found again among the snow-peaks, valleys and high passes of the Hindu Kush and Karakoram.

Jamie Clarke's vivid recollections of Arabia and the Himalayas have reminded me of the varied peoples I encountered and the magnificent sights I saw during my travels in these contrasting, still remote worlds.

Wilfred Thesiger
Fall 2000

about Sir Edmund Hillary, K.G., O.N.Z., K.B.E

"I looked anxiously up..." Edmund Hillary wrote in *High Adventure*, his account of the 1953 climb that brought him and Sherpa Tenzing Norgay to the roof of the world. Knighted for the achievement, Sir Edmund went on to co-command Sir Vivian Fuchs' Commonwealth Trans-Antarctic Expedition, 1955-1958, and to travel the Ganges by jet-boat in 1977. Deeply moved by the landscape and people of Nepal, Hillary was instrumental in forming various Himalayan Foundations, which serve the causes of health, education, and humane modernization in Nepal.The Sir Edmund Hillary Foundation of Canada can be contacted at:

> 222 Jarvis Street
> Toronto, Ontario
> Canada
> M5B 2B8

Sir Edmund's writings include his latest book, *View from the Summit* [Pocket Books:2000]. Young and old readers alike may also enjoy *First to the Top of the World: A Photobiography of Sir Edmund Hillary*, by Broughton Coburn and Mingma Norbu Sherpa [National Geographic: 2000].

about Sir Wilfred Thesiger, C.B.E.

"I went to Southern Arabia just in time," writes Sir Wilfred Thesiger of his journeys 1945-1950. The last of the great western explorers to have trekked the desert, Thesiger also became intimately acquainted with the last generation of the tribal Bedu to practice the traditional lifeways of nomadic camel herders. *Arabian Sands*, his best known book, gives a vivid account both of journeys and of people following a vanishing material culture. Thesiger's other destinations encompassed Kurdistan, Kenya, the Hindu Kush, the Karakoram, and the marshes of Iraq. Others of his writings include:

Among the Mountains [Trafalgar Square: 2000]
Crossing the Sands [Motivate Pub.: 2000]

Michael Asher's *Thesiger* [Penguin: 1995] provides a fine, detailed biography.

Published in Canada by Azimuth Inc.
201 18 Avenue NE
Calgary, Alberta, Canada T2E 1N3.
Telephone: (403) 230-2760   Fax: (403) 230-2773

Canadian Cataloguing-in-Publication Data
Clarke, Jamie, 1968-

Everest to Arabia

Includes bibliographic references.
ISBN 0-9687491-0-0   hardcover
ISBN 0-9687491-1-9   paperback

1. Clarke, Jamie, 1968—Journeys—Rub'al Khali.
2. Rub'al Khali—Description and travel.   I. Title.
DS237.R82C52 2000   915.38   C00-911186-7.

Azimuth Inc. website address: www.jamieclarke.com

Printed in Canada
by Friesens, Altona, Manitoba.

2 4 6 8 9 7 5 3 1

Front cover: photograph of Jamie Clarke—photograph by Bruce Kirkby; photograph of Mount Everest—photograph by Jamie Clarke.
Back Cover: Jamie Clarke on ladder—photograph by Bruce Kirkby.
Inside front cover: Jamie Clarke on summit of Mount Everest
—photograph by Lhakpa Tshering Sherpa.
Inside back cover: photograph by Doug Baum.

Editing: Leslie Johnson; Bradley Harris.

Book design by TrueColor Media, Calgary, Alberta.

To my wife Barbara, to the love we share
and to the family it will create.

To my team...

My thanks to Sandy Pearson, Karen Harris, Erin Linn, Tracy Sachkiw, Dominique Keller, Danielle Doiron and George Achilleos—the staff of Azimuth Inc. They protected my time so I could work, and they encouraged me through the long hours of the writing process. One afternoon, near the end of the book while I was working on Chapter 17, they all burst into my office yelling and jumping. Dominique rang a bell. Karen held a sign above her head that read ROUND 17. George wrapped towels around my neck while Sandy pulled off my shoes and massaged my calves. Someone turned up the stereo and Sting's *Desert Rose* blasted. Tracy gave a basket of snacks including her marshmallow bars—my favourite. Erin offered a bowl of fruit she had cut up—complete with Arabian dates—and started to feed me while Danielle massaged lotion into my hands and arms to fight carpal tunnel syndrome.

Aromatherapy mist shot into the air. My face was wiped of sweat. Karen gave me a mouthful of Alpine Snow Gatorade, which George made me spit it into a bowl. "You can take this chapter!" he shouted. More fruit, mist, shoulder massaging, Gatorade and yelling. *Watch your run-ons. Be witty and precise*, I was coached. *Stay light on the keys, man* and *Keep your puns up*. Everyone laughed and someone, overexcited, poured Gatorade on my head.

I'm lucky to have them in my corner and to call them colleagues, and I'm grateful to know and care for them as friends. Thank you, team.

I owe special thanks to two of the Azimuth team. Sandy, with Dominique, led the book project. Repeatedly, deadlines came and went that I couldn't meet, but Sandy still managed. Her faith in the book's value never faltered and for this I thank her.

It's a tricky business singling out one person's effort in a team of many, but no one would argue Dominique deserves extra accolades. Her research and fact-checking added layers in the text that I would not have been able to create alone. She managed the entire editing process and more than anyone else made the book possible and the process enjoyable. Through this project I was witness to her considerable talents. Her criticism of my writing always came with suggestions for improvement. She worked on this book as if it was her own and in many ways it now is. I was impressed with her sharp wit, her research savvy, and her eye for detail. I know with certainty this book was worth the effort due to the time it afforded me to spend with Dominique. In the stress and long hours I came to know Dom better—not just as a sister, but as a friend.

Leslie Johnson and Bradley Harris edited this book and pulled the scattered and fragmented thoughts of my diary and dictaphone into something readable. More importantly, though, they took the time to teach me while we were en route to the last draft and forced me to become a better writer—for this gift I thank you both.

Ian Clarke worked with me on my first book and again on this one. Together we tossed around ideas and laboured through some 300,000 words of the first draft. This book, like the last, was another good excuse to spend time together. Thanks, Dad, for giving shape to the story, for editing my awkward thoughts, for fighting for my voice to remain intact, and for your well thought out advice throughout. Thanks also to Kim, Hannah and Phillip for accommodating so many late nights.

Thanks to the rest of my family and friends for their patience with my absence for yet another self-involved project.

Thank you to our sponsoring corporations who have become friends—Harold Miltsch and Pat Langmaack of NEC Technologies, Jeff McLean of Bausch & Lomb, and Robin Ingle of Ingle Health.

Acknowledgements:

Thank you:
Sir Wilfred Thesiger and Alex Maitland
Sir Edmund Hillary and Zeke O'Connor
H.H. Sheikh Zayed bin Sultan al Nahyan, President of UAE and Ruler of Abu Dhabi
H.E. Sheikh Mansour bin Zayed al Nahyan, Director General of the Office of the President
H.H. Prince Turki bin Sultan bin Abdul Aziz
H.H. Prince Sultan bin Salman bin Abdul Aziz
H.H. Prince Saud bin Naif bin Abdul Aziz
Mohammad Ahmed Al Hossani of The Office of the UAE President
H.E. Daniel Hobson, Canadian Ambassador to the Kingdom of Saudi Arabia
H.E. Stuart McDowall, Canadian Ambassador to the United Arab Emirates
Wanda Slipp
Ian Shaw, Canadian Second Secretary in Riyadh
Stephen Reeve, Canadian Third Secretary in Dubai
Chris and Heide Beal and the staff of Heide Beal Tours
André Lemarre
Thomas E. Valentine
Douglas Valentine
Doug Baum
David Alloway
Calgary Board of Education
Bankers Hall Health Club
QLC Communications
Darlene Cook, our transcriber
Giovanni De Maria for his Arabic lessons and transliterations
Nader Salloum
Roberta Evans
Mike Wetherley
The crew at ABL Photo
TrueColor Media's Steve Agar and Chris Davis

Thank you to the team whose members are the form and substance of this
book:
Ali bin Salim
Bruce Kirkby
Leigh Clarke
Musallim bin Abdullah
Salim bin Musallim
Manaa Mohammad
Tuarish bin Salim and Salim bin Ali. The Al Mashali family and
the entire Bait Kathir Bedu Tribe.

Preface

A desert adventure is one challenge. Writing well about it is quite another. I was reluctant to write this book, thinking the memories better left to the privacy of those who experienced them. I was worried about how I would be portraying my teammates and whether I could even do justice to the experience. Something compelled me to try.

I have made an effort to get past the obvious drama of the story into the deeper reality of the experience. The book is written from my experiences as I recorded them on my dictaphone and in my diary at the time, not so much as I feel about them now. I depended heavily on my notes to convey events and thoughts. I have not ignored disagreement or confrontation nor our need and ability to compromise, but, only included them where they add meaning to the story. I am grateful to Leigh and Bruce for their input on the final draft.

It should be noted this story is mine only in voice. It is also Leigh's and Bruce's, Ali's, bin Ashara's and Musallim's and others' as well. I thank them for entrusting me with it, though I didn't give them much choice. Without these five men there would be no story worth sharing. I am grateful for what they brought to our time together in the desert, and though they may not be represented with equity, this is not intended to reflect on their contribution to our amazing journey.

Readers will note that the English renderings of Arabic correspond to no particular orthography. Rather, my team and I have tried to simply render Arabic in a manner accessible to general readers, while endeavouring to remain true to Arabic phonology and syntax as well as to custom and politeness.

We have elected to drop two symbols found in Arabic from our phonetic translations. 'Ain, represented by an apostrophe, would normally occur in a name like Mana'a. We have dropped it for simplicity. 'ghain is a tricky letter that sounds like a guttural r and is written phonetically as gh. It is difficult to pronounce for English speakers, and luckily there are few uses of it beyond the name of Thesiger's companion bin Ghabaisha.

Any errors in this book are my own responsibility. I apologize if, in any inadvertent misspelling or mishandling, I have offended anyone. We would be grateful to any Arabic scholars and speakers, and especially my Bedu friends, if they would exhibit patience with my imperfect familiarity with language and custom. With Giovanni De Maria's guidance, we have adhered to a consistent transliteration of all the Arabic terms and have tried to preserve the Arabic spoken by Ali, Musallim and bin Ashara.

A few liberties should be noted. The term *Bedu* has been chosen over the more familiar English word *Bedouin*, which is actually a double plural. Many writers, including Thesiger, use *Bedu* when referring to the nomads of southern Arabia for both singular and plural, and I have chosen to do the same. Liberties with other plural words have been taken. We have simply added an "s" on many words to convey the plural. A single camel stick is called a *yad*, numerous camel sticks are *ayoodi*; for clarity I have simply written *yads*. Although this book is Canadian to the core, we have chosen to convey measurements in imperial terms for two reasons. First, I have found that most people who understand metric also comprehend imperial. The converse is not necessarily true. Second, there is a literary value still inherent in imperial measures. *Sir Wilfred stood before us, all 170cm and 76 kilograms of him.* or *Sir Wilfred stood before us, all six feet and 165 pounds of him.* For convenience, a simple table of rough conversions:

1 mile/1.6 kilometres
1 foot/.305 metres
1 inch/2.54 centimetres
1 US gallon/3.79 litres
1 quart/0.95 litre
1 pound/0.45 kilograms

To convert from Fahrenheit to Celsius use
the following formula:
$C = (F - 32) \times 0.56$

Prologue

The roof of the world. Ten feet below the summit. I stopped climbing to look around and ponder my next steps. Mountains wrapped in snow and ice spiked upward from below. Beneath them, clouds snaked through valley floors. Where thunderclouds boiled, flashes of light caught my eye. The morning sky was magenta blue and, looking up, I could make out a few faint stars.

Then, as I had dreamed for years of doing, I kicked my crampons into the snow and stepped onto the very pinnacle of Everest. For nearly an hour we stood on the small patch of windblown snow and savoured the view from the mountain's peak. Reluctantly, my Sherpa friends and I tore ourselves away from this magical place and began our long descent toward the deep valleys.

On my return home there were many questions to answer, but the most frequent was not so much what it meant to stand at the highest point on earth, but rather, what was I going to do next? This last Everest expedition had been my third. Two prior attempts on Everest's north face had ended in failure. The missed summits had made my answer to this question easy—I was going back to try again. This time I had reached the summit. What could I possibly do after that?

At first I didn't answer the question, but secretly I was contemplating a return to Tibet for another go on the north routes. Deciding on another mountain instead, I started planning an expedition to K2. But my heart wasn't in it. There was somewhere else I needed to go. I'd had enough for a while of the endless up-and-down of climbing and longed for something low, flat, and hot.

My brother Leigh and I had been to such a place in 1990. Touring Africa's east coast and up through the Middle East to Turkey, we'd visited Jordan's Wadi Rum. The Wadi offers some of the world's most stunning desert scenery, much of it captured in the film *Lawrence of Arabia*.

While Leigh and I trekked across the sand, I imagined Lawrence surprising the Turks in Aqaba during the First World War. He and his Arab companions had walked below the same rounded mountains we climbed—mountains such as Al Khazali and the Seven Pillars of Wisdom made famous by Lawrence's book of the same name. Lawrence must have wondered, as we did, at how marvelously the mountains caught the sun's last light. It was here I became enthralled with the desert, and with the people who inhabit it.

The Bedu, whose ancestors are reputed to be the Semitic people mentioned in Genesis as the offspring of Noah's son Shem, hosted Leigh and me during our short stay. We were invited to sit in the sand under the shade of the Bedus' camelhair tent. Through the flames of the fire, the smiles of our nomadic hosts put us at ease. We sipped coffee, ate dates, and drank sweet tea while women busied themselves on the other side of the tent, preparing food behind a wool blanket. Leigh and I shared with the men what Arabic we knew and we much enjoyed our time. We were fed and were offered generous invitations to stay. By then we had already been traveling for months, and had planned only a few days in Wadi Rum. When we left, I knew I had to return. Now, the dream of Everest realized, it was time to return to the desert and its people.

I put away my maps of the Karakoram and took out a world atlas, seeking Jordan. I flipped pages and surveyed some of the world's deserts. The Kalahari and the Sahara were appealing, but the landscape calling me was one of endless rolling dunes of sand. The Kalahari supported too much vegetation. Mountains broke the Sahara's dunes. I became passionate about a desert journey, but unsure exactly where to go.

I called Leigh to see if he was interested, wanting to travel together again and needing a break from his legal career. He was. So too was Bruce Kirkby, who'd managed our Base Camp during the last Everest expedition. Bruce was in my office at the time, sorting his superb photographs from that trip, but he had plans for a river rafting adventure. I told him more about my desert dream and he became enthusiastic. After some exciting meetings with

Leigh and Bruce, we decided I should begin the hunt for sponsorship money to fund the expedition and to pay Bruce to continue the desert research. Leigh would begin work on a project to chronicle the desert in film.

Our research yielded several options for a desert crossing. Bruce presented them all, including a trek to Timbuktu and a journey along Sudan's Forty Day Road. But the vivid descriptions of the desert in Sir Wilfred Thesiger's book *Arabian Sands* had already seized our imaginations and fuelled our passion. Sir Wilfred's account of his epic adventures in Arabia, more than any other factor, deflected us from returning to Jordan and sent us investigating the southern end of the Arabian Peninsula.

Sir Wilfred, one of the last classic explorers, is one of only three westerners known to have ventured across Arabia's great desert by camel. Covering nearly 400,000 square miles, this spectacular sand desert is the size of France, Belgium and Holland combined. Biting winds blow regularly and temperatures exceed 120 degrees Fahrenheit in the summer, quite prohibiting human habitation. The Bedu have lived at the desert's edge for thousands of years. These ancient nomads roamed Arabia and believed the oceans and seas occupied one half of the world. The quarter of the world in which they lived formed the fringes of the desert, and the balance of the world—the last quarter, the heart of the desert—was thought to be empty.

Sir Wilfred Thesiger traveled through this little-known region fifty years ago, and his historic journeys were the last made by a westerner. No one on record has crossed this desert by camel since. Here was all we were looking for in a desert—an ocean of sand. Still largely unknown. Rarely traveled. Steeped in mystery and richly textured in the misunderstood Bedu culture. Our proposed adventure would be formidable as Everest, in its own way, and a fascinating contrast to the mountain world. I had discovered my answer. In the Bedu tradition, we would attempt a camel crossing of Arabia's Empty Quarter, the Rub al Khali—the world's most expansive continuous sand desert.

Chapter One

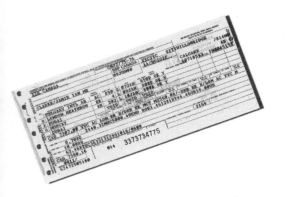

٢١ رمضان ١٤١٩
January 9, 1999
London, England

"I doubt you will be able to complete this journey."

Sir Wilfred's words hit us hard, though he speaks them softly. Here before us is the only westerner who's done what we are about to attempt, and he thinks it now impossible. I'd come to expect this sentiment from officials in the Prime Minister's Office or from businesspeople who claimed intimate knowledge of Arabia. In fact, I'd come to expect it from most anyone with whom I shared our desert dream. But how sobering that Sir Wilfred Thesiger, of all people, would react the same way. Worse still, his reasons for doubting our success at crossing Arabia's Empty Quarter are more valid than all the others.

We sit, a little dazed after his prediction of failure, with the man who has become the very inspiration for our adventure into the Empty Quarter. Bruce has gone to great lengths to secure an audience with Sir Wilfred in the idyllic little town of Meadow Hill in Coulsdon, Surrey, in southern England. We are here to meet and take the mark of the great old adventurer himself, and I am as thrilled about this meeting as when I met Sir Edmund Hillary.

Leigh and Bruce start in with questions while I ponder the moment's meaning. Sir Wilfred sits bolt upright, dressed immaculately in a tweed three-piece suit. His polished shoes seem large for his five-foot-ten frame, but they are certain evidence of his original stature. The man's skin hangs loose on a chiseled face. The mole on his chin and his aquiline nose give depth to his face and lend him a striking profile, which I study while he speaks to Leigh. His thick, silvery hair looks recently combed. Sir Wilfred is lean, but not thin. Despite the life he has lived, he is a vital eighty-eight year-old gentleman. He welcomes us warmly.

Leigh had planned for a *National Geographic* crew to be here in advance. Thesiger is known for his disdain of the media, and I worry their presence may poison our time together. We had called Sir Wilfred last night about the filming and he was not keen, wanting us to "get to know each other" before the crew materialized. That didn't happen. Now, we are here, with three members of the *Geographic* crew buzzing about.

The parlour of Sir Wilfred's retirement home has been turned inside out to accommodate lights and camera gear. The cameraman floats, collecting shots from varied angles. This distraction causes Thesiger occasionally to lose his train of thought, and he needs prompting to recover. I begin myself to resent the filming, thinking the experience would be better without its being recorded. But we are caught in the obligation to commit the adventure to celluloid. I resolve to ignore the crew as best I can, focusing instead on the meeting.

The four of us begin to pore over various maps of the Empty Quarter. Recent ones make little sense to Sir Wilfred. He is more at home referring to older maps of the region, maps based on Thesiger's own journeys between 1945 and 1950. As he scans a map, his hands jitter with the Parkinson's disease subtly manifest in his handwriting.

Sir Wilfred is legendary. He remains to this day the only westerner to have traversed the difficult eastern sands of the Empty Quarter. We have the temerity to hope we might follow. David Attenborough, the English filmmaker, describes Sir Wilfred as one of the very few people in our time who could stand alongside the great explorers of the eighteenth and nineteenth centuries. Yet here he is, sharing with us freely his intimate and exclusive knowledge of the desert. Thesiger seems a time traveller from a colonial age that should have ended years before it did. He appears a man who might have come to us from the plains of the Serengeti, one who might moments before have been chastising servants for tepid tea, though this was never Sir Wilfred's style.

A more accurate assessment of Thesiger can be gleaned from his *Arabian Sands*: "When I had traveled in the desert there I had always tried to break through the barrier that lay between me and my companions...I was only anxious for them to treat me as one of themselves."

Thesiger is impatient, slightly eccentric. He never took a wife or fathered children. Sir Wilfred clearly feels that adventuring is no vocation for a woman. In his youth, Thesiger forswore female companionship for fear it would distract him from his passion for travel. The memories of his journeys are now locked away in his mind, but his eyes light and a smile comes to his face when he retrieves one. Sir Wilfred seems unusually animated—excited to be talking with people who want actually to retrace his footsteps, not just to ask idle questions about them.

We spend a magical time going over his old maps and our new ones. We look through photographs, check our route, and seek his advice at crucial points. Throughout our time with him, Sir Wilfred repeats one warning: "The most important thing is to spare the camels all you can. Your life depends on them."

After exhausting our trove of questions, we all go for lunch at the neighbouring Woodcote Golf Club, where everyone knows and asks after Sir Wilfred. He orders chicken kiev and leek soup for all. He eats his soup, but little of his chicken.

Following lunch, the four of us walk back together—three self-appointed adventurers and one genuinely great explorer. Sir Wilfred's retirement home in Surrey is a comfortable and surprisingly inviting stone structure. Pleasant gardens offer a place to walk, for those who still can. Though the area is densely populated, the sense of the English countryside is strongly ingrained here, and the golf links add that manicured touch so important to the English sense of nature. Sir Wilfred has lived a life of exploring and, though he mourns the passing of the great age of exploration, he accepts his own aging with grace. Sir Wilfred takes my arm for extra stability and shuffles a bit on the pavement.

He comments on the damp air biting through his clothing. The sky has darkened since we arrived, and the green lawns give the only real colour under the flattening light. I feel melancholy to see Sir Wilfred struggling along the street, when once he had trod the sands of the world's great deserts. All three of us know that we are in the presence of greatness. This is an irreplaceable day.

Toward the end of our visit, Leigh asks Sir Wilfred which, among all the places he had been, he would most wish to revisit. "I cannot answer that question," the explorer replies. "It was not the places I have been, but the people I was with." This puts into an entirely new perspective the prospect of meeting our Bedu friends in Thamarit.

The *National Geographic* crew interviews the others while I settle into my own personal time with Sir Wilfred. Leigh had pointed out that the old adventurer does not suffer fools gladly, so I am flattered when he makes it apparent he wants us to stay longer. Clearly, he is enthralled with the possibility of what we seek to do. Sir Wilfred does not merely offer yet another account of his time in the desert but extends himself back to the sands. He gives information we know will be vital to our success, if not indeed our survival. Sir Wilfred's face wears a look of concern as I hold back my questions. I want him to dictate the direction of our conversation.

"The camels are no longer of the stock able to cross the sands," he says distantly, as if back in Arabia perusing a herd. "They're bred for racing, now, and won't have the stamina to get you across. Spare them all you can."

I nod.

"Keep an eye to the Bedu. You'll have Rashid, I presume?"

"Bait Kathiri," I say.

"The Bedu are no longer of the desert," Sir Wilfred says. He speaks softly, so I move closer, wanting not to miss a word. He talks not so much to me as to himself: "The worst event in human history—the invention of the combustion engine." Moments later: "Those were the most important five years of my life, and they were because of the companionship of bin Kabina and bin Ghabaisha." Sir Wilfred is speaking of the trusted and loyal companions who accompanied him through much of his Arabian travels.

"Did you know it at the time?" I ask, knowing he'd had many great experiences after his five years in Arabia.

"No. I didn't know it at the time—only upon reflection," he says. Sir Wilfred's words come slower now, as fatigue attenuates his melancholy thoughts. His longing for his past saddens me. I wonder to myself whether my best years, like Sir Wilfred's five in Arabia, have already passed on Everest.

The tyranny of an airline schedule drags us away from Woodcote and, after a group photograph, we all reluctantly begin to say goodbye. The film crew wraps up, but before disappearing they produce *Arabian Sands* and other books for the author's signature. Sir Wilfred leads us to the door, leaning heavily on his prized Zulu walking stick. I offer him a light handshake, which he returns solidly, and I regret thinking him frail. He says a cheery goodbye, but there is a distinct undertone of caution. I have a decided sense the great adventurer worries not for our success, but for our lives.

* * *

The cab races through charming English villages, fieldstone walls bracketing their frighteningly narrow streets. Unaccustomed to left-hand driving, I am constantly looking the wrong way on the cabbie's behalf as he negotiates the traffic. The sky is relentlessly grey, the light dead flat. A penetrating drizzle hangs in the air. I am chilled.

I feel faintly sick from the cab's motion and am preoccupied with the enormity, the uncertainty of what awaits. Leigh stares out at the passing world. I am excited, but apprehensive about sharing this adventure with my brother, older by two and a half years. He was my first hero, and it was his travels out of high school that inspired me to lead the life I now live. Leigh said he had lost his spirit of adventure somewhere during the pursuit of a law career and was coming to the desert in hopes of rediscovering that spirit.

Sitting beside Leigh, Bruce looks out the other window noticing the British lads out playing football on the local pitch, reminding us it's Saturday. But the day concerns us little now. At last, we are beyond the deadlines that have stalked our departure. The tedium of expedition organizing is behind us now. Bruce and I forged a fast friendship during the 1997 Everest expedition, where he took stunning photographs of the mountain and anchored the team in base camp. Bruce is a part-time river guide who gave up a promising career as an engineer years ago to become an outdoorsman and photographer. The three of us know our time in the desert will teach us about each other, about ourselves—though what, exactly, no one is sure. We will join three Bedu companions and twelve camels to form our caravan across Arabia.

* * *

We dole out some sterling to the cabbie, who drops us at Croyden station, where we hop the train to Victoria and on to Heathrow. We haul our seven bags of gear through the airport to catch our flight to the Gulf. The departures area is busy and filled with people pushing precarious mountains of baggage on wobbly carts. The luggage here is anything but western—an endless stream of boxes, taped and roped together, slathered with labels in foreign scripts signifying destinations I have never seen. The airport's walls are covered in signs selling travel, cosmetics, perfumes, Christian Dior, Chanel, Gucci. The models are cool and elegant, chatting on cell phones or draped over cars. They are utterly incongruous, standing as they do above the real world that floats around their feet. The stress level in the airport is palpable, betraying itself in the smell of nervous sweat. A couple of babies are crying, and both sets of parents argue, which does nothing to stop the tears. A number of children have found one another and play tag amid the baggage, while bored adolescents retreat into their Discman players.

* * *

Businesspeople race past everyone to the first class lounge, dragging designer bags they should have checked rather than let crowd the aircraft. A group of energetic Germans talk loudly together and exhale choking clouds of smoke from strong cigarettes, which provide a pyrrhic relief from the body odour pervading the building. Trash cans overflow. One can receives attention from a maintenance worker who takes absurdly long breaks to survey the crowd or talk to passing colleagues. In the midst of the chaos, a young couple sit together on the floor looking every inch the part of seasoned travellers, enjoying the new relationship they have found on the road.

* * *

Surrounding me are men and women dressed in the traditional garb of Islam, restrained by its strict moral codes. The men wear red *masar* wrapped skilfully about their heads. The women are fully clothed in black *abayah*. Even their faces are veiled, only their eyes showing. The Quran clearly commands that women wear modest dress: *Oh Prophet! Tell thy wives and thy daughters and the women of the believers to draw their cloaks close round them when they go abroad. That will be better, that so they may be recognized and not annoyed* (33:59). Muslim women vary on the precise extent to which they cover their heads, necks and faces. What is essential to a Muslim is not the extent to which a woman covers herself, but rather that the principle of modesty be upheld.

We work a deal with the check-in counter staff and are allotted 200 kilos' baggage—twice the norm. As we approach the weigh scales, we mingle our own nervous sweat with the thousand others who stream through the departures level. The little LCD reads 199.7 kilograms, and we are free to board. At the departure gate the excitement intoxicates us. I have never quite lost this childlike anticipation of flight to distant lands and exotic cities, despite thousands of miles logged. Thesiger resents planes and automobiles, preferring ships and trains, but I am hooked on the smell of jet fuel, not coal smoke.

On the flight through Dubai to Masqat, I have time to think about our visit with Sir Wilfred. I remember how he struggled to sign the books everyone put in front of him, hand shaking as he worked out each letter. Sir Wilfred's elegant penmanship, which we see in the original hardcover, has been lost to Parkinson's. I wanted his signature but felt uneasy about thrusting a book before him.

I never did take the opportunity to speak with Sir Wilfred about this other end of adventure—the business end. I had wanted to pursue this topic with him, particularly his fundraising efforts, though I was not about to query him on the £800 yearly stipend he received in inheritance after his father's death in 1920. To help with funding, Thesiger cleverly took advantage of an entomological rationale for his expeditions into the Empty Quarter, looking for potential locust breeding grounds on behalf of the Middle East Anti-Locust Unit. Thesiger himself says, "I was not really interested in locusts. I certainly would not have volunteered to go to Kenya or the Kalahari to look for them, but they provided me with the golden key to Arabia."

We do not have a scientific basis for our expedition as Thesiger did. We are simply seeking adventure. "What we get from this adventure is just sheer joy. And joy is, after all, the end of life." So said George Mallory, who was among the first to attempt Everest in the 1920s.

Any adventure worthy of the name requires great labour. We have worked for eighteen months. This was a shorter time than the three-year planning of my Everest trips, but it has seemed more challenging. Bruce faced the heady task of securing permission to enter countries that don't easily welcome tourists. He battled through the incomprehensible government bureaucracies of Oman, Saudi Arabia, and the United Arab Emirates to get us access to a route approximating the path traced across southern Arabia by Thesiger fifty years before. Bruce encountered roadblocks at every turn, but after two diplomatic missions here last year, and with help from our Everest contacts at the Prime Minister's office and Canadian Foreign Service, we have our entry.

While Bruce sought permissions, Leigh finished a deal with *National Geographic* to buy *Above All Else*, the documentary I filmed on Everest. The film helped us build relationships with producers at *National Geographic*. This in turn enabled us to negotiate a co-production deal to film and later broadcast on CNBC the desert crossing. Leigh also handled these negotiations with "Nat Geo."

Then he organized the film gear and worked with Bruce on organizing expedition equipment. On Everest in 1991, I dreamed of shooting my own films one day, and of working with or for the Society. Now, I am in charge of the filming in the field, and since this is only my third substantial documentary, I still consider myself a hack at the art and harbour concerns about the quality of the footage we will shoot. Regardless, Leigh and I will be responsible for assembling footage for the film.

My greatest responsibility, though, was to raise money to fund our crossing of the Empty Quarter. To motivate the others and to give me a goal that would propel me into action, I personally guaranteed to the team that I would either raise enough money or come up with $50,000 of my own cash to cover basic costs. Leigh and Bruce then agreed to commit $10,000 each on the chance we would be forced to underwrite the trip with our combined accounts. I didn't have fifty grand. They didn't have ten. The trip was going to cost far more than seventy anyway, and I wouldn't sleep till we had the money in hand.

If fundraising isn't the most difficult part of an adventure, it certainly is the least liked. For Everest, Alan and I had little trouble finding people to plan and organize, but finding companies to invest money was much more of a challenge. This has always been the case since the dawn of exploration. The renowned Norwegian adventurer Fridtjof Nansen wrote this of fundraising in the early 1900s:

> When the explorer comes home victorious, everyone goes out to cheer him...How many of those who join in the cheering were there when the expedition was fitting out, when it was short of bare necessities, when support and assistance were most urgently wanted? Was there any race to be first? At such a time the leader has usually found himself almost alone; too often he has had to confess that his greatest difficulties were those he had to overcome at home before he could set sail. So it was with Columbus, and so it has been with many since his time.

Unfortunately, things haven't changed. My search for money started with relationships I had built with companies that hired me to make presentations about Everest at their corporate gatherings. These paid inspirational talks have formed the foundation of my adventure business for nine years. Although it has happened more by accident than design, the cycle is simple and effective: I go off on an expedition and later return home to share the stories with corporate audiences. Speaking provides seed capital for adventures, and adventures provide exciting subject matter for speaking.

If someone from my speaking audience showed interest in the desert project and I had earned the right to approach them, I presented a sponsorship proposal and worked to negotiate a deal ensuring an acceptable return on investment. Even though I had momentum, after raising funds for two Everest expeditions with Alan Hobson, I made little progress in the first six months. Invoices came and credit card bills ballooned. I took funds from my company to keep us liquid and to move ahead with logistics planning. The expedition budget grew faster than I could raise money—we now needed more than $300,000. I couldn't keep pace. I was stressed, irritable, and hard for my wife Barbara to live with. Everest was an easy sell by comparison. The Empty Quarter is largely unknown and holds little public profile compared to the universally recognized brand of Everest. In meetings with potential sponsors I often had to point out where, on a map, the Arabian Peninsula was.

I made phone calls, flew to meetings, and faced rejection. Learning from mistakes, I started over again, unwilling to quit. During one meeting in Boston with NEC Technology's Director of Corporate Communications, Harold Miltch, things turned. I shared the desert dream with Harold, an adventurer in his own right, and outlined what we could offer—media coverage, photographs and more speaking presentations. Harold took up my passion and agreed to supply computer equipment and capital. With the first major sponsor in NEC secure, the second came more easily. I sat in another meeting with Jeff McLean of Bausch & Lomb, and found in him a desire for his company to manage our eye care needs in the harsh sun and damaging sand. After this, more companies came to the table. I put $370,000 in the bank. And started sleeping again.

Once oral agreements were made, Leigh stepped in to execute the legal contracts. Our work was still not done, however, as any sponsor must be well taken care of, with constant phone contact and regular face-to-face meetings. Although our desert expedition was to be only three months in duration, our relationships with sponsors would last three years.

Ernest Shackleton, who struggled to find money for his polar expeditions, also saw the value of sound sponsor relations, but took his to a higher level. He was known to charm rich widows to generate funds. On one occasion he began a liaison with Elspeth Beardmore, wife of the wealthy industrialist William Beardmore. Elspeth encouraged Shackleton to solicit her husband to support his expedition. Mr. Beardmore, who suspected his wife and Shackleton were having an affair, decided he would fund the trip, thinking this a small price to pay to be rid of the unwelcome explorer.

Human relations are not only reserved for fundraising, but for permission-seeking as well. With the promise of money coming, I continued to bridge-finance the expedition, enabling Bruce to continue with plans for a trip to the Middle East. In Saudi Arabia he would meet with the Canadian Ambassador and the Embassy's Second Secretary to discuss our expedition. Bruce would go on to the Eastern Provinces of Saudi and speak with Prince Saud bin Naif bin Abdul Aziz, whose grandfather was Abdul Aziz, founder and King of the Kingdom of Saudi Arabia (KSA), all of whom had to grant us permission before we could enter. Bruce would complete two separate trips like this, including visits to Dubai in the UAE and to Masqat in Oman. Each stop followed Saudi's similar hectic routine of meetings and permission-seeking.

٢٢ رمضان ١٤١٩

January 10, 1999 Masqat

A beautiful, gentle landing wakes us. We taxi to the gate. The door opens to a rush of desert air. It's just after seven in the morning. The temperature is already in the mid eighties, and a little humid. This is a surprise to me, but shouldn't be, since Masqat is a coastal city. It's a lovely place, sheltered from the excesses of the nearby desert by the coastal mountain range surrounding the city on three sides. The mixture of warm Gulf air and diesel fumes is reminiscent of another distant place—Nepal's capital, Kathmandu. Its smell is intoxicating, and for me it is always associated with commencement, the beginnings of other expeditions into the Himalayas.

We enter the Seeb International Airport. Rich red sand surrounds whitewashed buildings, topped with the domed roofs symbolizing for Muslims the belief that there is but one God.

It is all quite a contrast from the lush green and carefully landscaped lawns surrounding Thesiger's home, where we were only eighteen hours ago. Sir Wilfred would be disgusted. He hates the idea that people can now travel such great distances in so little time. "It takes the worth of the journey away entirely," he told us in England. "Much of the challenge is the travelling before you begin." When he returned to Africa in his twenties, he took a ship from England. Only yesterday, Thesiger told us about this long voyage and what he had learned aboard ship. The skills and experiences he gained at sea proved as important to him as what awaited him at his destination. We laughed at his description of the captain's criticizing his steersmanship. "Come on, man, keep it straight," the captain had shouted. "You could break a snake's back with the course you're keeping!"

Our modern group of three adventurers longs to capture a sense of what Thesiger experienced when he set out across the unknown southern desert, living as the Bedu lived. But as much as we want to do this trip in the old way, changes might make that impossible—changes such as the switch from the camel to the jeep as the major form of transport for the Bedu, or the transformation from their nomadic lifestyle to one that is sedentary. With these kinds of changes, can Bedu culture, which Thesiger so wonderfully described and which propelled us to start this adventure, endure? Thesiger believes "all that is best in the Arabs has come to them from the desert: their deep religious instinct, which has found expression in Islam; their sense of fellowship, which binds them as members of one faith; their pride, their generosity and sense of hospitality; their dignity and the regard which they have for the dignity of others as fellow human beings; their humour, their courage and patience, the language which they speak and their passionate love of poetry." Has a sedentary lifestyle robbed the Bedu of their past? Sir Wilfred thinks so. "I went to Southern Arabia only just in time...if anyone goes there now looking for the life I led, they will not find it."

Are Thesiger's grim assessments and predictions true? Are the traditional ways of the Bedu lost? Is it in fact now impossible to cross the world's largest sand desert on camel? We are about to find out.

Chapter Two

٢٢ رمضان ١٤١٩
January 10, 1999
Masqat

We're on the ground. Our bags examined, we clear customs. Chris Beal, an English expatriate, is our Gulf Coordinator. He meets us at the airport, his assistant Ali in tow. We load our gear and drive to the hotel. Bruce and Leigh ride with Chris, Ali and me in the other jeep. Chris's history is rather foggy and he prefers to keep it that way. He has lived in the region with his wife Heidi since serving with British Special Forces here in the seventies. Chris and Heidi run a tour company catering to high-end business travel into Oman. Bruce found Chris and Heidi on the internet, and we have depended heavily ever since on their contacts and their expertise in local customs and politics.

I ask Ali to shut down the air conditioning and open the windows. Imagined or not, the sweet smell of frankincense cuts through with dry breezes rolling in from the south. It blends with humid air off the Gulf of Oman in the middle of Masqat, the capital. The highways and the local streets are immaculate, and lined with manicured hedges, palm trees, and flower gardens with scattered bougainvillea. Lying in its mountain cradle, Masqat is a friendly city even through *Ramadan*, the month of fasting from dawn to dusk. Of Oman's million people, 350,000 live here in this shipping town. Everyone seems to have a car, and the streets feel unusually congested, given the population. High whitewashed walls surround newly erected buildings, the walls smooth and thick, more to keep out the harsh climes than any unwanted visitors. The sky is lined with power and communications cables, all above ground. Masqat sits entirely on a foundation of bedrock. To the northeast, the ocean shows itself occasionally beyond the mountainous enclosure.

Ali and I talk about the heat and the conversation turns to our desert adventure. In halting English, Ali asks me why I want to do this. "For the adventure," I tell him.

But this is not much of an answer for Ali, and he changes the subject. "This is the National-Oman International Bank. Golden door, because of money keeping, you know."

"Do you have money in there?" I ask just to keep the conversation going.

"No, sorry. I don't have. My money in India, not here."

Ali seems to be racing Chris—either that or he's excited by our arrival and shows it in his driving. I want to talk but say nothing, not wanting to distract him from the road. He can't resist. "You are Jamie."

"And your name is Ali."

"Yes. Ali Sevi."

"Ali Sevi. Is that it?"

"That's enough."

"Of course it is. And where are you from?"

"South India, Kerela. You not be anywhere?"

"I've been a few places, but never there. Never even to Masqat."

It's not unusual for Indians to find work in the Gulf region. Non-residents do much of the labour involved in running the city and its households. Hired help comes from Africa as well, Somalia and Ethiopia, and it's mostly men who come. They leave their homes for years on end, returning only every other year for a visit. Since salaries are far higher here, the money they earn in Oman supports large extended families back home. Like Ali, many of the Indian population hail from Kerela Province. I wonder how long it has been since Ali has been home, but lose the chance to ask as he exits the freeway on to a busy thoroughfare and slices through traffic.

"Why you go Rub al Khali?"

"Well, I want to see the desert and live with the Bedu and be with the camels."

"Camel whereabouts...I don't know."

"No, no. Ride the camel in the desert."

"Camel is..."Ali bounces his hand on the steering wheel.

"Very awkward?" I guess.

"Not good for two months. One month okay."

"Yes. But we have three months."

"Ha, ha, ha. Let's see."

"Yeah, we'll see."

Ali asks me my occupation and I try to explain I am an entrepreneur, a bit of an author, something of a filmmaker. But, mostly, someone who loves adventure.

"You are famous," Ali tells me.

"No."

"Yeah. Famous. Because maybe this go and this come." He holds up six fingers, one for each person on our team starting the adventure. Then he holds up five for those returning.

"I hope not."

"Yeah. That's the problem, you know." Ali holds up six fingers again and folds one away. "Right away everybody knows. Magazine, newspapers, everything. That's good. Famous. Not bad."

"I want six people go and six to come back and no famous."

"We'll see."

٢٤ رمضان ١٤١٩
January 12, 1999 Masqat

We awaken to a monstrous breakfast buffet. Hommous and pita bread accompany every meal, as do garlic and olives, which then accompany me. Leigh and Bruce—champion eaters both—think there's no better place to feed than at a good buffet during *Ramadan* after sunup when they are suddenly alone with all that food.

The act of fasting or *Sawm* during *Ramadan* is one of the five pillars of the Islamic faith. The other four pillars: *Shahada*, or the witness statement that "There is no God but God and Muhammad is the prophet of God"...*Salat*, the act of praying five times a day...*Hajj*, the commitment to make a pilgrimage to Mecca if at all possible...and finally, *Zakat*, the dedication of a part of one's wealth to the relief of poverty.

The Muslim *Hijra* calendar contains twelve lunar months, each beginning with the actual sighting of the new moon. Because the months are lunar, the Islamic year contains 354 days, so annual feasts occur thirteen days earlier in each successive year, in relation to the Christian calendar year. This year *Ramadan* falls in January. Muslim men and women abstain from food, drink, and sexual intercourse from daybreak until sunset for the entire lunar month. Character building and an unobstructed connection with Allah are the fundamental benefits of observing *Ramadan*. Through fasting, Muslims learn they have the power to control all material pleasures. Faith alone, they come more clearly to understand, is sustenance enough.

After eating, we tour the offices of government officials and pressure them ever so subtly to let us undertake our little adventure. I thought these logistic details had been dealt with by Bruce during his pre-expedition planning trips here in December, and so did he. During one trip Bruce e-mailed a report that everything was going well:

> Of primary importance on the trip was the imparting of information regarding the expedition to the host countries and the final securing of permission to travel in their restricted areas. In all three countries involved in our crossing I received a warm and enthusiastic welcome. Not only were all our permissions assured (largely thanks to the efforts of Canadian diplomatic staff abroad), but a deeper involvement and interest was sparked in the countries.

We're worried now that the Omani government will deny its consent and our crossing of the desert will be over before we start.

Later in the day, we meet for coffee back at our hotel with Sheikh Said bin Ali, one of our main Bedu contacts. We learn from him that permissions are not our only concern. The *sheikh* explains that our team of camels is not ready. In fact, one of the Bedu working with Sheikh Said, Manaa bin Mohammed, is actually in Abu Dhabi now, searching for hardy camels to form the herd—work that was supposed to have been completed more than a month ago. I press Sheikh Said. When I ask why the camels have not yet been procured and trained, he offers no response. Bruce sits back and shrinks in his chair, uncomfortable with my questioning. I feel at ease, as this is often the way of the Muslim world. Leigh and I discovered, during our time in the Middle East in 1990, that among the Arabs it's important to raise any concern. We were initially intimidated by their willingness to confront issues, but we soon learned to enjoy it.

This cultural characteristic is rooted in the Quran, which calls upon Muslims to express their opinions, as it is their duty to speak out. The Prophet Muhammad himself said, "He who remains silent about the truth is a dumb devil." The Bedu are known to delight in debate. As Thesiger observed, "For one entire day bin Kabina and Muhammad argued about the money I had given them two years before at Tarim...the argument went on and on, angry shouted interruptions checking but not halting an endless flow of repetition. It only came to an end when we stopped for the night. They then sat contentedly together baking bread."

As with Thesiger's companions, we finish the discussion amiably and pose for a group picture. Sheikh Said says he will be in contact with Manaa. There is little for us to do now but wait and see what happens in Thamarit once the permissions come through.

٢٥ رمضان ١٤١٩

January 13, 1999 Masqat

Though we have enjoyed Masqat, we are eager to get into the sands. In the desert we will escape the hustle of the city and get our first taste of the life Thesiger wrote about so passionately. Just as we go to bed in preparation for the morning's early start, Masqat comes alive with an entire population who, under the rules of *Ramadan*, are now free to head for the cafes and restaurants, parks and seaside picnic grounds to eat, read from the Quran, and share time together. Most shops are closed during the day. They open after evening prayer until one or two in the morning. We will be fast asleep when the city settles down, but for now our minds are racing with what awaits us. It is the unknown that has brought us here, and the time to step out into it has finally come.

٢٦ رمضان ١٤١٩
January 14, 1999 Ghaftain

It's Sunday, a little after ten o'clock, and we're on the move. The city is long awake. In Muslim countries Thursday and Friday constitute the weekend, with Friday being the holy day. We drive through town in our rented Toyota Land Cruiser listening to the Tragically Hip. We stop at Chris Beal's place, an inviting home of smooth concrete walls, to pick up maps. Leigh takes the maps in the back and navigates. We pass the Seeb airport along the Qaboos Highway. Heading southeast on Highway 31, we travel through the Jabal al Akhdar or Green Mountains, but there is no green here—just endless tans. The road follows the natural course of several *wadis* or open drainage systems. We stop for gas, and pick up some olives and roasted chickpeas for snacks. With the 26 gallons of fuel in the Land Rover's dual tanks we can cover 265 miles. Chris has instructed us to drop the tires down to 20 pounds per square inch once we reach the sand, and on the asphalt, he cautions, "Try to keep it under the natural limit of seventy-five miles an hour," sounding rather like "Q" cautioning James Bond.

While we drive, we talk about differences between travelling in the mountains and the desert. "It will be hard to photograph the desert because everything looks the same," Bruce says. I think of the mountains where, around every corner or with each upward leg, a beautiful scene unfolds, providing ample subject matter.

Shadows and contrast, textures and depth play before your lens. Mountains provide natural relief and give a sense of progress. But there is none of that here in the desert—just open sky and tabletop land stretching as far as the eye can see, endless sand and gravel, uninterrupted sameness.

A hundred plus miles out of Masqat, we stop to stretch. The flat expanse surrounding us makes the Canadian prairie seem like rolling hills by contrast. Bruce muses, "People fall in love with this place and write endless books about it." And here we are—Canadian boys with a feel for snow and cold places, and seasons to mark the passing of the year. We know little of this place but somehow the land pulls us.

The midday heat is suddenly oppressive, though we know it's only a warm-up to what we'll soon face—and with no air conditioning to retreat to. We guess it is over a hundred degrees—a temperature sometimes reached at home in Canada, but here with a physical impact unlike any I have ever felt. The heat pounds my head and face. We stand together looking out at waves of heat rippling along the flat horizon. I inhale a deep draught of the desert air through my nose. The smell of a heated desert is one of my favourite scents. It's igneous, clean, bare, essential. Unlike a jungle's air, humid and laced with floral perfume, this land smells bleak and thirsty. Foreign. Unforgiving.

It has been nine years since Leigh and I first breathed this air in Jordan. Some of my favourite time on that adventure was spent in Aqaba by the Red Sea, where we lived on hommous and pita, baklava and chickpea salads. Leigh and I visited Petra before trekking into the Wadi Rum, as we followed our interest in T.E. Lawrence. There is an unconfirmed family legend that Lawrence was involved, however briefly, with my great grandmother Hope, during a time of convalescence. This romantic connection, even just imagined, made the place all the more tantalizing.

Our little walkabout in Wadi Rum and our time with the Bedu nine years ago had planted the seeds for this journey across the Empty Quarter. I learned then that the desert had something to teach. I'm now ready to find out what. The desert's subtle beauty, its light, its colour, and its smell intrigued me then, but I didn't understand them. Until today, nothing could match Jordan's scent. Now Oman offers the desert fragrance I long for—hot, not burnt, apparently devoid of life, but not dead. I plan to savour it for the next three months.

"I read somewhere that the desert is like a mirror, reflecting your character," someone says, breaking a silence so pure we can almost hear the heat rising from the packed sand. We jump back in the vehicle and drive on.

Leigh looks up from the map and asks whether we have passed any landmarks. I laugh and look around at the surrounding emptiness. Frequently we pass CAMEL CROSSING highway signs, and, on occasion, a camel availing himself of the safe passage the signs seem to offer. The signs are triangular and outlined in red. In the middle a camel strides forward with great purpose.

Meanwhile, back in the Land Rover, the music plays and the miles click away on the odometer. We roll into Ghaftain, low on gas and hungry. Ghaftain's landmark is a mosque, which Bruce and I will photograph against the setting sun and the silhouettes of two other buildings. One is our hotel. When we arrive there is no one about, save a man working among the few trees that surround the property. He stops his work when we approach, and smiles when we ask him in Arabic if we can have a room. When we talk he tells us in English he is from India—Kerela, to be exact. I'm impressed by the care he gives his trees and shrubs, the pride he takes in cultivating life in such a place. For those who live here, plants like this may be equally aesthetic and symbolic. In the heat of the peninsula's summer, little can survive on this arid plain without considerable coaxing.

For sixty dollars we get a couple of rooms and settle in for dinner. Our Land Rover is the only vehicle in the parking lot; our dinner orders are the only ones placed in the restaurant. We are the only guests in a hotel built to accommodate two hundred.

As Bruce and I photograph the mosque at sunset, a game of volleyball starts up behind the hotel among the locals. It is difficult to tell where the players come from, but two teams of six form easily. Their cheers and laughter echo off the hotel's smooth walls. Worn powdery like the paths of a ball diamond back home, the ground at their feet is soft and clear of stones. The rallies are long, and the players show remarkable skill at the game.

We return to our rooms. Bruce reads a book, I write in my journal, and Leigh works on the camera gear. I am grateful for his continuous efforts to keep the gear clean, a necessity under the constant threat of sand. It is similar to talcum powder in its fine consistency and, driven by the wind, it penetrates everything. The cold and snow of mountains can also disable camera gear, but even they are more forgiving than the sand. Clear the snow and ice, and the camera will likely dry out and function again. But once sand penetrates the camera's body, it's there to stay unless high-tech cleaning equipment is used. Even then its sharp erosive powers can end a camera's useful life—quickly. We have only brought two video cameras with us, and in light of our contract with *National Geographic*, we are tense about having so little margin for error.

٢٧ رمضان ١٤١٩
January 15, 1999 Thamarit

One-thirty a.m. I sleep fitfully, my snoring roommate nearby. As I lie on my side in the heat, a single sheet pulled up to my waist, something suddenly runs up my lower back toward my shoulders. I am instantly very much awake. I reach back to brush it off. It has a weight and substance that concern me. At first I think it is a cockroach or large beetle. I grab a headlamp from my backpack and track it into the bathroom. There on the concrete-and-tile floor sits *Androctonus crassicauda*—a black scorpion. Its abdomen is the size of my thumb. I can see its venom-filled telson or tail probe curl above its back in the light of my headlamp. There are eleven hundred species of scorpions worldwide, twenty of which harbour venom toxic enough to kill a person.

It darts behind the toilet. I will get no sleep knowing it might be scuttling around our room in the dark. We were fairly sure that the scorpions we'd encounter on this trip would not be lethal, but they could be incredibly painful. The end of this fellow's tail is pear-shaped and tapers to a point. Acting like a hypodermic needle, the sharp, hollow tip would easily push through my skin to deliver several neurotoxins, enzymes and other compounds. This would produce a sting like a bee's at best, or allergy-induced anaphylactic shock at worst. In terms of toxicity by weight, this is one of the most venomous creatures alive. It evolved to its current state over 400 million years ago and is regarded as remarkably aggressive.

I approach respectfully, sandal in hand, and drive it away from the toilet. The scorpion dashes for the shower, and I jump, startled by its speed. It changes course, heading for the door. Like Pooh Bear stuck in Rabbit's hole, the scorpion's tail protrudes, leaving only its head protected. Its stinger, the size of a leather needle, repeatedly strikes at the door, searching for vulnerable flesh. Standing naked in the dark with only my headlamp and my sandal, I am becoming increasingly nervous and decide to dispatch the little creature with a couple of well-timed blows. Although he moves faster than I anticipate, he runs into the lip of the shower where I can finish the job. I leave the evidence for morning.

Still I cannot sleep, convinced a hundred scorpion relatives lurk just outside the door to exact revenge. My only hope is that they will hit Bruce first, warning me of their attack and ending his snoring. I welcome the morning and am awake well before the alarm sounds.

By eight, we're on the road. Finally, Thamarit comes into view. It's a town of perhaps two thousand, built in the late 1950s to support aggressive new petroleum exploration projects and the construction of the highway. The town's paved roads look to have been built first and the homes second, and it appears that the roads meant little to the builders. One asphalt road leads to a traffic circle that ends with one exit to a group of stores in the middle of a gravel field. Rutted trails fan out in all directions, leading to clusters of houses in no recognizable pattern. Though this is a relatively new town, the Dhofar region has been home to the Bait Kathir since biblical times.

An American military installation of some size sits outside the town. Although the base could house hundreds of people, I see no soldiers in Thamarit. In 1980, Oman agreed to allow the U.S. a military presence. In turn the U.S. provided economic and technical military assistance to Oman. The arrangement proved especially valuable during the 1990 Gulf war.

Chris Beal has arranged for us to meet young Ali, one of our team, "at the hotel with the gas station." Ali is a member of the Bait Kathiri tribe, which is closely related to the Rashid, both of which groups travelled with Thesiger. Each is part of the Al Kathiri and descends from the same Yemeni tribe.

There is only one gas station in town, but there is no hotel attached to it. We drive around on the paved and gravel streets which criss-cross between the houses, connecting small stores and several mosques. Convenience stores, each the size of a North American living room, spill their contents onto the street. Plastic buckets, children's bath toys, brooms, camel sticks and cigarette posters make flashy displays. There is a tailor, next to a laundry, next to an ironing shop, all manned by folk from India. Further down the road another cluster of buildings contains a hardware store, barber, and tire repair shop. Two men, dark from work under the sun, sit on the concrete porch of the tire shop digging nails from tires. They pause from their work and stare as we pass.

We ask around for Ali, but no one knows him. Word travels that strangers are in town, and before long Mohammed Sudani finds us. Mohammed works for Manaa, who will coordinate both our Bedu personnel and the organizing of our camels, and who may still be in Abu Dhabi looking for camels. We follow Mohammed out of town past the camel racetrack to a makeshift camp three miles southwest where, according to plan, Manaa has set up the headquarters for our camel training. Mohammed speaks, and he tells us to rest at the camp while he goes off to pray and have a nap. "Ali come see you," Mohammed assures us. "You wait here."

Our camp is basic, built in the lee of fifteen-foot bluffs for shelter from the westerly winds. It consists of a barbed wire corral, two water tanks (a large, rusted vessel and a white plastic 600-gallon igloo-shaped one), and a green canvas military tent that would sleep twenty. The tent offers the only shade in camp and is not unlike the Chinese tents we used in Tibet at Everest Base Camp during our first two expeditions to the mountain.

The water tank was put in place for training the camels raced at the two-mile track next to our camp. In the traditional Bedu world, the camel was used for food, transport, clothing and raiding. With the introduction of the automobile, the camel lost its monopoly on desert travel. In the mid-seventies, Bedu who could no longer sell their camels or use their traditional skills voiced their concerns to Sheikh Zayed, president of the UAE. On television, in response to these complaints, Zayed said, "Look after your camels well. A day will come when they will be worth millions." Shortly after Zayed's famous speech, the sport of organized camel racing came into being. Today, top camels are worth a great deal of money, and ironically a car is now a popular prize for first place winners.

We hoped to see twelve camels, perhaps some retired racers, awaiting us in camp. According to the original plan, the camels should be in the final stages of a two-month training regimen to harden them for the long marches ahead. A special high-calorie diet of oats, honey and eggs, and lots of dates was developed to strengthen the animals for the rigours of the trek, food for which we had already paid. We have expected to be greeted by our Bedu teammates astride powerful, well-fed and well-trained mounts, ready for the desert. During his final planning trip not two months ago, Bruce was to come here "for [a] final check with the Bedu," his e-mail said. "And a visit to our twelve camels now in training for the desert traverse."

As Sheikh Said had warned in Masqat, rather than a herd of twelve we find only two ill-tempered camels, and not a single member of our team. What had Bruce seen when he came to observe the training? Why had he not shared this bad news? I want to ask him but there is something odd about this situation and I think it better left alone for now. While on Everest with Bruce in 1997, I gained considerable respect for his knowledge, talents and his personality. He possesses a positive attitude and a willingness to try anything. This previous experience encourages me to think we'll work this problem out.

I am leaning on my 1994 Everest experience. In Tibet, we discovered that much of our advanced planning had little connection to reality. We'd plan for thirty yaks to arrive on a certain date to transport our gear closer to the mountain. The day would come and go with no sign of the herd. Then our Tibetan team would arrive, four days late, with only eighteen yaks. With this perspective, it's easier to take these glitches in stride, but Leigh is becoming increasingly concerned as he realizes just how little is ready.

Another truck arrives within our first hour in the Thamarit camp. The five year-old Toyota looks twice its age with faded paint and dented panels—the result of hard desert driving. On the other hand, it is rust-free. Three young men jump out and confidently approach us.

"*Salaam alaykum!*" they shout from forty feet. *Peace be with you.*

"*Alaykum as salaam!*" Bruce answers back tentatively. *With you be peace.* One introduces himself as Ali. "Ali Salam?" we ask, checking to see whether this is the Ali we are looking for.

"*Aiwa.*" he answers. Good—he's the one.

Ali bin Salim bin Hazaar al Mashali el Kathiri is small and wiry. He is nineteen years old and carries himself with an athlete's grace, something my intuition tells me we'll come to appreciate. The Bedu are neither large nor tall, as a people. Those who have not been seduced by abundance and new sedentary lifestyles remain sinuous and powerful. Singularly well muscled, Ali has a small frame with broad shoulders and thin hips. His long *dishdashah* shirt drapes straight down from his developed shoulders.

Ali stretches out his hand to me with an easy smile and boyish good looks. He wears a white head cloth in a loose wrap, barely containing his rambunctious black hair. In his eyes, I can see a penchant for mischief, but no malice. Ali walks with the confidence, even the mild arrogance, of a young man who feels invincible. He is warm, instantly liked.

It is just after noon, January 16th, and we have finally made contact with part of our Bedu team. Ali will ride with us across the desert. Our meeting with him seems reminiscent of Thesiger's meeting with Salim bin Kabina, the young Rashid whose loyalty to the famous explorer was the stuff of legend. Bin Kabina, who was the only provider for his family, had recently lost his only camel to old age. Without it he had little hope of supporting his mother, younger brother, and infant sister—a heady responsibility for a sixteen year-old boy.

Thesiger met bin Kabina at a well, where he volunteered to help Thesiger's party retrieve water. It was a critical point in bin Kabina's young life, and he said so to Thesiger. "God brought you, and now I shall have everything."

Of his new friend, Thesiger wrote: "He announced that he was coming with me and the Rashid *sheikhs* advised to take the boy and let him look after my things. I told him he must find himself a camel and a rifle. He grinned and said that he would find both and did. Already I was fond of him."

Ali jumps back in the jeep and takes off as quickly as he had come. Bruce thinks he's said he'll be back. We stand in a circle, unsure of what to do next, and walk over to the camels. "That one looks really upset," I say. "It'll be for Bruce."

The camels are tethered to bags of sand in the centre of the corral. We approach gingerly, wanting to begin a friendship of sorts, but they will have no part of us, jerking their heads and making nasty noises as we come near. We retreat.

Leigh takes a nap on the bedrolls amid the gear. Bruce and I sit and admire our new beards in the mirrors of our compasses and try to relax. We have been told to grow our beards so as to distinguish ourselves from women. A beard also offers a Bedu man protection against the harsh sun and wind of the desert. Musil, a famous anthropologist who lived among the Rwala Bedouin of northern Arabia in the twenties, tells of raiders cutting a captured man's chin beard. For the Rwala to cut a man's facial hair was a worse insult than cutting off his head. Bruce and I decide that our beards are coming in nicely, and we sit back and relax, basking in our renewed masculinity.

We finish the water we carry, apply liberal doses of sunscreen. Hang out. I kick off my sandals in favour of boots to protect my feet from the sun and skittering scorpions. Bruce and I go back to the camels, both female, to feed them some straw in another effort at relationship building. One has become entangled in a careless loop of the corral's barbed wire so we work to free her using the cutters from our repair kit. Luckily, the wire hasn't damaged her hide. She is a dark-coloured dromedary camel. All of our camels will be single-humped like her. We move about her with some confidence thanks to the camel training we took last summer back in North America.

Doug Baum, our instructor, lives with his wife and daughters in Uvalde, Texas and is an expert with camels. Bruce, Leigh and I spent a week riding with Doug and his herd of Texas dromedaries—a dozen of the 1200 camels in North America (most of which are privately owned, and not in zoos as we had thought). All Doug's camels are Australian imports and he normally uses them for his private non-profit placement program for at-risk youth and for other educational events. The basic idea of the program is for young offenders to learn life skills and develop compassion by caring for something other than themselves. While Doug's primary interest is in helping troubled kids, he is also the only person we could hire to help us with our camel training.

Doug—with his huge heart, his rare expertise, and his sense for our fear—moved us along gently. We started with camel care basics: Feed them oats for strength and carrots for friendship, approach slowly from the side where they can see you and never stand between a thirsty camel and water. Later we became versed in their habits and temperaments. The camels towered above us, weighing twice the average horse, and were utterly intimidating. I have no real history with large beasts, having only ridden horses a few times, but slowly we began to feel better under Doug's encouraging tutelage. Within days, we were walking among the camels with relative ease.

Doug taught us what a wonderful specimen of environmental adaptation the camel is. Long, thin legs keep the camel's mass high above the ground, away from the radiating heat and exposing them advantageously to cooling breezes. Viewed from above, the camel presents the smallest possible surface area to the sun, minimizing heat absorption. The hair is thick and dense at the apex of the hump and in the mane along the top of the neck, providing partial insulation from the sun's beating.

The hump, which lends the camel its striking profile and is often thought to be a water reservoir, is actually a mound of concentrated fatty tissue—a remarkable energy storehouse which, under optimum conditions, enables the camel to go a week or more without food or water. When the fat is metabolized for energy, it produces a reciprocal degree of hydration.

On the same trip, we entered the Chihuahuan desert in west Texas with David Alloway, a desert survival expert. David taught advanced desert craft, including water procurement and how to make inedible vegetation edible. We ventured so far as to try baked cactus, a dish that required a healthy appetite to stomach. No worries—we knew there are no cacti in the Empty Quarter! David did show us how to catch birds and lizards, and the latter we knew we could find in the sands. We decided to train in Texas in July to try to approximate the heat we might face in the Quarter. It was 105 degrees in the shade, considerably more in the sun. We felt lethargic and struggled to concentrate. Luckily we could escape to air-conditioned quarters at night to sleep. Here, because of the heat, we begin seriously to doubt our ability to endure the sands.

The heat so far has been tolerable, but this won't last for long with summer's approach. A breeze blows through camp, with an invitation to take a walk. To the east and a little north lies Thamarit, a couple of miles away. Light clouds fill the sky over the town. South lies a collection of sand and rock debris, not so much deposited by wind as distributed there by some past flood. Most of the obvious erosive forces on this plain appear to be water-based, though it has obviously been some time since any rain has fallen. In the distance sit hoodoo formations where hard rock caps protect the strata beneath, while wind and water eat at the base. A dozen line the horizon, some the size of a kitchen table, others broad as a football field.

We are in an open drainage system—a *wadi*. The tawny ground is composed more of gravel than sand. Chunks of fractured rock lie everywhere. Living vegetation is limited to scrubby gorse, though other plants, long-since dead, are also present. I sit beside a wizened acacia whose dark, thin branches curl at their ends, conjuring gruesome memories of a dead climber's hands high on Everest. This acacia's branches have become those blackened fingers my Sherpa teammates and I had seen hanging in the tangle of ropes that clutter Everest's Hillary Step just below the summit. The climber's palms had turned the colour of porcelain, darkening toward fingers that closed into claws. Wind and sun had ravaged the climber's body for a year. He had been one of the last mountaineers to reach the summit during the spring season on Everest in 1996. When I reached the dead climber's terrible perch on my 1997 summit attempt, American alpinist Peter Athans was already there, working awkwardly at the ropes with a knife to free the unfortunate climber from the macabre scene of his final hours on the mountain.

Other climbers had passed him, but none till Athans had stopped to help. Did the fact of his death pull him past the point of compassion? He seemed to have fallen headfirst down the rocky Step. His hat had fallen off. His light hair still waved in the wind. Eyes stared vacantly behind his goggles. Had he hit his head hard against the rock when the rope arrested his descent? Or had he simply paused for a break, too tired to be careful now that he had completed his long climb up? It was likely dark, then, and the numbing cold perhaps had penetrated his boots. His toes slipped beyond feeling, his hands just blocks at the end of arms that would not respond to his mind's command. Cold would have added to his lethargy, robbed him of dexterity. He had been sleepy, perhaps, thinking the fatal thought that a little rest would do him good. He had most certainly forgotten what no climber can afford to forget—that the fatigue he had felt was half physiological and half psychological. He had been too high on Everest—too high too late in the day.

Dead almost a year to the day by the time Athans and I stopped, the climber's face had become blackened by the arid wind under a heatless sun. I saw the last strands of sun-decayed rope cut, finally freeing him from the mountain's cold. Committed to the mountain that had claimed him, his empty form was taken by the wind and swirled away.

The dead climber was British journalist/photographer Bruce Harrod, who had been climbing with a South African team. He had risked everything to make the top. As his body slid down the south slope, I turned away, my heart in my throat, and continued the climb to my own summit. It was less than an hour ahead for me, but an eon behind poor Harrod.

Now, here in the desert, the twisted branches of the acacia have awakened these memories. At the base of the dead tree, a hole the size of a small shoebox is cut into the sand among the roots. There are no tracks at the mouth of this burrow, but small dried droppings lie everywhere—the kind you can use to kindle a fire with a magnifying glass. A rabbit has deserted this home. I look about for something to help change my mood, something alive. Vibrant green saltbushes grow close by. They make good camel feed when water is abundant and look similar to the Nepali juniper we burned at Everest base camp during *Puja* religious ceremonies in memory of dead climbers. I walk on, needing further escape.

Ali and Mohammed have returned to the tent. Leigh and Bruce greet them as I walk back. Mohammed is only dropping Ali off; he is not staying. We start a conversation with Ali, who laughs warmly at our struggle with his language. Another vehicle arrives and a man with a young boy steps out to meet us. Sheikh Salim bin Mohammed al-Toof introduces himself with much enthusiasm. His peppered beard is evenly cut, his clothes crisp and clean. His voice is as smooth as his brown eyes are rich. Compared to the three of us after our day in the heat, he smells freshly "washed" in the smoke of some wonderful perfumed resin, which I have seen burned in the custom of the Arabic world. Sheikh Salim laughs at our reaction to his sweet aroma. Along with Ali, he is only the second Bedu from Thamarit we have met. Both of them are openly friendly and show none of the reserve we were told to expect from Arabs. There is little pretence, no façade. While we speak with his father, Salim's twelve year-old son makes a fire and prepares some tea with obvious pride.

Since Salim insists that we accompany him to his home for dinner, we all leave and follow him into town in our jeep. He pulls over at one of the cubbyhole shops we saw earlier when looking for Ali, who now walks home. We have stopped at a clothing store. Here, we pick up some head wraps with Sheikh Salim's aid—chequered squares of cloth called *masar*. Under Salim's direction we size up light rectangular cotton sheets called *wasir*. These, we're told, are like underwear that we will wrap around our waists like a sarong. This is entirely unexpected, as we have been advised many times that the Bedu community is closed and that we would not be easily welcomed into it ranks. "You will be kept at arm's length," we've been told.

Sheikh Salim measures for each of us a bamboo camel stick called a *yad*, cutting them the full length of our arms with a knife hidden on a belt on top of his *wasir*. We walk a few doors down to the tailor's shop, where four men are working. Sheikh Salim orders one to measure us. The gentleman wraps a measuring tape around our necks and then our chests and shouts out some numbers. No one writes them down. Next he stretches the tape to the length of our arms, then measures from our shoulders to our ankles. The shop is the size of a modest dining room. Bolts of fabric lining the walls from floor to ceiling make it even smaller. We stand in what room is left between two padded tables on which sit heavy scissors, bundles of cloth, and cushions of pins and needles. The floor is slippery with discarded strips of fabric. The air is thick, humid with the smell of men at work, deep in concentration.

The tailor shouts more measurements and a man notes them on a pad. There is struggle with pronouncing our English names, and Sheikh Salim declares that we must forget these names and be given Bedu ones. He speaks fast, with continuous hand movements. We understand little of the specifics but get the general meaning. The tailor is sizing each of us for *dishdashahs*—the traditional dress of all Arabian men. Made of silk and cotton, they are similar to dress shirts but they are long enough to reach the floor. This style of dress for men is common throughout the Middle East and has changed little in centuries. The *dishdashah* finds its ancient roots in the *abayah*, mentioned in the Bible as the attire of the Hebrew prophets. Through the ages it has functioned well for men, its loose fit allowing for free limb movement while protecting the body against overheating, blowing sand, and blazing sunshine. Beyond the practical value of the *dishdashah*, which is easily constructed, the garment maintains its currency because its wearing is not only culturally accepted but supported by Islam. I wonder whether we will feel out of place wearing this traditional dress.

A price dispute erupts between Sheikh Salim and the tailor while we select material. We look for the lightest weight because of the heat ahead. Bruce suggests a dark colour to hide the dirt. We decide on two tan shades similar in colour to the sand. We also order two of each, one each shade, provoking another dispute over price. It is settled when Sheikh Salim appears content. Each *dishdashah* costs $50, and all six will be ready in two days. I cannot wait.

We drive to Sheikh Salim's home, where we sit in his backyard under a corrugated metal roof supported by four beams. We stretch out on blankets and prop ourselves up on cushions. A fire burns on a thick bed of ashes in a metal pit. I look around and try to absorb all I can, so grateful for this invitation to Sheikh Salim's home. Numerous children peer at us from inside the house, not yet daring to venture out. The son, whom we met at the camp, produces coffee and brings us dates and a delicious doughnut-like dessert. The setting sun vanishes without warning. Cool air immediately bites at my back, while my face throbs in the heat of the fire. Our numbers begin to grow as more men join the gathering. Each slips off his shoes before stepping onto the carpets under the permanent canopy. They pepper us with questions in Arabic.

"*Limaza enta huna?*" Why are you here?

"*Antom nassarah?*" Are you Christians?

"*Kam marra tussallee?*" How often do you pray?

They ask about money, a favourite topic among the Bedu.

"*Ma thaman haziheel saat?*" How much does that watch cost?

"*Kam dafaat thaman zalik el hiza?*" What did you pay for those shoes?

"*Kam dafaat lee Manaa?*" How much have you paid Manaa?

However long they stay to chat, all sip a little coffee beside the fire.

The children gain confidence and now run about in the dirt courtyard between the two-storey house and us. A young boy yells from the door and announces that dinner is ready. The rest of the men leave, save three who may be immediate family—brothers, perhaps. The house is alive with the voices of children. I leave the room to wash my hands and return to silence. Back in the room Leigh and Bruce sit behind untouched trays of food, their eyes wide with what is unfolding before them. I freeze at the door, unsure of what to do. Our Bedu hosts stand in a row, shoulder to shoulder, facing toward a corner. Their hands are crossed at their chests, and Sheikh Salim whispers. Leigh waves to caution me so I cut in front of the group to get out of the way. Salim stops me with a shout and points his hand to his back, indicating that I should not pass in front.

All Muslims pray facing the city of Mecca in the southeast corner of Saudi Arabia. The city houses a centrally important mosque—the Masjed al Haram—at the centre of which rests the *Kaaba*, a hollowed-out cube of rock draped in black fabric. The *Kaaba* has been rebuilt many times and is the most sacred site in all Islam. Muslims face the *Kaaba* when they pray. Central to Islam is the concept that Muslims are directly and intimately connected with God, and to facilitate this relationship there is no official priesthood in Islam. Had I walked in front of the praying group, I would have come between them and the *Kaaba*, and, more importantly, Allah. I sheepishly circle around and find a seat.

The group drops to their knees, pauses, and bends forward until their foreheads touch the ground, symbolizing complete submission to God. Their hands reach slightly forward. They sit back on their knees and together share prayers. Leigh, Bruce and I sit frozen as though we are witnessing something we shouldn't. I have never been in the company of a Muslim at prayer and I feel awkward, wondering at our imposing. It is part of the cultural briefing that we should have studied more intently. But the Bedu appear comfortable with our presence and pay us no further attention.

The young boys are as focused as their father, following his every action. In one fluid motion they all take to their feet again, and the only sound is the swish of their *dishdashahs*. One boy scratches an itchy foot with the toes of the other, maintaining complete synchronicity with the group. Down to the knees again and to the foreheads—up and down, up and down—and all the while melodic prayers fill the tiny room like the sounds of the meditating monks of Tibet. They turn toward us, then away, marking the end of the prayers.

After re-wrapping their *masars* they join us at the trays, and the buzz of happy noise returns to the rooms beyond. Silently we eat rice and meat stew, hommous and pita bread, olives and very odd red pickles. We return outside to the fire, where conversations criss-cross, leaving us confused as we struggle with the local tongue. A few more hours pass quickly. With a couple of high signs to Leigh and Bruce, I grab a blanket for sleeping and Sheikh Salim nods approval. What a day we've had. This morning seems as though it was a week ago with all we've seen today wrapped in Sheikh Salim's hospitality. This morning he asked us about our religion, but after learning we were not Muslim held nothing back of his fatherly care. This man we met just today has given us all his time and given freely of his knowledge. I knew generosity to be an integral part of Bedu character, but until one is the recipient it is hard to fathom. Whether riding in a modern vehicle today or on camelback as in the recent past, a guest benefits from the Bedus' deep tradition of hospitality. The *sheikh* helped us buy clothes and protected us by negotiating a fair price on our *dishdashahs* and now, after feeding us, he welcomes us into his home to sleep. I wonder if an Arab visitor to North America would receive such a reception?

Strangely, I already feel at ease and welcome in this new land. I am thrilled to be here. I lie down near the fire. Sheikh Salim pats my shoulder and smiles before I fall asleep.

Chapter Three

The household awakens before sunrise for a pre-fast breakfast. We are still in the final days of *Ramadan*. The tradition of fasting in Islam began with Muhammad, Prophet and Founder of Islam, some 1390 years ago, when it was Arabic custom for those with religious interests to participate in an annual retreat. The purpose of this retreat was to meditate and pray. Muhammad spent the ninth lunar month of every year, known as *Ramadan*, away from Mecca meditating in a desert cave. His dedication was so intense that often he forgot to eat. One year, while meditating, Muhammad was visited by the angel Gabriel, who revealed to him the word of God. These revelations, continuing over a period of twenty-three years, form the basis of the Quran. In honour of Muhammad's fasting, Muslims throughout the world replicate his devotion.

The Bedu feel a particular connection to Muhammad. When little more than a week old, Muhammad was given to a wet nurse who hailed from one of the neighbouring nomad tribes—probably Bedu—where he spent the first five years of his life. The Bedu believe that Muhammad kept close contact with their people and gained from them his sense of social justice and humanity. Much of the teaching that guides a Muslim reflects the rhythms of desert life. The prayer schedule of any Muslim while travelling, for example, is much less demanding than when at home, and those who must travel during Ramadan can postpone their fasting until they arrive at their destination.

After our modest pre-sunrise meal, Sheikh Salim escorts us on another tour of town in our Land Cruiser, offering colorful commentary on all that we pass, though we understand little. He knows and waves at everyone as we drive about. Salim insists on driving and has no time for Bruce's Spice Girls cassette, asking us whether we have any Arab music. We are no longer to listen to English music or even to think in English anymore. He tells us we are now Bedu.

"Inglisee khalass!" he shouts. *English finished!* He laughs as he speeds about, going nowhere in particular. After the confusion with the tailor yesterday and in light of our new Bedu designation, Sheikh Salim insists we take Bedu names and sets about trying a few for each of us. Looking at Leigh and then to Bruce and me in the rear view mirror, he says: *"Mohammed? La."* No. Mohammed won't do. *"Ahmed? La."* He looks at me and fires off a few more names, not finding any he likes. He looks at Leigh. *"Yamis. Mumkin Yamis. Enta Yamis La, la, la."* Sheikh Salim needs more time to get to know us before he can pick any good names. We, on the other hand, have already decided to call him "Sheikh and Bake." Entirely appropriate, we think, to his colourful personality.

Hours later we end up back at the encampment to water the camels. The *sheikh* stays with us through this chore. He has an opinion on everything, and holds nothing back. Before he jumps in his truck to leave, he declares that of the two camels we have, the light-coloured one, is strong, a good and useful animal, but the dark coloured one is *"Mafi zein."* He leaves us with that thought and a cloud of dust.

We settle in for a rest and wait to see what happens next. Of our team we have still only met Ali. We have yet to meet Musallim and bin Ashara, our two other riding companions. Manaa, our fourth Bedu team member, with whom Bruce has been arranging ground logistics, has also yet to arrive. Manaa lives in Thamarit, but has not been by the camp that he has organized for us. His name no sooner rolls off our tongues than another Land Rover pulls into camp. Out steps a man of robust build in a rust-coloured *dishdashah*. He finishes a call on his cell phone and returns it to the pocket of his *dishdashah*. His pockets hang heavy with keys and extra batteries. Bruce knows Manaa from their previous meetings and rises to meet him. Bruce and Manaa share the roles of leader—Manaa of the Bedu, Bruce of the Canadians. We are soon sitting with him around a new fire while Bruce asks questions about our plans. Manaa is in his forties, with curly salt-and-pepper hair which he keeps trying to push under his *masar*. His facial hair is sufficient only to support a moustache and goatee, which he pulls while speaking.

A reminder of the region's Ohotari tribal rebellion that began in 1965, Manaa had been seriously injured, losing an eye and three fingers on his right hand. As a young boy in 1971, Manaa and his cousin found a high-calibre ammunition round in the sand left over from the fighting. Curious, they started hammering. The round exploded, tearing Manaa's hand apart, damaging his eye and leaving other scars. His injuries are hard not to look at, especially when he examines me with his one good eye. I try to keep my gaze locked on his left eye, wishing not to offend. Though he can see nothing with it, the damaged eye moves with the other. It is badly scarred, with an opaque cornea. Manaa shows no self-consciousness about his eye, or the hand he waves about, punctuating his speech. Along with the three fingers, he is also missing a portion of his palm, making the index finger appear long and claw-like.

Manaa smiles. There is an air of confidence about him, though we are all a little nervous about our first meeting. We sit enjoying tea as more trucks arrive at camp, some loaded with camels. The animals are sitting and only their heads and necks can be seen. They seem more curious than anxious as the truck backs up to an embankment for unloading.

A host of local Bedu get to work. Everyone shouts orders that no one follows. Leigh and I pull out the video equipment—part of our commitment to the film for *National Geographic*—and we tape the unloading against the setting sun. Wonderful silhouettes fill my screen, but I feel detached from the scene and wish I could be free to participate, not just observe. I lie on the ground, and this angle makes the camels look even more dominant. In the background I can hear the motor drive on Bruce's camera as he captures image after image for our photo archives. When the camels are unloaded, Manaa shouts at us to take them.

Even in broad daylight, the sight of these animals had worried me. Now, in the dark, they loom, large and sinister. Under my breath I plead with them not to crush me. The camels are stiff and sore after their long rides from various locales around the peninsula. They stomp their feet and swat their tails at the ever-present flies. They smell of stale manure, long matted to their hair, but it is their breath that is most foul—a combination of partially digested feed and the nastiest plaque imaginable.

Darkness descends and though the Bedu are now released from the day's fast and are free to eat, they choose to stay and finish the job of unloading our herd. None of the men has had water, let alone food, for twelve hours.

Eleven camels are tethered to sandbags in the corral. As soon as the meanest is secured, we stand about admiring our new group. Manaa has taken a couple of hard kicks during his struggle to undo the lasso used to secure the last camel. Though he has sidestepped most of them in the dark like some kind of Bedu Jedi Knight, two hard kicks have landed solidly on his arm and thigh. Like a young Bedu awaiting his rite of passage, through circumcision, I begin to dread my first kick. It's only a matter of time.

The excitement over, we are hungry—especially the Bedu, who are now irritable under the demands of fasting. We drive to Manaa's home to eat.

His one-storey house is basic, matching most of the other town homes, with slight variations. Shoulder-high cinder-block walls surround the home, all the walls finished in fine mortar and whitewash. Manaa's house typifies Islamic architecture's relative disregard for outward appearance. Its high, windowless walls and low doors present an exterior stark by western standards, the house's focus being on the interior, symbolizing family.

Male guests are not allowed to venture into any rooms of the house other than the seating area dedicated to receiving us. We enter the room, which is dead square. Though it is attached to the home, we enter from outdoors via the courtyard. Manaa sends orders to the kitchen and joins us. Several shaded lights on the ceiling illuminate the room. Two fans hang dormant between them. The floor is covered with two wool carpets of complex geometric patterns in deep primary colours. On the floor along all four walls is a thick foam cushion, a foot and a half wide. Densely packed individual cushions line the walls. Cushions and foam are covered with a thin matching cotton fabric featuring elaborate pastel floral patterns. The room is homey and welcoming compared to the harshness of outside. A beautiful core, where the family interacts, is paramount.

Tea is served, and we await the food. Dates are laid out in the middle of the room, which we taste, careful to use only our right hands. In Arabic culture, the left hand is reserved for bodily functions, and people do not touch food or others with it. A young woman of Asian descent, perhaps from the Philippines, appears periodically from the courtyard to check on the tea. She is employed by Manaa as a maid. Like the rest of us, she enters unshod. She is the first woman we have seen since meeting our Bedu companions. Though she tries to hide her interest, she eyes us thoroughly.

At one point Manaa's helper enters, carrying a large heavily laden metal tray above her shoulder. She walks to the middle of our circle and places before us an impressive assortment of food, including oranges, bananas, apples and dates. There is also a large bowl of doughnut-like desserts. They are heavy with oil, and as addictive as doughnuts back home. I dig into what I think is a scrambled egg dish with spices and chilies and bits of unidentifiable meat. This dish is a favourite and disappears quickly.

Manaa dishes out soup. It looks harmless in my bowl until I give it a stir. Suspicious bits of meat float to the surface. I decide not to examine the spoon's contents and instead just shovel it in. The soup is the gathering place for everything left out of the other dishes. It has the viscosity of Chinese sweet and sour soup, but not the familiar taste. The main ingredient, I learn, is goat tripe. Leigh flashes me a twisted grin as he slurps his down. Manaa picks up on our struggle with the soup, asking what's wrong. Wanting not to offend, I take up the bowl again and work down more of the now cold and congealing concoction. As foreign as the taste is, I wouldn't trade it for any meal back home. This experience is why I have come.

After a day in the sun and a large meal, it is all I can do to not stretch out my numb legs and fall asleep. This would be entirely unacceptable, however, as the Bedu sit on their feet with their knees together and bent. This kneeling/sitting position is painful even when I am on the cushions. Accustomed to this practice, the Bedu wonder why we can't sit still. Thesiger also had a hard time adjusting, writing in his *Arabian Sands*:

> While I was around the Arabs I was anxious to behave as they did, so that they would accept me to some extent as one of themselves. I had therefore to sit as they did, and I found this very tiring for my muscles were not accustomed to this position. I was glad when it was night and I could lie down and be at ease.

How little certain things have changed. These Bedu now live in houses and do not camp out in the sands as they did in Thesiger's time. But in so many ways our experiences seem to parallel those of Thesiger. Leigh, Bruce and I suffer through these sitting sessions in thinly disguised discomfort, constantly tempted by the cushions surrounding us and the comfort they could offer. I cannot understand this most uncomfortable of sitting positions, but it is the basic position that the Bedu assume during prayer.

Unable to comprehend the swirl of Arabic around me, I turn my attention to the complex, abstract print in the carpet and escape the foreign conversation. I am in danger of falling asleep where I kneel, heady with the smell of incense burning in the corner and the fragrance of the desert cooling beyond the door. Then my head drops and my eyes close. Sometime later, Leigh taps me on the shoulder and tells me to stand up. The three of us struggle like arthritic old men. We wince at the formality of it all and the discomfort that results from our desire not to offend.

A new man has appeared at the door. We all stand to receive him. He is unlike the others. Everyone jumps to his feet with a sense of urgency. The man's gait is smooth, balanced, and slow. He holds his camel stick in his left hand as though it is floating beside him, not actually being held. His *dishdashah* is well pressed and the colour of sand, unlike the white *dishdashahs* of the others, tinted with a dye made from the *abal* bush. Traditionally, the Bedu have used the russet colour of the *abal* dye as camouflage in the open desert. Thesiger dyed his own clothing with the resin from this bush when he first crossed the sands.

The shoulder cloth of the new man's *dishdashah* is sun-faded and thinning at the elbows. The cuffs of his sleeves are stained, the hemline threadbare. The neck is tight to his throat, forcing his thin, dark skin to roll over the edge. The tassel from its single button is unusually long for this region. I guess from its style that he comes from west or north of here.

The man looks to be about eighty-five—much older than most of the men who visit us. His head is covered in soft white hair. A thick, fastidiously groomed white beard graces his face. His sideburns drop steeply from his temples and swoop along his jaw line, then upward to his moustache. He keeps the hair on his upper lip half the length of the rest, and he has trimmed a perfect arc of hair below his nose. Not a single hair touches his wrinkled lips. His white hair frames the darkness of his face perfectly.

The elder, a Kathiri *sheikh*, takes his seat at the head of the room and is offered drink and food—here in the desert, the offer of drink always comes first. He accepts only coffee and exchanges greetings with everyone. Normally, a new visitor will walk the circumference of any gathering, greeting everyone with a handshake and often a mutual nose rub. The *sheikh* stands his ground while all in the room walk to greet him with a kiss to his nose. Giving a nose kiss is most appropriate when greeting an elderly man or a *sheikh*. The junior man actually kisses the bridge of the senior man's nose. Equals might merely touch noses. Since non-Arabs are not expected to perform this type of greeting, we simply shake his hand.

With little trouble, the new man drops into the traditional sitting position—the daily routine of prostration before Allah seems to keep the elders supple and agile, a nice physiological benefit to their spiritual pursuits. Manaa talks with him at length. From what I can piece together, the elder predicts our crossing will prove impossible due to the length of the drought and the lack of grazing for the camels. Our Bedu team listens closely to this respected *sheikh*. He plays with the hair on his chin, rolling it between thumb and index finger while talking to the others. His predictions of our failure must weigh heavily on the Bedu. How will this affect their commitment to the journey?

I earlier asked Manaa how one attains the designation *sheikh,* and he explained that it is most often inherited, but blood does not guarantee the status. A son whose father is a *sheikh* gains respect through consultation with the village elders—learning from them and so earning his right to assume the role. There is no shortage of *sheikhs*, but this does not dilute the respect given them. Every group of Bedu, whether clan or tribe, has a *sheikh* as a leader.

This elder is visiting relatives during *Ramadan*. For Muslims the idea of close family includes three or four generations. *Ramadan* is the most important time of the year to be with relatives. Given that family is central in Muslim culture, it is not surprising that we are meeting so many of the Bait Kathiri elders. Unfortunately, their predictions of failure are eroding our confidence, but we are well advised to heed them.

The *sheikh* pays little direct attention to us, simply glancing over periodically and then asking questions of the others. I struggle to position my *dishdashah* modestly. Since Muslims value modesty, I want not to offend the *sheikh* by revealing more of myself than is acceptable. At the same time, I work the fabric loose on my back to stop the neckband from choking me. Losing a little weight on the trip will help my *dishdashah* fit more comfortably.

As familiar as he was with the culture, Sir Wilfred battled with his *wasir*, which he called his loincloth. "My companions always kept their loincloths on even when they washed at wells," wrote Thesiger. "At first I found it difficult to wear a loincloth with decency when sitting on the ground. Bedu say to anyone whose parts are showing, 'Your nose!' I had this said to me once or twice before I learned to be more careful."

We return to camp and I marvel at this being only our second day, thinking of all the wonderfully rich experiences we have already enjoyed. Time to file a report back home. We have come to the desert in full partnership with our new sponsors, but others are interested in our progress. NEC Technologies has supplied one of the critical elements of this adventure—the communications system that will enable us to take our partners' employees and thousands of schoolchildren into the desert with us.

From this remote place, we will send regular digital photographs and reports with help from one of our other partners, the Calgary Board of Education. Reports will be posted on our website www.alwaysadventure.net. It has been loaded with thousands of dollars' worth of school curriculum created for grades one through twelve, containing information relevant to subjects from social studies to science, all themed on our adventure. The Empty Quarter web site will allow us to share many moments of our adventure with teachers, their classes, and anyone else who is interested enough to link up with us. We want to share the spirit of our adventure, enabling others to accompany us in "real time" across the sands. If some of these electronic adventurers derive any form of inspiration from our effort, if they gain a greater understanding of the region and the culture, if they draw some sense of adventure into their own lives, then we will have succeeded, whatever the outcome of our expedition.

I first connected with school children from my alma mater in this way from Everest in 1991. The profound effect it had on students was evident when I later met with them at school and saw their enthusiasm for what they learned and what they dreamed of doing in their futures. This inspired me to repeat the effort in 1994 on Everest, on a larger scale, reaching more students. In 1997, we tapped into the power of the internet and connected with thousands of children. Making sure the satellite equipment in Base Camp functioned to send the reports was a challenging part of Bruce's role on the mountain back then. The desert offers another perfect opportunity to connect with thousands more children and their teachers and provides us a sense of giving a little something back.

Before going to bed we organize the satellite gear to file our first report from the desert proper, but battery trouble gives us little time to correspond: "At camp in Thamarit. Doing great. Trying an initial satellite linkup. Cheers—the team" is all we manage to send.

٢٩ رمضان ١٤١٩
January 17, 1999 Thamarit

We are up early this morning, keen to face another desert day. The Bedu have all slept in their homes in Thamarit. Although they invited us to stay with them, we remained out here in our tent quarters, not wishing to impose. We like it out here under the desert sky, amid the camels and the quiet. One reason we have arisen early is to practise the Bedu art of coffee making—an essential skill for social acceptance, since the Bedu take their coffee and tea making seriously. The fire must be started in a small sand depression, using minimal kindling.

A simple metal pot is dedicated to this use. The pot is filled with water and placed on the coals, which are coaxed into flame with a hard blow. This is the easy part. As the water comes to a boil, either four teabags or a handful of loose tea is added. The tea is black, imported from India. Moments later, the water fully aboil, a healthy handful of sugar is added. Depending on whose hand is used, the tea is often either too sweet or not sweet enough. This is the critical moment. Once the sugar has been added, only thirty more seconds on the fire is needed. But the boiling must be ferocious, and the fire must be worked to maximum heat. At just the correct instant, the tea is pulled from the fire, then set in the warm sand for two and a half to three minutes of steeping. If everything is done just so, the right flavour and drinking temperature is achieved. The tea is then poured with fastidious attention, as one might pour a martini at an exclusive club. But the stakes are higher here. We have already seen one pot of tea angrily thrown into the sand when a young Bedu did not make it properly.

We rehearse the tea-making procedure in our effort to master the craft before we attempt to make a batch for our Bedu friends.

64

Inshallah! If God wills! We sample our brew. Though it tastes good to us, we are certain it would not satisfy our colleagues, without really knowing why. We sit close to the warmth of the fire, eating dates. The dates don't cut our hunger so we dig through our food box to find a few of yesterday's ash-covered flatbreads and warm them over the fire.

We are uncertain when the Bedu will materialize and decide to get the camels some water after their trip. The crazed camel that kicked Manaa last night is unhappy this morning. Its leg is still tightly lassoed from last night's encounter, and it favours the now swollen foot. The camel protests as soon as we get close even to offer water. Distressingly, the camels are already suffering—something we wanted to avoid. In our incompetence, there is nothing we can do for her.

We mill about the herd, using our time alone with the camels to work out our anxieties. If last night is any indication, the Bedu are not as patient with our fears as Doug Baum was. Had we not had the camel training time in Texas, I'm certain we would not even be able to water these animals without placing ourselves in a fair amount of danger.

About two and a half hours later than we anticipated, Manaa and the local Bedu who helped us unload drive up in two worn trucks, skidding to a stop. Among them is a new man in his forties. I talk to Manaa about the camel's swollen foot. Manaa turns to the stranger, who then walks calmly to the corral, all of us in tow. The man approaches the agitated camel without hesitation and convinces it to sit, using soft commands and gentle touches. After tying her front legs to prevent further movement, the man stands back surveying the animal. He is handsome, with a greying beard. His face displays concentration as he continues to work around the camel with more prodding. This exposes the lassoed back foot.

With the camel unable to kick, the slipknot is addressed. Too tight to pull apart, it may have to be cut, but the swollen flesh bulging over the rope would surely be damaged and the tendon would be at risk. He tries one more time at the knot then pulls an eight-inch knife from under his *dishdashah* and slides it across the rope at an awkward angle. The rope springs free. A small bead of blood appears, but nothing more.

The man says nothing and returns to the fire, tastes our tea and discards the remains to brew another batch. Only now does Manaa introduce us to Musallim bin Abdullah bin Rubat el Kathiri—our second riding mate. Perfect. At forty-one, he is married and the father of eleven children. Musallim is a reputed camel doctor in the region. He is also a renowned poet, we are told. If his poetry is anything like his camel skill, we should be well entertained at the fire in the weeks ahead.

Happy to sit a moment, and feeling much more confident now that two thirds of our team is here, we pass an enjoyable time watching our new Bedu friends socialize over the new pot of tea. All of us sit tight together, shoulder-to-shoulder, on straw mats around the fire. The sun sets and the drinking begins. There is no shortage of enthusiastic conversation. Perhaps the caffeine has something to do with it.

Someone has brought from town a small pot of coffee—*gahwa* in Arabic. As it is the host's privilege to provide coffee to his guests, three boys in their early teens, all sons of men who have arrived, push and shove each other for the right to serve it. One wins out and begins. A little red bucket rests near the blaze. It is half full of water, a couple of inches of sand at its bottom. In the water are six small, thick porcelain cups, without handles. The coffee ready, the proud server stacks three cups in the palm of his right hand, passes by the fire to retrieve the coffee pot with his left hand, and circles the fire in front of the group. The oldest man in the group is served first. The boy pours each cup half full before the recipient and hands the gift forward before moving on to the next. Once three glasses are given out, the boy returns to the bucket for more and repeats the process, all the while keeping an eye on the contents of each distributed glass. The moment a glass is empty, he offers more, taking the glass in his free hand, refilling it and passing it back. Anyone who is satisfied gives a triple shake of his cup to send the message to the server.

It is an insult to the host to refuse the first round of coffee, and guests are encouraged to take several refills. A well-mannered guest will drink an odd number of cups—one, three or five. I drink three, which appears to be the habit of most of the men around the fire. The coffee is bitter, and though it smells nothing like the coffee back home, its aroma is wonderfully unique. The Bedu soften the brew's sharp edge with shaved cardamom, but never with milk or sugar.

Used cups are returned to the bucket for a quick rinse, then cycled back to the group for anyone who has missed the first round. This continues until the group of eight is finished. It has taken forty minutes. All the while the server sits or stands at attention, waiting to offer more coffee. Tea drinking is a recent addition to the Bedu tradition. The tea ceremony is similar to, but not nearly as elaborate as, the coffee ritual. For instance, it is acceptable to place a cup of tea in the sand, but never a cup of coffee.

There is unusual harshness in conversation and gesture among the Arabic-speaking Bedu, and so this sensitive drinking ritual is a welcome contrast. I wonder whether the Bedu hold to this ritual so passionately because of the harshness of the desert against which it is set. Clearly, drink in any form symbolizes survival for these former desert wanderers. It is not hard to see how the practice of drinking coffee would have become so ritualized in the Bedu culture, performed in an environment as unforgiving as their character can be.

٣٠ رمضان ١٤١٩
January 18, 1999 Thamarit

Our training continues with further camel familiarization. One of the animals is rocking back and forth, dance-like, from hoof to hoof. We name it Dancer. Leigh takes a liking to a tall Sudanese camel, the only white one in the herd, and the largest in stature. Seeing them more docile in the morning, the camels are not nearly as frightening as they were when we were trying to subdue them in last evening's darkness.

We receive saddlebags, handmade for us by Bedu women. Six of our camels are now getting accustomed to saddles and one to being ridden, but the rest are not. Though these other camels will be used as pack animals, they still need some training with the loads of gear. We Canadians keep a respectful distance, uncertain which is worse—the frightful physical battle between Bedu and beast, or the terrible screams it produces from the camels. They are actually in little pain, but protest anyway, seeing the packsaddles and anticipating a day of work. We are humbled by the skills of our Bedu companions and can offer little help.

Taynoonah, the most crazed of the herd, escapes and loses her saddle. Six men have been trying again to teach her to sit. Even with everyone holding on to her she breaks free and is quickly out of camp. Two jeeps race off in pursuit. We strain to see through the wall of dust kicked up by the jeeps, when the camel bursts back suddenly through the cloud, the jeep in hot pursuit. As the camel darts away from us, one of the Bedu, a young man whom we have not formally met, jumps up from the fire and runs after it, hiking up his *dishdashah* on the fly. Amazingly he gains on the camel, barefoot across the ground full of thorns and sharp rocks. The jeeps have stopped and the group now watches the foot race, cheering the runner.

While I am amused by the scene, Leigh has realized the gravity of what we are witnessing and scrambles to videotape it as the Bedu boy reaches the running animal. The boy grabs a clump of its mane and tries to jump on, misses and lets go, but does not give up. His arms and legs blur as he continues the chase. Up close again, he grabs another clutch of hump hair, skips a few steps, and throws both feet forward, planting them in the sand. His body stiffens, and like a pole-vaulter he launches himself upward onto the camel's back to the cheers of the crowd. He leans forward to grab the single rein and pulls back on the rope, immediately slowing the camel to a trot. He jumps to the ground, then walks back toward us, the camel in tow, both boy and beast obviously winded from the sprint. The young man's name is Salim Ali, and we are indeed impressed.

After a day sorting gear in camp, we are invited to Manaa's home for dinner. Again, we sit in the small square room with the cushions. The food has just arrived from the kitchen. There is more of the dreaded soup, with some rice and the tasty egg dish. The sun is still up so we choose not to eat. As the consummate host, Manaa tells us to dig in, but we prefer to wait until the Bedu can join us. A large pot of tea has been poured, and family and friends sit with a full cup before them, still unable to drink. A bowl of half-mashed dates is being passed about and each man takes a small piece, massaging it between his thumb and forefinger. Still, no one eats. Again today the Bedu have not had a drink of water, let alone a morsel of food, since sunrise.

Without warning, the call to prayer comes from the mosque a hundred yards away. The sun has officially set, and the fast is over for the day. With the call still ringing in the air, the children have already eaten their dates and drunk most of their tea. The three little ones struggle the most with the fast, and dive into the rice and eggs as though they hadn't eaten for days. Prepubescent children are not required to fast, and their parents encourage them to nourish their growing bodies. Yet they all try their best to join their parents in this symbolic gesture of faith. The frenzied meal lasts only a few minutes, and now everyone heads to the mosque for the *Salat al-Maghrib* evening prayer. We are suddenly alone, our mouths open, our hands dripping rice. I immediately pour my soup back into the serving bowl, much to the disgust of Bruce and Leigh. As a child, I would hide despised vegetables like brussels sprouts or yams under the edge of my plate, removing the evidence later when I cleared the table. The habit is hard to break.

١ شوال ١٤١٩
January 19, 1999 Thamarit

Manaa, Musallim, Ali, and a host of local men and boys put the camels through their paces. Half the camels will be used for riding, the other half to carry our supplies. The Bedu survey each camel and assign its role. The training of each camel starts with teaching the animal to sit or "couch"—to lie prone, legs tucked underneath. Along with calloused knees, the camels have a thick pad of cartilage covered in callous on their chests. On this pedestal of sorts they rest and sleep. Camels are born with this chest pad, which keeps the more tender skin of their bellies off the hot ground and away from thorns and sharp rocks. Once couched, the camels are very content and will remain like this for hours chewing their cud. Convincing the camels to couch is not easy.

Leigh, Bruce and I are assigned to our riding camels. Leigh to Labian—the tall white one he likes. Bruce to the crazy camel that rocks back and forth all the time, the one called Dancer. And I to a muscular camel we've named Mr. T, for the T-shaped *wasm* or brand of his previous owner. We lead our haltered camels from the corral to couch them and learn to attach their saddles. Following the Bedu example, we tug downward on the rein, saying "Khkhkhkhkh." There is no literal translation for this command, but I assume *Please, camel, sit down* is close. Often, to add emphasis, one taps the ground while pulling and *Khkhkhkh-ing*. If this yields nothing, a few taps to the camel's knee helps encourage it to drop to its front knees. I try this with Mr. T. He pays little attention to me until, after twenty minutes of unrelenting effort, he obliges—but not before scaring me with a well timed roar close to my ear. Once kneeling, Mr. T can then bend his back legs and set his great mass—twice that of a medium-sized horse—down on his chest pad and tuck his hind legs in too.

Once couched, Mr. T can then be saddled. Theoretically. As soon as I move to start placing the saddle, he jumps up. I couch him again and, having asked him nicely to stay seated, reach for the saddle, whereupon he promptly stands up. Ali teaches me to tie a rope around one of T's front legs to keep him down. Thinking the camel secure, I reach again for the saddle, and once more T jumps up. But this time his tied leg is bent under his chest, forcing him to hop away on the other three free legs. I give awkward chase, couch him and tie both front legs this time. As I move to place the saddle he lifts his rump and spins in a circle away from me while I run around behind.

Leigh and Bruce aren't having much more luck. An entire day is consumed in this struggle, and under the heat we all become disheartened. Musallim comes to help. The Bedu are patient with us only to a point, as we fumble along, until they can handle our incompetence no longer and take over each simple task themselves.

The skilled man couches Mr. T, who cooperates without protest. Musallim tosses on the saddle, secures the confusing web of line in minutes, and walks away. T looks back at me with all the smugness of that Warner Brothers frog who sings opera for its owner but never for a crowd.

I inspect the secured saddle and rope system—it bears little if any resemblance to a horse saddle. The Bedu of Southern Arabia use a lightweight saddle comprised mostly of blankets—unlike the saddle used by tribes further north, which incorporates more elaborate frames built of cedar poles. The Omani riding saddle is much smaller than its northern counterpart. The northern Arabian saddle is placed over the hump, while in Oman the rider sits behind the hump. The Omani saddle is built around a wooden anchor, held in place with straps and padded with blankets.

The anchor of the Omani saddle is the cedar-made *hadut*. The V-shaped *hadut*, which sits like the roof of a house over the spine of the camel just in front of the hump, is tied in place with two long hand woven girth hitches called *zwars*. One hitch passes behind the chest pad and bears most of the load, while the other passes in front of the chest pad to add extra security. The *hadut* is ornately carved with geometric patterns and is padded with woven date fronds. Manaa tells us emphatically that only natural fibres like wool and date fronds should ever be in contact with the camel lest its fur be worn away and the skin exposed to the sun.

Behind the hump and tied to the *hadut* sits a semi-circular pad of fibre just above the camel's rump. It is secured with a long black strap of woven wool called the *betan*, which passes around the girth of the camel in front of the rear legs but behind the camel's penis. Two wool blankets are rolled together and curled on top of the semi-circular pad, creating a dip between the hump and the blankets in which we will sit. Over the hump, wool saddlebags called *khar*, with two compartments, hang from either side, and carry gear. On the back portion of the saddle and over all of the blankets a sheepskin or *soof* is added, giving the final padding. The remaining length of the wool *betan*, securing the semi-circular pad, is then pulled over the blankets, the saddlebags and *soof*, around the *hadut*, and back again to the rump, where it is tied off.

Many of the animals have never been ridden or used for packing gear. Manaa tells us that when purchasing the camels, he looked for the strongest he could find, unconcerned about their prior training. One of the camels, Taynoonah, has never been trained at all. A group of boys spend the day teaching her to couch. It takes six of them to manage her.

Before our first ride, Leigh, Bruce, and I steal away behind the tent for a long drink of water and a couple of boiled eggs that we had cooked before everyone arrived. We feel some guilt, but know we need the nourishment and hydration to stay safely focused on what we are doing. We finish our snack and rejoin the group.

Manaa takes the rein of my camel and motions for me to get on. I grab some hump hair, but as soon as I swing my leg over the saddle, T jumps up, tossing me to the ground. Manaa shouts at me to be faster and couches T again. This time I seize the hair and jump into the saddle. Before my butt hits, the *soof* is up and I'm almost thrown forward to the ground. On the back of the camel my head is eleven feet off the ground. There is little to hold onto so I squeeze my handfuls of hair till my hands ache, slippery with sweat.

Musallim mounts his camel gracefully, jumping lightly into the saddle and holding nothing but the rein loosely in one hand and his camel stick in the other. Somewhere behind me, Bruce and Leigh mount up with the help of the others. Manaa ties T's rein into Musallim's saddle, then does the same for Bruce. Leigh, on Labian, is tied to Ali, and we're off. It takes all my concentration to hold on let alone steer the camel—I am relieved to be tied in. The camel's awkward gait rocks us from side to side while throwing us slightly fore and aft. It becomes apparent why camels are called "the ships of the desert"—not only do they carry cargo across seas of sand, but they move with the sway of a vessel on open water.

I hope Musallim has arranged my saddle blankets incorrectly—if he hasn't, then this saddle is inherently an instrument of torture. Without stirrups, my weight sits heavily on T's spine, which I can feel through the saddle. His wide girth spreads my legs like some frightful yoga position, and with each step something strange happens in my lower back. During our time in Uvalde, Texas, the only place we could train with camels in North America, we never learned how to sit on a camel Bedu-style, or how to find any comfort on a Bedu saddle. The Bedu of Oman ride with their legs tucked up beneath them. This position requires great flexibility and feels precarious to the unaccustomed rider.

We ride a mile around camp and return. The camels are couched and we get off in the same manner we got on. After the ride my legs have gone numb, and the supposedly soft *soof* has torn away a couple of layers of skin on my seat, leaving two dime-sized sores. A dubious start. How will we manage 700 miles like this?

The saddling and short ride has consumed the whole day and nearly the whole of our energy. While I rest on a bag of feed inside the tent, Bruce sits in the doorway. It is his turn to file a report to the students. He works on the laptop, describing the highlights of our activities and outlines our plans for the next few days. The computer screen throws blue light on his face, beard and head wrap.

A hundred feet beyond Bruce, the camels stand silhouetted. Only their jaws move. Behind them, the horizon bursts with colourful emotion. Red and purple splash upward, filling the wide desert sky. There is not a whisper of wind, and only my own breathing and the sound of Bruce's fingers on the keys interrupt the silence. Even the flies have stopped buzzing. They sit oddly clustered on a bit of red rope that hangs from the two roof poles.

My breathing is audible, deep, meditative. A welcome feeling of peace overtakes me. I look at my hands holding my diary. They are already tanned and worn. The nails are worked short. My wedding ring has become loose enough to fall forward against my knuckle, revealing white skin normally hidden from the sun. My feet are bare in the sand and equally dark. Their soles still burn from the day of walking about on the rough ground, and I wonder whether they will ever toughen enough to make this journey barefoot as the Bedu insist. The last splashes of colour fall like tears on the horizon. Some are caught in the night's cold and crystallize into stars. The difficulties of the day disappear.

Today was *Eid el Fitr*, the holiday ending *Ramadan*. Earlier, a group of enthusiastic Bedu arrived at the desert camp, many of them new to us. They have brought fruit and drinks for a suitable feast and have slaughtered a goat, which is now cooking. Tonight, our sighting the little silver slipper of a crescent moon will mark the end of fasting with three days of feasting. It is an image of this moon that sits atop the mosques.

I hear trucks approaching. Bruce packs up the NEC laptop. The calm is broken. Three sets of blinding lights bounce toward us. They stop in a cloud of dust. The magic of the night sky is obliterated and once again our camp becomes a small circus as people unload goats for slaughter. The celebration begins. We settle around the freshly stirred fire and begin eating. Manaa tosses me an orange. When I start to peel it he tells me to eat it like an apple—rind and all. I laugh at the suggestion, thinking it a joke. Manaa says something in Arabic. Something about the future. Something I don't understand.

Our Arab friends, with Sheikh Salim's encouragement, give each Canadian a Bedu name. In the Arab tradition, a boy's first name is followed by his father's first name. This is followed by a third name for the family, then a tribal name. For example, Ali's name is Ali bin Salim al Mashali el Kathiri (Ali, son of Salim, of the Mashali family of the Bait Kathir tribe). A woman is named as the daughter of her father and grandfather, and her name will not change with marriage. Bruce has been given the name Salah bin Kanada el Mashali el Kathiri—Good Son of Canada—because he is a good person. Leigh, as the eldest, receives the honour of being named after Manaa's Grandfather, and is now Abdullah bin Kanada, al Mashali el Kathiri. I have been given the name of Suhail bin Kanada, al Mashali el Kathiri—Easy Son of Canada, of the Mashali family of the Bait Kathir tribe. "Easy," I'm told, because the Bedu think I have a positive spirit and laugh easily.

Some thirty Bedu soon join the circle in waves of singing and dancing. Groups form up, ten abreast, and march out of the darkness toward the group at the fire, drowning them out, now tired after twenty minutes' hard singing. Rifles are spun overhead. Everyone is talking, singing, dancing. Leigh, Bruce and I join in.

We choose to twirl our camel sticks because we have no guns. I toss my stick into the night sky and find it again in the sand near the fire.

٢ شوال ١٤١٩
January 20, 1999 Thamarit

In Canada, a party like the one last night might have ended in a drunken blur for many. But here there is no alcohol, according to strict Islamic code. The lack of drunkenness and the clear thinking that came with it is refreshing. In Arabic intoxicants are called *khamr*, a term meaning *to cover*, and any substance that masks or alters the mind is forbidden by Islam. Our Bedu friends return bright-eyed and ready for another day of training with the new loads of gear. I, however, ate something last night that upset my stomach, and spent the night ridding my system with violent vomiting. I am still not well today and spend it trying to recover.

٣ شوال ١٤١٩
January 21, 1999 Thamarit

We return from our six-mile ride at 12:40 p.m. In the shade of the tent we finish up some meat from last night's dinner. The temperature is 115 degrees Fahrenheit and our energy is sapped. The sun's brilliance bleaches out all features of the surrounding desert. There are no shadows. There is no breeze, and the air feels thick and oppressive. The buzz of flies accompanies the rippling waves of heat, which rise from the baked sand and distort every view. Flies have gathered in a dense cloud at the peak of the tent, too dazed by the heat to escape, too obsessed with the smell of meat to want to.

Manaa and I recline on a wool carpet, our heads resting on our hands. A few flies crawl between us.

"You see how the fly puts its hands together," says Manaa. I look closely at the fly, see it rubbing its forelegs together as if it were washing. "The fly was like the bee. The fly give honey. The Prophet Muhammad, God bless him, can speak with the fly and asked them for some honey."

In a high voice, impersonating the flies, he wails, "Weeee have no honey."

"The Prophet ask again and still fly has no honey. But the fly do have honey and the Prophet understand this. He get angry with the fly and punish this fly for not giving honey. They not tell the truth. Now fly has no more honey and only shit."

Manaa leans forward and points to the fly, continuously rubbing its legs together like hands, back and forth.

"You see the fly doing like this?"

Manaa hunches over and rubs his hands together as if to beg or pray and in his high fly voice says: "Pleeeeease, Prophet—let us work in honey and not shit."

The message of the story is clearly in support of *Zakat*, or almsgiving—one of the Five Pillars of Islam. Generosity is a principle of life for these men out here in the desert, as we have seen so often in the meals they share with us. *Zakat* means *purity*. It symbolizes the dedication of a person's wealth to relieve poverty. The Bedu combine this with the moral code of the desert, which dictates that all guests share lavishly in provisions. The flies were wealthy in honey. Yet they refused to share with the Prophet. In the result, they were condemned to a life spent crawling in the camel's manure. Islamic tradition not only encourages hospitality and generosity, but demands it. Rules have evolved through the centuries which guide Muslims on giving. For example, an owner of camels must give one sheep for every five camels, up to twenty-five camels, for the work of the faith. The owner of twenty-six camels must give one camel. Today, many salaried workers give two and a half percent of their annual income, a payment due at the end of *Ramadan*; but whether a Muslim pays is a matter strictly between him and Allah, for there are no civil laws enforcing this practice. As the Quran reads: "In the name of Allah, the Beneficent, the Merciful. Hast thou seen him who belies? That is the one who is rough to the orphan, and urges not the feeding of the needy (107:1-5)."

Back in his normal voice, Manaa says: "This is a good story for the children, so they not be greedy." He looks at me making certain I understand his English. I thank Manaa for telling me the story, grateful for this glimpse into his culture. I promise to myself that I will share this story with my future children.

Manaa takes his *masar* from his head, covers his eyes and lies back on the mat to sleep. I shoo away the flies and do the same.

Chapter Four

٥ شوال ١٤١٩
January 23, 1999
Thamarit

We are still missing a third of our riding team—the region's most renowned tracker, bin Ashara. So far, there's been no sign of him, save conversations around the fire. We are told that bin Ashara's tracking skills are founded on a photographic memory in which he stores the footprints of five thousand camels. Though the tracks of camels in the sand all look alike to me, they offer something more to the highly trained eye.

Bin Ashara is exceptional amongst the modern Bedu as he knows vastly more than do others. Today, these skills are less important to a Bedus' survival, but apparently bin Ashara still employs them with the camels he keeps. I thought there were no more men like Bin Ashara, and I am thrilled to meet this man of the past, someone Thesiger says no longer exists. It sounds as though he is one of the "wolves of the desert" whom Thesiger so vividly describes in his writings. If everything said about bin Ashara is true, he will be an astonishing addition to our team, contributing not only to our chances of success, but also to the cultural texture of our journey.

I suggested Manaa might take up bin Ashara's place on the team if need be, but Manaa is committed to managing the ground logistics and says he is not fit enough to ride with us in the desert. It has been longer than he can remember since he has ridden a camel any distance. "I should learn to ride again," he tells me, "so

I can teach my sons." Manaa also has undertaken a construction project that he wants to monitor—he is building some condominiums in town. Though Manaa no longer rides or lives in the desert, he shares with us all that he knows. So far he has been a great source of advice.

"You catch camel strong. Then like baby, soft, soft touching, soft talking"—this is Manaa's latest direction. One lesson is built upon another, and our knowledge grows each day as he adds more complexity to our training. Each time I work with my saddle the lines that pass behind T's genitals are still a source of trouble for the two of us. Ali comes to help with a broad smile, amused with my struggle. While we laugh together he helps me organize the lines without further agitating the camel.

Our rides have been only ninety minutes long, so far, which is plenty for us as we slowly become accustomed to the camels and the awkward riding. Leigh is making the best progress with Labian, whose name comes from *laban*—the word for milk. Bruce and I still struggle badly with Dancer and Mr. T.

Two *gerbers*—goatskins—arrive from the Nizwa in northern Arabia, where an elderly Bedu woman has taken weeks to fashion them. The old art of making these traditional bags for transporting water is known to few and is no longer common practice. We will have eight in total, but only these two for testing. Each *gerber* is made of an entire goat hide. Once slaughtered, the goat is carefully cleared of its innards through its rectum. No cut is made to the hide except at the end of the legs and at the neck, in order to optimize water volume. The hide is stripped of its hair and rubbed with fat. The entire skin is then turned inside out and all the openings, save the neck, are sewn closed. Manaa fills the two *gerbers* and hangs them on the tent. The bags leak profusely but, once the leather is saturated, they will seal. The leaking water smells foul.

Wanting to travel in the most traditional fashion possible, we are using *gerbers* in place of plastic jerry cans. In any event, Manaa explains, plastic containers are no good for our purposes. The plastic is prone to cracking, and deteriorates rapidly burning under the pounding sun. The containers are also difficult to store when empty, while the *gerbers* can be compressed and rolled up.

We finish a dinner of chicken and rice, and learn songs to sing to our camels. One is to be sung at night to relax them; another in the morning to wake them gently; yet another when watering them. Each song is quite distinct. The nighttime tune is calming, even to the singer. Arabic can seem harsh to the English ear when spoken, but the Bedu sound almost angelic when they sing to their camels. The songs we sing now condition the camels for later. For example, we may come upon water that is too brackish even for the camels to drink willingly. If we sing the familiar drinking song, the conditioned response of the camels will be to drink when otherwise they might not. The nighttime calming song was very important to past generations, as this is the song they would whisper to their camels during a raid to keep them calm and quiet for the approach.

The songs seem complex. The Bedu love to use intricate language, laden with adjectives. The Bedus' dedication to complicated verse dates back to pre-Islamic times when oral rather than written communication was used to convey messages over long distances. Says anthropologist Allan Keohane, "In comparison to the modern spoken Arabic of the cities, Bedu Arabic, especially in Southern Arabia, is much closer to the style of the Koran. It is a difference as great as that between modern colloquial English and Shakespearean verse."

All this makes the songs difficult to learn. The Bedu will teach us other songs for watering the camels and for feeding them. We will learn yet another to pace the camels when we are riding and to help us pass the time. Two are enough for now. The flies retreat to their evening perch on the camel ropes in our tent. We nestle into the fire's warmth while the last of the day's news is passed through the flickering light. When the flames die, the Bedu go into town, leaving us alone. Tomorrow we ride again.

The camels stand stoically in the corral. Most are chewing their cud. All of them are quiet except for one, who is scraping its teeth together with a high, loud pitch—a sign of distress.

Manaa points to a large camel whose knees have been damaged in the truck ride from the UAE, and the Bedu examine him. The camel must have come in a truck without padding and has therefore suffered for the sake of our adventure. Manaa wants the camel to couch, as it has not slept since his arrival. If it does not do this, it will be unable to rest, and this will further tax its system.

Manaa uses warm saltwater to wash away the dirt on the camel's knees. Sores twice the size of a silver dollar on each knee reveal themselves as the dark blood dissolves. The wounds are not deep, but the exposed flesh is clearly tender, since the camel kicks violently with every splash of water. Manaa is undeterred by the threat, and I marvel at his courage. He always shows great love for the camels and talks to them and touches them softly. Once dry, the wounds are rubbed with coconut oil. If the camel does not heal, he will not go with us, and we are keen on taking him since he is one of the stronger and better-behaved camels in the herd.

While the doctoring continues, Leigh, Bruce and I take the truck to Mohammed's house to re-pack. Our perspective about what we need and do not need is changing dramatically. We have 400 pounds of gear, and must cut it in half to make the loads manageable for the pack camels. Any redundant gear must be cut. This includes all comfort items. We discard hand cream, shampoo, conditioner, razor blades, shaving cream, aloe vera gel for sunburns. And deodorant. We will share one tube of toothpaste—sparingly. Each of us gets one pair of socks but we take only one pair of boots among us: Leigh's. They are a little big for me and a little small for Bruce—the perfect compromise. Each of us has the luxury of three pairs of underwear. We will each take one *dishdashah*, one polypropylene top and one pile jacket for cold nights, which may approach freezing. We keep our light sleeping bags and a half ration of sunscreen.

After much contemplation I decide to take two sentimental items: the balaclava and the Yoda Pez dispenser I took to the top of Everest. As a concession to childhood passion, I ate a lemon Pez on the summit. I take one packet of lime Pez for the desert. To this bit of clutter, I add my diary, a pen and pencil, a dictaphone, ten hours of recording tape and one extra 9-volt battery.

My personal gear now weighs twenty pounds and fits into a large stuff sack. The shared gear, including satellite communications equipment and cameras, yields one haul bag of equipment—170 pounds. The lighter load is emotionally liberating as it might have been for Thesiger as well, who had brought only a sleeping bag and one set of clothes—

> a coloured loincloth and a long shirt...My shirt was girded in at the waist with the belt of my heavy silver Omani dagger, so that I had a natural pocket between my shirt and my skin where I could carry my compass, a small notebook, and anything else I required...I had my rifle and cartridge belt. Inside my saddle-bags were spare ammunition, my camera, films, an aneroid and thermometer, a large notebook, a volume of Gibbon and *War and Peace*, a press for plants, a small medicine chest...and several bags of Maria Theresa dollars.

I finish some modifications to the Sony PC10 digital handi-cam Leigh and I will use to shoot while riding. The camera—$6000 of our precious expedition funds—is the size of a healthy paperback novel, but three times the weight. It is the same model I used shooting footage from the summit of Everest. It will be mounted on a telescoping pole for interesting angles from the back of Mr. T.

When we return to camp, Manaa busies himself spraying purple medication on the injured camel's knees, the camel protesting with kicks. Camels have surprising dexterity and a large range of motion with both front and rear legs. They can kick anywhere within a five-foot radius and, though their feet are softly padded, long toenails curl over each pad, adding sting to their kicks. When the can is empty, it is tossed aside. Its Arabic script is undecipherable. The nozzle smells of mercurochrome. This camel *has* to be named "Purple Knees." Manaa heads to the corral. Tapping his camel stick on the ground and lightly pulling on the reins, Manaa convinces Purple Knees to couch. For the first time in the eight days he has been with us, the camel is prone. Manaa ties his legs to keep him down, but it hardly seems necessary since the camel is fast asleep, his head stretched out on the ground ahead of his body. The camel will now rest for a few days while we continue to train.

"Manaa, you've helped the camel. Good job," I whisper.

"*Aiwa.*"

"What's its Arabic name?"

"It has no name."

"I think we should call him 'Purple Knees.' From the medication."

"*Aiwa*...Now we go for overnight ride."

"*Aiwa. Bokrah?*" Tomorrow?

"*Mafi Bokrah. Al ahn.*" Not tomorrow. Now.

I run over to Leigh and Bruce to announce the new plans. Bruce and I laugh as we run, gathering sleeping bags and cooking pots for the trip. Leigh isn't laughing.

The Bedu are keen to get going and yell at us to ready our camels. Leigh, following up on our deal with Nat Geo, wants to tape the departure, and tells me to wait for him to prep the gear. "*Suhail, taal, taal!*" Manaa bellows at me to get ready. The Bedu have little patience with the videotaping aspect of the expedition, but Leigh and I shoot what we can. I make videotaping motions to Manaa as if I am playing charades, and laugh at the awkward moment.

"Come on, Leigh, let's shoot the next one," I say, running off to get my camel.

"Hey! Are we shooting a film here or what?" he barks back while leading Labian.

"Look, they told me five times to get my camel."

We shoot a little and get ready.

Our scramble to prepare lasts about twenty minutes, and by four we are underway. Manaa has given Leigh, now the best rider among us, control of Labian. But the camel refuses to respond to Leigh's command to move faster in order keep up with the others. Still unable to control our own camels, Bruce and I are attached to Leigh's saddle via our camel's reins. This is our first overnight trip, and a crowd of visitors has joined us from Thamarit. They are now well ahead of us. Some are on camels, most in jeeps. All are out of sight.

Forty minutes into the ride, I mount the camera on the pole and film around the camels in an effort to familiarize them. Bruce's camel is suspicious, but seems okay. Mr. T twists his head around and is a little startled. He begins to buck and run, but Leigh gets Labian under control, and we slow to a stop—not the success I hoped for this first filming test.

We enter Wadi Dawkah, which runs into the *wadi* where we are camped. Dawkah cuts a shallow trough extending over a hundred miles to the northwest. It has more vegetation than our campsite, in the form of fern-like *saf*, and acacia trees that throw circular shadows with their perfect canopies.

As the adrenaline dissipates from the bucking episode, my muscles begin to ache. I also realize, uncomfortably, that I have torn my buttocks on the saddle, which is wet with blood. All I can do now is distract myself from the burning soreness by concentrating on the passing beauty. We ride among scattered acacia trees much older than their growth suggests. The severity of this place stunts their growth, as would the harsh environment of high mountains, where dwarf-like trees are found. A short growing season, limited nutrients, and little water slow their growth. The larger trees have branches that reach out horizontally for only three feet before thinning and bending toward the earth. There is inherent sadness in the way they droop to the ground. I quietly shoot our own phantom images undulating over the boulders and across the sand in the glare of the late afternoon sun.

By six we arrive at the new camp. It is only a two-hour ride, but I am thankful to see its end. The open lesions from the hard ride are a painful reminder of how frail we are in this desert. One's rear end is not a good place for an open sore, as constant riding would prevent it from healing, and an infection here could incapacitate me, causing delays in the whole expedition. I impose on my brother to inspect the hidden sores. He pronounces them "minor" and leaves me alone to self-medicate. I silently hope he never asks me to return the favour.

Just as I drop my *dishdashah* back into place, a couple of trucks join us and two goats materialize from within. The group assembles, facing Mecca to pray. Five young men, who'll have to pray later, chase after the goats, pinning the shrieking animals to the ground. The boys manoeuvre the animals until their throats face Mecca, the direction the group faces to pray. The knives are held by two of the older boys in such a way that the goats don't see them. Together, they make deep cuts across each neck in unison and dedicate the action to Allah. There is quiet again, save for the murmurs of men praying.

Wood is gathered and two fires lit. The group splits to gather around them. One fire is dedicated to tea-making and socializing, while the other is dedicated to serious cooking. The business of sipping tea and sharing the news proceeds while seven or eight Bedu move around a large pot containing the goats. It's interesting to witness the camp's organization. Everyone is enthusiastically engaged in getting a job done. The Bedu are impressive to watch, once they decide to undertake a task. The group is tightly focused, though there is no clear leadership. This contrasts with my own western experience, where an individual usually takes the lead and assigns tasks. In the thirty minutes we've been here, prayers have been completed, the goats slaughtered and now cooking, the tea has been prepared and consumed, and the news has been shared.

I watch the fire and see its orange flame twisting with each new blast of wind. When it does blow, the wind gusts for a few hours each day in the late afternoon. The Bedu have specific terms to describe wind character and direction. Wind in general is called *habob*. A north wind is called *shamal*. This is what we have tonight. This evening's *shamal* has a little more power than usual and disturbs the tranquility of our evening gathering. It fans the fires, pushes the smoke toward us, and leaves our eyes teary and smarting. Still, the *shamal* is not strong enough to blow away the flies. What little has been left behind of the two goat carcasses—skin, hooves and a few glands—teems with flies engorging themselves. When I try to drag them away from camp, Musallim tells me not to worry. "Perhaps a wolf will come and eat them in the night."

Surrounding acacia trees are outlined against the darkening sky as the light fades to black, and the desert day suddenly ends. In the distance, I can just make out a stray camel standing beneath a tree. It is not one of ours. Stretching its neck upward, it chews on the branches: the reason why all the branches grow to a uniform height above the ground—camel topiary. This must be frustrating for young camels not yet tall enough to reach these pruned branches. But, then, little is easy in the desert.

A brilliant half moon illuminates the ground, a pale but welcome imitation of the harsh light of day. We are camped next to a patch of hardy reeds that sway in the wind. The smooth, waxy surface of each strand reflects the moon when a strong gust of the *shamal* bends it far enough. The rustle of the reeds softens the harsh voices darting across the fires. The cooking fire, as distinct from the other, social one, seems to be the locale of the most animated conversation. Though no one stays around it for any appreciable length of time, the cooking fire is always surrounded by seven or eight people. Someone is always cycling from the social fire to add their culinary direction to the amorphous group attending to the boiling goats. The cultural tradition of speaking one's mind pervades all aspects of Bedu life, including cooking. No one seems to be in charge, but everyone has something to offer and an obligation to do so. When someone is satisfied with the progress, or disgusted with it, they head back to the chat sessions at the other fire.

The Bedu frequently remove the lid of the cooking pot to taste the broth and inspect the meat. This always sparks an impassioned debate and the addition of rice or spices to the brew. The amount to add is hotly contested. Some shout for more, others for less, but in the end the man with his hands on the spice bag listens to no one and controls the amount himself. When the lid is replaced, the conversation continues with a flourish of hand gestures toward the pot. Several new people from the other fire join while others head back to it. The new cooks always take up a fork or a stick and want to look into the brew. This creates more controversy, sometimes ending in another peek into the pot. Conversation and arguments rise and fall seamlessly, uninterrupted by silence.

The words tumble out of their mouths so fast I recognize one word in a hundred and guess at the rest:

"Musallim, add another stick—the fire is too low."

"No, you fool. That will burn the rice."

"But we need more heat for the meat to cook."

Someone else: "What of the salt, let me taste the broth—I'm certain it needs more salt."

"Leave it be. We can add salt once the rice has time to cook."

"In the name of God, will you let me taste the broth?"

"More water is needed."

"Are you mad? We must add more rice."

The lid is finally removed and the broth tasted by four men.

"Onions! Where are the onions?"

"No, no, no. Tomatoes. It needs more tomatoes, not onions."

"Pull out that log—it needs to simmer to cook the marrow."

"Any more simmering and I won't eat the rice."

After another taste: "Ah-ha! I told you this needs more salt. Give me the salt."

"In the name of Allah, not a grain more salt."

The cooking goes on like this for another twenty minutes, then the food is pulled from the fire and dished out onto the pot lids. Two groups circle around the food.

"Bismilla," we all say and dig in. *Praise be to God.*

The rice is perfect—well cooked but still firm. The meat is tender and flavourful. I have eaten nothing since my dates at breakfast. We waste little time. No one stops to talk. Everything is eaten—brains and tongue, intestines and stomach. The intestine is particularly interesting, not in taste, but in texture. It is like hollow spaghetti, cooked al dente. Stomach is not my favourite because its taste is that of grass and its consistency that of squid. But I enjoy chewing bits of the smooth cartilage found deep in the hip socket.

We wash the pots with sand. Not a single grain of rice is burned at the bottom of pots. The camels finish the last of our rice from the pot and then work the sand beneath them into a soft bed for the night. The crowd gathers about the fire for coffee. Our party of six has now swelled to twenty-eight, and our eleven camels are now outnumbered by jeeps—all driven by friends of our team. Many come from Thamarit and Salalah.

Manaa tells us a story. Kindly, he shares each section in both Arabic and English. "I was young boy, same like Tanuf [his son of seven]. My father and me come to this wadi. Our no-good camel is here. Very, very mean and strong. This is the camel for my father for many years."

The group sits and listens quietly. Someone asks a question and Manaa answers in Arabic. I think his father had caught his errant camel three days before, but it escaped again after a bout of kicking and biting.

"He try control this camel very hard." Manaa works his arms as if he is wrestling the camel. "But still he run away. Again we try to catch this camel with food. Soft, soft. Slow, slow." Manaa starts whispering and moves his body and arms like a cat sneaking up on a mouse. "Slow. Soft. Like baby."

He returns to Arabic, his face aflame in the yellow light of the fire. With a flurry of arms, Manaa shows how his father had grabbed the camel. *"Manaa, taal, taal!"* he shouts, mimicking his father, who needs a rope to hobble the camel. "Now we have the camel and my father gives to me for hold. He get other camels and I wait. My father goes one kilo and is gone from camel's eyes. Now camel go crazy and want to kill me," Manaa says, lifting his arms to protect his head from the blows of the camel. The group is now too large to sit around the fire in a circle. Some stand and lean forward on their rifles. Sparks rise up and illuminate their attentive faces, then swirl away in the breeze.

Manaa continues. "The camel try to kick me and I run, but the camel come in front of me and stop me. Then I run to the small hill to get away, but he get in front of me again. I was crying and running and running and yelling for my father. One hour my father comes back and shout and the camel sit down fast. He hit the camel and tied it to a tree. We leave it there all night. The next day he comes back and loads this camel with water and equipment to punish it. He ride it out into the desert. This was a very strong camel. My father come back in three days."

"Why did the camel want to hurt you?" someone asks.

"My father hit him the first time and the camel remembers. He is angry with my father want to kill me." Looking at us, he adds, "Be nice to your camels. If you are angry, they remember. If you are soft, they remember."

This story of a camel's memory makes good sense to me. Male camels will try to return to the place of their birth, and female camels will seek the place of birth of their first offspring. For this reason, a female that has not yet given birth is more valuable than one that has, as the latter will forever run from its new owner to return "home."

My homing instinct feels equally strong at this moment, but home is much further away, and the level of activity here leaves little time to dwell on it. Here we are governed by the rise and fall of the sun, by our thirst and hunger, by our need to study the ways of the Bedu. I suspect Sir Wilfred was quite right when he wrote: "No man can live this life and emerge unchanged. He will carry, however faint, the imprint of the desert, the brand which marks the nomad." What mark, I wonder, will it leave on us?

Chapter Five

The wind has blown all night, and this morning we are cold and miserable. No one moves much, and everyone seems tired from last night's long conversations. The Bedu are all wrapped tightly in their blankets, no one wanting to move from the fire, which Ali refuels with a twisted branch.

There is no evident schedule to the morning. It starts with much talk and more tea drinking. The Bedu telegraph no signs of impending action. There are no leisurely stretches, no *Well, we'd better get going*. One moment they sit, sipping tea, looking as if they might fall asleep and the next they are in a panic. Suddenly, there is great commotion, and everyone is up, hurrying to get underway. I am accustomed to the mountain way. Morning departures from mountain camps are usually calm affairs, conducted in silence. On Everest there were no braying animals to manage. Everyone knew what to do, and when there was confusion our Sherpa friends spoke softly in typical Buddhist fashion.

The Bedu, on the other hand, have only two gears: full stop and full speed. Once the decision is made to move—I'm not sure by whom—everyone sets forth in a great rush. I have been caught off guard on more than one occasion, watching the entire Bedu crew mount up and make headway in the time I take to brush my teeth. Though stressful, these cultural differences delight me, and I don't want to impose my own cultural perceptions about the use of time. If we are to truly live among the Bedu, we must be prepared to surrender to their ways.

This morning, in the effort to adapt, I set myself a steady pace of preparation. I keep careful watch on the group at the fire to note any abrupt action that could mark the race to leave. This is a little nerve-wracking. I have yet to master saddling Mr. T quickly. Neither have I mastered how to pack my saddlebags, or how to determine precisely what gear to take with Mr. T and me, and what to leave on the pack animals. In previous panicky departures, I have left without my camel stick or sunscreen or even crucial parts of my saddle, like the *soof*—the sheepskin on which I sit for padding. In time, I imagine, this all will become second nature. I might even sit about the fire at one with the Bedu. But for now I fuss.

My gear finally ready, I have some coffee and dates with the group. They still appear to be far from leaving, so I relax and warm my hands on the hot glass cup. Bruce and Leigh are here, and Bruce tosses one of his date pits into the fire. Manaa speaks to him in Arabic. "You should never throw the date pits into the fire," Manaa says as he leans forward and works the pit out of the coals with a stick. Thesiger was told the same by his Bedu friend Tamtaim, but he never explained why. Manaa does: "You know Mary? She is the Mother of Jesus. She birth Jesus and is very, very tired. After Jesus is coming, Mary sit by this fire to be warm. This fire is under a tree. Mary is very tired and hungry. Very tired and hungry, no more strong. God sees Mary and shake the tree."

Wrapped in blankets, Manaa leaves only his face visible. But under the wool I can see his hands helping to tell the tale while he tries to keep the blanket tight around his head. I carefully toss a pit beyond the fire and keep listening.

"From the tree fall *tamar*, brown like the sand and the camel. So easy to eat and full of *sucre*." Manaa has taken French lessons and often uses French words when speaking English. "These are good for bad stomach and full of good for you. Mary eats the dates and become good again. God told Mary this date has a stone in the middle. 'Never throw in the fire,' God said. 'Put them in the floor so can come other trees and more people can eat.' So, Salah, you be like Mary and put this in the sand."

I am thinking about what I can learn from the lesson in the story—do not break the circle of life; enter it and leave it, but never harm it—when, as expected, the group abruptly adjourns the breakfast social and loads up. In minutes we are underway.

For the six miles back to the main camp, Bruce and I are tied into Labian and Leigh again. Musallim is already gone, and Ali is coming behind us. Manaa is packing up his truck and will follow. I think about what I need to do with my gear when I get back to camp. Suddenly, Labian is running. I don't know whether something has spooked him, or whether he is still angered at the yelling yesterday, or maybe tired of the camels tied on behind him, but off he goes carrying us along in his fearsome rush. Labian becomes more and more agitated. He bucks to the side and accelerates. In seconds we are at a full gallop. Just holding on is a struggle. Leigh hollers at Labian, hoping to slow him, but the camel does not respond. I pull on T's reins with all my strength, but he, too is upset and refuses to slow down. Labian pulls T along regardless of what he wants to do. I bounce up and down in the saddle, holding as much of T's mane as I can gather in both hands.

I shout to Bruce, who is slightly back to my right, but he doesn't answer. Looking over, I see he is barely holding on. Our speed is frightening, the ground now only a blur beneath us. He bounces so hard I can no longer breathe properly. I lean forward and try to cushion the bounce with my arms.

Leigh uses both his hands to hold on. He can no longer get an arm free to pull the reins and slow Labian down. The bouncing is too violent to hold on with one hand, and he would need two hands on the reins to pull Labian's head back enough to make him stop.

Our camels are right behind Labian. If Leigh loses his hold, he'll be injured by the fall itself or by the camels' trampling. My arms are burning; I am weakening rapidly. T cuts left, then right, bucking as he runs. I fall off one side and then he cuts back again. This catches my fall and throws me to the other side. Through no effort of my own, I bounce back on top.

"I can't hold on! I'm gonna fall!" Leigh shouts.

"Hang on. Hang on. Hang on. You can do it," I'm shouting at myself as much as at Leigh.

I look back to try to see whether the Bedu have seen our plight, but the bouncing makes it too hard to discern whether they are behind. I look left to scout for soft ground, thinking jumping the only option. But it is still all boulders off the trail, and I cannot leave Leigh.

I call out, "They'll get tired! They're gonna stop!"

Suddenly, Ali is waving his arms as he chases after us on his camel. The truck! Manaa is in the truck, swerving through the sand fifty yards behind us to the left.

"Leigh! Hold on!...Here...comes Manaa!"

I check for Bruce only to find he is gone. He has fallen off. I can see him in a blur behind us as he rolls on the road. Alarmed by Bruce's fall, I can only hope he has not broken anything in his fall on the rocky ground.

Manaa's truck engine roars when he catches air, bouncing across the wadi in time with us. He is trying to get up front to cut off the camels.

My head snaps forward and smacks on T's hump. My arms are too tired to protect my face any longer. I am losing the feeling in my hands and arms. My groin slams against T's hump, the pain producing a new nausea.

The truck is beside us now. The engine roars again, and the truck fishtails through the sand. Manaa guns the vehicle, steers the truck across the shoulder of the road and pulls in front of us. The camels stop running.

I sit frozen atop T, breathing heavily, trying to calm down. Bruce is now walking toward us, and thankfully shows no sign of damage. Leigh jumps down and walks around. He shakes out his legs and clasps his hands. I stay on board, not wanting to have to get back on again later.

"Is everybody okay?" Bruce asks, his voice shaky. We nod but say nothing. Manaa is upset and is already lecturing Leigh for not controlling Labian. Ali is speaking soft Arabic to Labian. I remember Manaa's stories of camels and their memories, wondering whether Labian's foul mood today is the result of our arguing and yelling around him yesterday during filming. Does he sense we were yelling at him?

Manaa suggests we make use of Labian's nose ring. Ali ties a thin rope to a ring through the camel's tender nose skin. This rope is long enough that Leigh can hold it along with the reins. By pulling on the rope gently, Leigh can get his camel's immediate attention. This will ensure that Labian will obey Leigh's commands.

Ali rides with us, giving us a little extra confidence, and we all return to the camp uneventfully, talking loudly of the escapade, flushed with nervous energy.

٨ شوال ١٤١٩
January 26, 1999 Thamarit

Each of us is a little crippled from yesterday's camel races. Foolishly, we tell Manaa we would have been all right, that the camels would have tired out and stopped. He looks at us, realizing the depth of our ignorance, and says, "No, no, no. These camels can go like this for three days!" We say nothing, returning sullenly to the fire.

Manaa changes our riding program without discussion, making no attempt to explain the changes to us. He seems quite fearful of another dangerous camel incident. He just keeps waving his hands above his head, shouting that we "need rest" or there will be "more trouble later," then leaves without further explanation. Perhaps he wants to give the camels a break from our inexperienced handling. I look to Bruce for some guidance about what we should do next. He shrugs.

Musallim goes to his truck, producing a faux leather rifle bag and a box of shells. He pulls out a .308 and sits in the sand near our tent and busies himself with his weapon. The three of us decide to nap before the day gets too hot. I find a spot in the tent where I can still see Musallim through the door. He sits with his back to me, the rifle in his lap, the leather rifle bag drooping lazily over his thighs.

Thesiger was surprised to discover that Bedu men always carried their rifles with them. He wrote that he was often concerned about the possibility of attack from the marauders who swept the edges of the desert from the more remote regions of Arabia. Like the Bedu, Thesiger soon became accustomed to carrying a gun himself. The rifle came late to Bedu society. Until the beginning of the 1900s, the Bedu largely engaged in hand-to-hand combat, often using the same *khanjar* knives they continue to wear today.

In the 1600s, swords imported from Europe or made by local blacksmiths became the favoured weapons. When the Bedu adopted lances, their camel saddles were engineered for greater stability to improve raiding efficiency. The Arabic word *shadad*—saddle—comes from *shadid*, meaning *firm*, which is how the Bedu raider needed to be anchored to his camel in order to fight well.

Rifles started arriving in the desert only in the latter part of the 1800s, and even then only wealthy townsmen and desert *sheikhs* owned them. After the Boer War ended in 1902, a trade of surplus arms passed through Masqat, transported on great caravans, two hundred camels strong, carrying as much as a thousand guns, into the desert for sale. After the First World War, rifles became widespread in Arabia, as did casualties. The mortality rate of raids and warfare dramatically increased. T.E. Lawrence described the huge casualties of desert warfare owing to the lack of natural cover provided in the desert. Raiding with guns might have wiped out the Bedu, had it not been outlawed by Abd al-Aziz ibn Saud, the ruler of Saudi Arabia in the early 1900s.

The new weapons made killing humans and animals easier. Ostrich, gazelle, and oryx become far more accessible to the rifle-armed hunter. Though bin Saud's prohibition may have helped the Bedu survive, it did little to prevent most large game animals from being wiped out in large parts of the peninsula.

Raiding is now nonexistent. There is no real concern among our team that we will encounter tribal bandits, as Thesiger might have, far into the sands. But there is concern for our safety, a concern fuelled by the killing last month of three Brits and one Australian in Yemen by a Muslim extremist group.

Jamie and Leigh explore Jordan's Wadi Rum, 1990.

Chomolungma Everest reveals her majestic
North Face—sunset 1994.

3

A weathered "wolf of the desert".

4

Elder with rifle—a vital tool of desert life.

5

Bin Ashara brews tea—his way.

6

Bedu woman in traditional attire.

7

Manaa listens to the wisdom of an elder.

Tying the **masar** —traditional headwear of the Bedu.

Nose kiss. This greeting between Bedu men is one of warmth, respect, and trust.

Sharing the adventure with students, via the internet.

The timelessness of the camel caravan—a scene evocative of ages gone by.

Salim Ali shows his expertise as he pursues and captures a runaway camel.

16

Leigh studies the route.

17

Jamie captures footage for National Geographic.

18

Omani camel saddle.

19

Jamie saddles up
Mr. T

Early days of training near Thamarit.

Jamie rests in the blistering midday heat.

22

Bruce and Manaa
ponder the path.

23

Leigh has a bad headwrap
day while sorting gear.

24

Feasting with Manaa's
sons, ending the fast of
Ramadan.

25

Ali makes **khobz**, a
Bedu staple.

Gahwa—coffee, served
Bedu style.

Crossing Arabia's Empty Quarter
1200 kilometers by camel
February - March 1999
Jamie Clarke   Ali Bin Salim
Leigh Clarke   Salim Bin Ashara
Bruce Kirkby   Musallim Bin Abdu

" No man can live this life and emerge unchanged.
He will carry, however faint, the imprint of the desert, the brand which marks the nomad... for this cruel land can cast a spell which no temperate clime can match."
Sir Wilfred Thesiger, "Arabian Sands"

A commemorative photo spread—for the sponsors.

A Bedouin World

Artwork from a schoolchild who followed via the internet.

Jamie visits with students.

Before coming to the desert, I had learned from my readings that Bedu males are attached to their weapons and carry them as if they were an extension of their personality. My own limited experience with arms came in high school as part of the trap and skeet club. With 4-10s and 12-gauge shot guns we destroyed clay pigeons flung from concrete bunkers. I was just an average shot, struggling in my general discomfort with guns, when a near-tragedy struck. Standing in line, unattended only for a moment, a student on the firing line swung around to laugh at a joke and his 4-10 discharged into a classmate's right shoulder. The school staff raced the wounded boy to hospital in a truck, leaving us locked in shock, staring at the bloodied ground. My eyes checked the earth again and again, tracing the path of blood to where it ended in the skid marks of the spinning wheels. Long after the roar of the truck's racing engine had disappeared, I could still hear it. The prairie dust drifted listlessly across us and my stomach turned.

My classmate lived, but only after hours under the surgical knife and days clinging to life in intensive care. If the pellet cluster had struck an inch to the right or if it had dispersed, my friend would likely have bled to death. We all knew it could have been any one of us. My interest in weapons was lost.

More than fifteen years after the shooting incident, the desert trek ahead of me, I still harboured the distant fears that day had provoked. I needed to get past them. The knowledge that weapons literacy would be useful for desert travel with the Bedu convinced me that I must learn how to handle a gun.

Ignorance—such as my ignorance of guns—breeds fear, and this was not a fear I wanted to feel. I paid for a thorough and professional arms training session in the southwestern U.S. before the expedition. Afterward I felt much more at ease with firearms, but knew also that if we got into a scrape, I would likely forget all that I had learned, thrash around in a panic, and be killed before I had a chance to take aim. I am hoping my new skills will not be tested. But judging by the way Musallim is fastidiously cleaning his rifle, I've a feeling I might be wrong.

The day is waning and it has become obvious that the Bedu are not interested in any more training sessions for the moment.

The three of us decide on some "R & R" in Salalah. After a helter-skelter jeep ride, we find the perfect beach. Bruce and I body surf while Leigh reads Tolstoy's *War and Peace*, the very volume Thesiger took into the desert for distraction. We find some delectable Omani fast food and head back to camp, not knowing what tomorrow might hold.

Chapter Six

١٠ شوال ١٤١٩
January 28, 1999
Wadi Dawkah

Yesterday's training went well. Leigh has bonded anew with Labian.

Though Manaa's original plan had us training here until the 24th, we're not overly concerned about the delay. Our camels' late arrival, and some real cultural and language barriers, are understandably causing change to the schedule. Our greater concern is for the whereabouts of our third team member, who has yet to appear. Bin Ashara, the desert dweller and renowned tracker, cannot be found. Even his son has been searching. Bin Ashara was to have been here a month before us, training the camels. He is known to go off into the desert to herd his camels for months at a time with little word to anyone. Bin Ashara is to be our chief navigator through 700 miles of the Rub al Khali. Without him, we are lost. We still hope to begin the crossing on the first of February—*Inshallah.*

Today is our last overnight training ride—we are off to Wadi Dawkah. We have become more proficient on the camels, and this ride is going much better than our last—a boost to our confidence. Our backs become more accustomed to the camels' pounding gait, but whether our thighs ever harden, or our seat muscles strengthen—these are other questions.

The sun is already sinking and the landscape's textures around us come to life with shadows quite absent in the full light of day. Airborne dust reddens the sky, and my camel casts an elongated shadow over the sand. There's a sense we are settling into the rhythm of desert life, sliding into circadian patterns, the rise and fall of the sun as our measure of time. In a report to the students, Bruce puts it nicely: "It's a wonderful feeling to drop behind all the worldly possessions that encumber us at times, and live only with the basics."

I've brought along one of our VHF radios to test as we ride. When the prearranged call comes from camp, the voice startles T and he bucks me off. Later a lizard skitters along beside the group, spooking T, who bucks me off again. After things have calmed down, I pull out my camera to shoot the sunset. When the last of the frames is exposed, the camera rewinds automatically. The sharp whirring of the drive startles the camels and we're off again. Not wanting to drop the camera, I hold the reins with one hand and again I'm sent flying, cradling the camera as I hit the ground and roll.

Near dark, we stop and unload the camels, collect firewood, cook some goat meat, and sit in the sand to drink tea while we make dinner. Six-thirty p.m., and we have ridden eleven miles. Once evening prayers are said, we begin to eat a rich stew. We all sit in a circle around the pile of food, pulling knives from our pockets to cut the larger pieces. I carve at the cartilage stuck to the hipbones, which I now quite enjoy. It tastes like hardened calamari. Musallim is my carnivore tutor. He's a master. I marvel at him in the light of the fire as he works contentedly with his knife. He takes a piece of meat from the fire, bites a piece in his teeth and gives it a pull. In his left hand he holds the thighbone, in his right the eight-inch knife he is never without. He carefully cuts the tendon stretched between mouth and bone.

I work on a femur, myself, till I'm certain nothing edible remains. Before I throw it beyond the fire, Musallim stops me and takes the bone. He cuts for another few minutes and pulls away more meat then he taps the bone steadily with his knife until it finally cracks. Applying his foot for better purchase on the bone, he uses his knife to pop the bone apart, revealing a long vein of marrow, which he slurps down like a spaghetti noodle. He follows the marrow with a date and some rice, tossing the spent bones back over his shoulder, completing the rough, hardy image of a desert-dwelling man.

Our little group around the fire breaks up when a truck full of visitors arrives unannounced. They have followed our tracks to find us in the desert. Immediately, Ali, Manaa, and the others stop eating, not because they are done, but because we have only brought enough food for ourselves, and they must offer their acquaintances something to eat. Leigh, Bruce and I also stand to greet the guests, who are given our places around the plate of food and begin to eat. They eat only half of what food remains and then insist they are satiated. Could this happen at home? Could visitors arrive at a North American house at dinnertime and see the entire family step away from their table? This Bedu generosity makes me feel I have never properly hosted anyone in my home before.

The group shares tea and a round of chat, largely in Arabic, which still escapes me, and presently our guests leave. We eat a little more and stare into the fire. Our team before the flames makes a desert tableau as timeless as the generous code of these people. Over my shoulders the camels sit in pools of grey shadow. A moth crawls near the fire, taking sudden flight in the smoke and rising heat. Manaa tells us we are ready to begin the crossing.

١١ شوال ١٤١٩
January 29, 1999 Thamarit

We are now certain of the three camels we will ride. All three are males, which is unusual. Female camels are generally preferred for riding, owing to calmer temperament and better endurance. Males are more aggressive and tire more easily, though they can carry larger loads for shorter distances. Because of their lesser value, most males are killed for food shortly after birth. Female camels are preserved and prized because they reproduce, eat less and, most importantly, give milk. Often the only nourishment for Bedu families during long marches in the past, camel's milk offers almost twice the vitamins and calories of a cow's. If a female camel is properly cared for, an owner can keep it in milk indefinitely and live on nothing else for months at a time. Outweighing the Bedu by fifty pounds each, Leigh, Bruce and I need stronger camels to carry us. The gelded males we ride may be the perfect compromise between strength and endurance.

We have added "Crazy" to Dancer's name because he still shifts or dances compulsively from leg to leg when at rest. We have begun singing while feeding them, since Manaa has told us camels like singing. At the start of each day I sing the same song to Mr. T, because the camels find comfort in familiar sounds. *Frère Jacque* is the song my French-Canadian grandmother, Thérèse, sang to me as a boy, so I sing it, assuming it will offer T the same comfort. Bruce sings the Huron Carol and Leigh, the musician, sings an eclectic collection of ballads for camel bonding, drawing on Neil Young as his main inspiration.

The Bedu say that when we become friends with our camels, they will become loyal and protective—even in the face of a threat from another human or a camel. "Be strong when you catch your camel," Manaa says. "But after, be very soft—like with a baby. Do everything slow, slow, soft, soft."

۱۲ شوال ۱٤۱۹
January 30, 1999 Thamarit

Tomorrow we leave for Salalah. Today, camels and humans alike enjoy a day of rest. We pack the rest of our gear and let our saddle sores heal. The Bedu express their doubts about our chances of getting across the desert. We're told the journey is impossible even by truck, let alone by camel, due to the twelve-year drought in the region. Normally, sporadic rains would produce enough patches of feed to graze the animals. Through the intricacies of word-of-mouth communication, the Bedu would share the news of grazing locations. As Thesiger discovered, the Bedus' thirst for news is insatiable—and justly so, as their lives depended on this information. The rumour mill grinds out information still today, and we learn there is extraordinarily little grazing in the sands through which we are to pass.

Our initial plan was to leave the coast at Salalah with all our supplies and to depend on the wells for water, without using outside assistance. This was a considerable stretch, as even Thesiger needed encounters with nomad families for milk and meat. But the chance of meeting a nomadic encampment in this part of the Arab world has vanished, the nomadic life long passed. The Bedu have supplanted it, for better or worse, with a more sedentary existence. We will encounter no one else this deep in the sands.

I begin to question the way we are operating here in the desert. We struggle daily to impose our will in the form of the plan, albeit agreed to initially by Manaa, on the Bedu and in fact on nature. Admittedly, the conditions in the heart of the Quarter will dictate how and whether we cross or not. Why do we think we can force our way across the sands? I never did think of "conquering" Everest. In 1994 our climbing team was beaten down by winds that could not be ignored without incurring insane risk. Even Thesiger acknowledged the supremacy of nature in determining the lives of the desert tribes: "A cloud gathers, the rain falls, men live; the cloud disperses without rain, and men and animals die."

Yet I struggle with my expectations, wanting them not to colour my experience so much that I lose the value of what we are able to achieve. Rather than becoming angry at changes in the plan, perhaps we need to learn instead that our expectations are just not possible, that we're being unreasonable.

The latest information we have indicates that the drought in the eastern half of the Empty Quarter is so severe that there are simply no pockets of vegetation for the camels. The Bedu want two trucks to follow us where the ground will allow, to guarantee food and water for the camels. We agree to this plan for the first leg of the journey, from Salalah to Shisur, a ruined city ninety miles northwest of Salalah, where we will take stock again. Doing this enables us to travel lightly through the mountain passes. Personally, I am just as happy not to have the camels loaded on the first leg, as our riding skills decidedly need more work.

Two young Bedu men who frequented camp during our training sessions have been selected by Manaa as the truck drivers.

Salim bin Ali is the fast-footed fellow who chased down the run-away camel Taynoonah. Tuarish bin Salim is the brother of our teammate Ali. They will shadow the first part of our journey in the trucks.

١٣ شوال ١٤١٩
January 31, 1999 Salalah

Though we are ready by eight, it's noon before Musallim arrives at the wheel of the truck. But before we begin loading the camels, Musallim announces he will not be coming with us. He tells us the three thousand dollars a month he is receiving to do this journey is too little for him. This is utterly unexpected, and conjures up my memories of our Tibetan yak herders threatening to drop our supplies a mile short of our Advanced Base Camp below Everest. The herders said the yaks were too tired to continue. Somehow more money gave the yaks new energy. This is classic posturing, and I have seen it everywhere from mountains to movie sets. While a teenager, I worked as one of the principal actors on an American BMX bike movie *Rad*, shot in Canada in 1985. In the midst of shooting the movie's climactic stunt, with a huge crew standing by, high-speed cameras in place, the stuntman balked. He pulled director Hal Needham aside and demanded more cash as he talked about added risks. The stuntman got his way.

I didn't expect Musallim to pull this stunt on us. He is a crucial member of the team, we tell him. And we very much want to complete the journey with him. But the deal is the deal, and we have no more money to pay. No sooner do we begin loading the remaining camels than another truck appears and out jumps a man. He looks at us and breaks into a welcoming smile. Ali runs to greet the man, shouting to us as he does: "Bin Ashara!"

Good timing, I think, still locked in shock from Musallim's announcement. I stride over to meet the famed bin Ashara, our team navigator. His shock of grey hair makes him look older than his stated age of 45 years. His skin is dark and weathered from the elements. Here is the renowned tracker, one of the very few southern Bedu who still lives a semblance of the old nomadic life. It is rumoured that he owns more than a hundred camels, though no one will say for certain, as that would bring bad luck.

Bin Ashara is just his nickname. Salim bin Musallim bin Haramarsh el Kathiri is his actual name. *Ashara* means *ten* in Arabic, and the nickname was given to him when he fathered his tenth son. Shockingly, this number does not account for his daughters, who often are not included when a man mentions the number of children he has.

Bin Ashara has had more children since gaining the nickname, but the name stuck. He is obviously a close friend of Musallim and Ali—they share affectionate greetings. Moments before, Musallim was filled with the gloom of his impending departure. Now he is filled with excitement as he talks animatedly to his famous friend. We approach the group, shake hands, and share names. Bin Ashara laughs when we announce our Arabic nicknames. When I meet him he holds my hand after shaking it and looks into my eyes. Though he is openly examining me, I feel no discomfort. There is a special way about him—bin Ashara is confident without being arrogant. Dignified. Calm. He offers no explanation for his late arrival, and sets about loading the camels.

The day is half over. It has been filled with awkward preparations and dizzying human relations. We can do little about any of it and learn simply to go with the flow. There is no wind and the temperature is nearly 113 degrees. Heat has finally beaten modesty. Everyone joins bin Ashara and strips to their *wasirs* to load the camels. We will take only half of the herd with us, leaving the pack camels to join us after the first training leg to Shisur. This way the pack camels will be spared the dangers of traveling through the busy streets of Salalah and we only have to attend to only one camel each.

Reluctantly, the animals take their place in the truck box. The truck box is lined with straw, so the ride should be soft, though unnerving for them. The work takes about an hour to complete. Then we all jump into the trucks and head off. When we stop for gasoline, the camels appear comfortable and are eating their bedding.

An hour later we arrive in Salalah and unload our special cargo on the beach, to the sound of crashing waves. Salalah was built upon the medieval city of Zufar, which thrived as a trade centre between the tenth and fifteenth centuries. It is the capital of Dhofar province, and some think it the region of "Ophir," mentioned in the Bible as a place from which Solomon's ships brought gold and jewels.

Thesiger described Salalah as "a small town, little more than a village [which] lies on the edge of the sea and has no harbour... The Sultan's palace, white and dazzling in the strong sunlight, was the most conspicuous building, and clustered around it was the small suq or market, a number of flat-roofed mud-houses, and a labyrinth of mat shelters, fences, and narrow lanes." In Thesiger's time it was not unusual to see Bedu returning from the desert to trade camel's milk for dates and coffee.

Little remains of the Salalah Thesiger knew. Navigating our camels through the maze of noisy paved streets to get out of town will not be easy. Many of the narrow streets, though now paved, were obviously never intended for automobiles, and any vehicle traffic causes congestion. For all its changes, Salalah remains a charming shipping town of 150,000. The city now sprawls along the coast, with several major roads running parallel to the beach connecting its neighbourhoods. To the west of the city the coast curves around to the Bay of Raysut, where we can see large ships docked in a modern harbour. Sailors have landed here from India and Africa over thousands of years. Members of the Omani Royal Family ruled Zanzibar, off the east coast of Africa, until 1964. Leigh and I visited Zanzibar during our 1990 trip. The people of this island of spices have intermingled with the Dhofaris, as can be seen in the physical features of both the islanders and some of the Dhofaris.

Just as it was for Thesiger, Salalah is our ground zero—the starting point. At two in the afternoon we drop the camels off on the beach, much to the amazement of several German businessmen staying at an adjacent condominium complex. The camels have traveled well and remain remarkably calm despite their new surroundings. They are oddly serene about disconcerting moments like this, but become tremendously excited at times of apparent tranquility. As well as much more, they are lovable for their enduring patience with our silliness.

The beach is chaotic, with our team unloading camels, saddles and bags of gear. I can barely contain my excitement, running about from task to task, settling the camels and leading them safely to the water for a bath and a stretch. Leigh, Bruce, and I take the camels to the water's edge and let the ocean wash their hooves. Some are fearful of the surf, others indifferent, and a couple even enjoy it. This seems so typical of their unpredictability and distinct personalities. Mr. T couches easily while I splash water along his flank to wash away the dust of the truck ride, and he seems to like the larger waves. I tell him that this reward awaits him again some 700 miles north on the other side of the desert. We then take the camels further along the beach, where we find a resting spot among date trees at the ocean's edge. The rustling leaves and crashing waves add a wonderful mood to our work organizing the gear.

The Bedu choose to sleep with friends in town. Instead of accepting the management's invitation to stay at the nearby Holiday Inn, we choose to sleep among the camels to keep an eye on them. Soon, we're under a moon so bright I can easily read the face of my watch.

I am beginning to feel more and more connected with these incredible beasts—sensing their moods, their complex personalities. I know now this comes only with time, and with patience. It's like trying to hurry a friendship—impossible. Quantity of time leads to quality of relationship. Unfortunately, one of the camels is filling the air with loud flatulence and a foul stench, a sign of its being upset from the ride. Crazy Dancer and Lucy, named for my little sister, are being extremely friendly. Mr. T is couched and sleeping, as is Kicker. Labian, whose stomach was also erupting during the truck ride, has finally settled and is near sleep.

Inspired by the desert walk Leigh and I took in Jordan nine years ago, and after eighteen months of planning this expedition, we are about to begin. Tomorrow we cross the plains of Salalah and camp at the base of the Qara Mountains. Next day, we pick a route through the formidable cliffs of this impressive coast range, and ride to the Pool of Ayun. There, we will take water just as Thesiger did, then step into the fringes of the Empty Quarter. Our desert adventure has begun.

Chapter Seven

١٥ شوال ١٤١٩

February 2, 1999
Divide of Qara Mountains

Day 1 — 17 00' N 54 08' E

Our hope for an early departure yesterday had been foiled, owing to complications with permissions, which Manaa is still trying to resolve. The local media also want us to wait a day, allowing them to pursue the story of our journey. We are being delayed again—more meetings, and more of the ubiquitous red tape. Though we've lost another day, we've regained our teammate. Musallim, offering no explanation why, has decided to rejoin the team. At the insistence of the Bedu, who view a man on the move as incomplete without a rifle, Leigh and I finally purchase two rifles. Although Musallim suggests a more powerful weapon such as a .30-06, we opt for a small .22 calibre, which costs us $250.

This morning we have fed the camels and they are ready to go, once the Bedu arrive from points unknown in Salalah. The early start has already been sacrificed to a press conference set for nine at the Holiday Inn, after which we'll begin the journey. I race about camp collecting gear and readying our saddlery. My arms feel weak and my stomach churns with the day's excitement and anxiety. We will soon have to ride through the crowded city traffic, with its honking horns, shouting people, and nothing soft to land on if the camels spook, which seems almost inevitable.

My saddle already at the beach, I lead Mr. T to the water. Both of us squint through the light reflecting off the immaculate white sand, clean as a glacier the morning after a snowfall. People greet us beside the hotel, as do a gaggle of confused guests, mostly expatriate mothers and children off to use the hotel's swimming pool. The team forms a circle, our camels standing behind us, to greet local government officials. Elders from the local Bedu population also come to see us off, wearing their *khanjars*, rifles, bandoleers, and proud smiles. Their presence encourages us greatly. They stand and nod as if to offer their blessing on what we are about to attempt. Then they encircle us, hold hands, and break into a song of good luck. The interviews are finished and we shake hands. A *shaybah*, an old man, offers me his valuable antiquated rifle. I feel quite honoured and almost obliged to take it until Musallim, sensing my predicament, steps in to save the moment by better explaining that I already have one. With the matter handled without offence to the *shaybah* and his generous offer, Musallim flashes me a wink and a smile.

There is much debate about what route we will use to get out of town. Bruce and I explain that we reconnoitred one possibility yesterday. But the Bedu have other plans, which we follow without argument. To get off the hotel compound we must walk the camels through a labyrinth of shrubbery. Musallim leads, and it is a challenge to stay ahead of T as he pushes to catch up. I keep his rein tight and try to hold him back, but T continually steps on my ankles, raking my Achilles tendons. Then he steps on my *dishdashah*, pinning it to the ground and causing me to fall. Were it not for the shrubs I could roll out of the way, but he steps on my back, planting me in the path. As I try to get up, he bucks, reefing hard on the reins still in my hand. He jumps over the hedge and, with a whip of his head, jerks me to my feet. I give him lots of rein to calm down and make a quick survey of my wounds—no dripping blood, some nasty scrapes down the back of my legs, and a welt on my back. Meanwhile, T is getting anxious about being apart from the group and tugs at me to rejoin them. Back on the path, the hotel's cleaning staff looks us over and moves nervously out of the way as we approach. The clatter of their cleaning cart spooks my camel and he starts bucking again. T knocks me down and kicks, but misses my head. His next kick whistles past my ear as I struggle to get up, but lands squarely on my thigh, actually lifting me off the ground and dropping me back down. Though the kick was powerful enough to propel me, it was less damaging than it could have been. I get to my feet and pull T along to join the others, examining the bruise on my leg through my *dishdashah*.

We finally take to the road, but the Bedu don't know where to go next. Bruce and I take the lead and to the dismay of the Bedu, who only want to move north, we head east. We try to explain about the route and the need to stay out of the city's heart, but the noise of people shouting and honking car horns makes this impossible. We thought the people in the town would be more familiar with a camel caravan. The stunned looks give them away. The camels are agitated, but surprisingly manageable, much to our relief. Perhaps it is not the camels which surprise the locals but rather the three Canadians who are leading them. Musallim insists that we turn north. It is, after all, his hometown. But we come to a traffic circle with no northerly exit. Bruce and I take the lead again and immediately head south to the beach to pick up our alternate route. This time the Bedu agree.

Once back on the beach, we mount up and ride for the first time. Within minutes Crazy Dancer has bucked Bruce off, but our caravan eventually calms. I can look around at the two- and three-storey houses lining the beach. The windows of every building are enclosed with ornately carved wooden shutters. The sun has bleached the grey plaster walls unevenly, evidence that the shutters aren't always shut. At ground level some of the wooden doors are elaborately carved in floral and geometric patterns. Lines of sand have collected in the deep carving of the wooden door, blown there by the onshore wind from the beach.

The lazy waves of the Indian Ocean wash up fine sand and then carry it back out again. I watch a Little Egret swoop along a wave crest and flare its wings for a soft landing on the beach beside us. Fishing boats drift on the deep azure of the ocean and fishermen stop to watch us as they bring their catch to shore. The boats are laden with crayfish and kingfish, sardines and lobster, and prized abalone destined for export from Salalah's refrigeration plant. We are destined for two months of dates and rice.

The remainder of our ride beyond the city limits is uneventful, compared with the chaos of the first half hour, even with the honks and shouts of passing motorists. We move past the city limits and onto the plains of Salalah, now opening up for us and offering a chance to turn north. The mountains of the Jabal Dhofar soon come into view, rising 3600 feet before us, a daunting barrier which we must cross tomorrow. These mountains encircle the plain. To the east they drop down to the ocean. To the west they continue into Yemen, creating a monstrous amphitheatre thirty-nine miles long. The unusual formation also creates unusual weather patterns. We will cross its deepest point, about six miles from the shoreline.

At 1:30, we stop for lunch at the side of the road that has finally taken us out of town. We have just entered the mouth of a large ravine at the foot of the mountains. Clambering down an embankment, we sit below our camels, which are tied in the shade of thick trees. Friends of Musallim arrive and he fires his gun into the opposite embankment, to their amusement. Rounds ricochet from rocks, taking haphazard trajectories before coming to rest in a little puff of dirt. Till the gun is put away, we feel a little tense.

The friends unload a variety of food fresh from a local restaurant, heavily wrapped in tinfoil, and smelling of delicious spices. A fire is lit to cook some meat at Musallim's request. The camels are fed alfalfa and watered from a trough of diverted water running from the canyon above.

In three and a half hours we have covered seven miles. According to at least one of our alternative plans, I could make camp here. A short day, but I would be happy to stop and get organized after our confused departure. Instead, we move on after a two-hour rest, leaving our generous acquaintances behind. The road fades as the canyon closes in. We ride along footpaths so covered over with vegetation that we are eventually forced to walk. The beauty of this valley is well concealed from the arid plains above. Here we have not a hint of the brutal desert beyond and we have left the city of Salalah behind. Because of the swirling weather pattern inside the bowl formed by the mountain range, this basin receives unusual volumes of rain. The special fog that rolls in off the ocean and thickens to produce a monsoon-like rain is known as the *Khareef*, and averages more than thirty-six inches of rain per year. The months of July and August are the rainy season here, making the region something of a mecca that attracts people from across the Gulf in hot summer months seeking slightly cooler temperatures. Surrounding us now are grasses, native plants and trees, sun-seared and hibernating in anticipation of the next season's moisture.

This is the only valley of its kind along the entire 1350 miles of the south Arabian coast. Date trees and the odd fig are also recognizable, and their size is evidence of the healthy growing season. Mr. T and I pass the distinctive desert rose, a plant used by the local Jabalies mountain people as medicine for various ailments. Cows and goats have heavily grazed the valley bottom, where it is clear of vines and entangling undergrowth. Our progress is slowed considerably through here, but it allows us some time to enjoy the passing beauty.

Farrah, a local man who joined us at lunch, claims to know the way ahead. The difficult terrain has dissuaded the other guests and it's nice to be away from the road and its noise. A few young boys follow us from their mountain homes. One is shy and stays about twenty feet up on the valley's side, keeping an eye on us. The canyon winds its way north in confusing twists left by the varying rock formations. Steep walls leave no way up. Even a rock climber would have trouble scaling these heights. Our current route was also Sir Wilfred's route through the Qara Mountains years ago. The spectacular ramparts echo our conversation.

We walk in the cool of the valley bottom, shaded from the sun by the summit ridge three hundred feet above. As we rise higher along the dry creek bed, the terrain becomes increasingly difficult. There is now no discernible path. I am forced to pick a trail for Mr. T along the uneven ground and around great boulders, trying my best to give him a route that will limit damage to the soft pads of his feet. He is accustomed to sand and gravel—not sharp rocks.

The valley walls begin to close in as we ascend. Though the summit ridge is now only 180 feet above, there is no possibility of climbing to it. The rocky outcrops are impossibly steep, and lush with succulents. They would make the climb too slippery. The conversation between Musallim and Farrah has increased in volume and intensity, making me wonder whether our guide is as familiar with the terrain as he had advertised. He pulls out a machete to clear the path, which has not seen use in years, and I laugh, thinking Thesiger himself was perhaps the last to pass this way. Looking to the top of the ridge, I spot some Jabalie who have come out at the news of our party. They are clearly curious, unaccustomed to such strange traffic. The Bedu yell a greeting, but the Jabalie shrink from the edge and disappear without a word.

We have come to an end. Steep walls block our advance. One wall forms the head of the *wadi*, the other forms the west face. The east wall is heavily covered in vegetation but is not as steep as the others. The camels are tied and left with Leigh and Bruce while the Bedu and I look around. I hike up the east face at bin Ashara's request, and after a short scramble find that it backs off enough for us to get through—*if* the camels can manage a steep initial climb.

Back with Leigh and Bruce, we untie the camels and lead them toward our only hope for a passage over the ridge. The ground is difficult, rocky, strewn with thorn bushes, and steep. The camels force their way through the foliage at our urging while our saddle blankets become caught and torn. Musallim's cedar *hadut* is snapped in two. His saddle contents drop to the ground. We each grab an armful and continue.

Leigh worries about navigation and is concerned for the safety of the camels. I have never known him to be an animal lover but his sensitivity for our camels is undeniable. The Bedu tell him that the camels are far more durable than he thinks. Leigh's concern at this point is for a fall or a torn footpad and he is upset about the risk in our going on. But there is nowhere to stop now.

Leading Mr. T is tiring work. I run around him moment by moment to navigate each step over the rocks and slippery roots. I lead his head under and around thick branches, always mindful of the clearance needed for his saddle. Once we clear this first section, the going becomes considerably gentler, and we find an animal trail that parallels the ridge we hope to gain. From here we work the hillside like the terraced mountain slopes above Namche Bazaar on the route to Everest. We work from one trail to the next, zigzagging upward, traversing northward and gaining as much height as we can with each transition.

Darkness is about to descend, as suddenly as in the southern tropics, so I look around through 360 degrees to get my last bearings before the light goes out. As with a mountain's false summit, the ridge we finally achieve is not the top, and we find we still face a long hike to get above the valley and past the divide—just how far we don't know, as the ridge and sky have blended into darkness. In the distance I can see the lights of Jabalie huts, the reflections of their reinforced corrugated aluminum roofs and reason we have a couple more hours of climbing.

A rifle shot! Musallim yells, then a voice calls out from the direction of the shot. It's a friendly response from a man who moments later walks out of the dark to meet us. After animated conversation, all the Bedu, along with Farrah and our new guide, join together for prayers. Leigh, Bruce and I hold the camels. This is the first real break we have had since lunch. It lasts only as long as needed to complete the ritual of prayer.

After another two hours leading our animals over troublesome terrain, we reach a substantial gravel road still below the crest. The road is easy going and we make good time, but it is also after nine at night. No one can guess how close we are to the top, so we stop at the only reasonable flat ground we can find, under a large tree. In the six hours since lunch we have come another five miles. The camels are unloaded while Farrah and I head up the hill to the lights above, looking for food and perhaps the top. I take a blanket to carry back what we might find.

Only 500 yards away we crest the top and encounter a police station. We enter the barracks. Our hunt for food ends at the barracks' supply store where we fill our carry-all blanket with supplies. We return to the group waiting at our camp below. Word of our arrival has spread quickly through the area, and no sooner have we finished settling in than twenty men arrive. The local *sheikh* has provided a goat for slaughter and Musallim sets to work without protest. He hangs the slain animal on a tree from its hind legs to dress out the carcass. Bruce and I watch closely, hoping to learn something from Musallim's artistry.

Our experiences with Bedu hospitality highlight the changes that have occurred since Thesiger's time. The explorer spoke of frequent guests while camped right here in 1947, but Thesiger was angered by their presence: "These unwanted guests never waited for an invitation before sitting down with us to feed," he wrote. "They just joined us and shared whatever we had for as long as they were with us." Our dilemma, on the contrary, has become the generosity of the Bedu and their perpetual desire to set a feast for us. Unlike Thesiger, though, we cannot count on meeting anyone once we penetrate the deep desert. The sedentary Bedu who now entertain us will retire to their homes, leaving us to trek the sands of an empty desert devoid of both aggressive raiding parties and hospitable fires.

The *sheikh* wants to slaughter a camel in our honour tomorrow and, like the others, he will not easily be dissuaded. Slaughtering a camel is not an everyday occurrence. It is an event accompanied by much ceremony, and a whole day of eating. We are barely underway, and while the offer is wonderfully generous, we don't want to stop now. After midnight, we finally settle on the gift of a large bowl of frothing camel milk, which seems to satisfy our host.

١٦ شوال ١٤١٩

February 3, 1999
Day 2 — 17 09' N 54 03' E

Musallim calls the crew to action at six. His shouts are as jolting as an alarm clock. I slip my head back into my sleeping bag to escape his yelling and the morning's cool damp air. The breeze penetrates my sleeping bag, as do the loud commands to pray. *"Salat! Salat!"* Musallim keeps yelling, walking among the sleeping bodies rolled like sausages in their camel blankets, feeling it's time for the day's first prayer or *Salat al-Subh.* "*Salat! Salat! Salat!*" he shouts again and again, poking his camel stick into the ribs of his sleeping Muslim victims. This morning I am oddly rested and ready for the day. I have managed only five hours' sleep on this sloping ground, but it has been a deep sleep and I remember none of my dreams.

Today we take no breakfast, lest it slow our departure. Bin Ashara is keen to travel during the cool part of the morning, and we're on the move by 7:30. Leigh, concerned about the burn I received yesterday, reminds me to take sunscreen. There is talk among us about how much to ride and how much to walk. Seasoned riders, Musallim, Ali and bin Ashara invariably want to ride the camels right away, while we Canadians, unaccustomed to the ride, would prefer a little walking to warm up the camels—and ourselves. Bruce and I defer to the Bedu, while Leigh says we should walk in the mornings to properly warm the camels. Leigh looks to Bruce for his support, and is unhappy when it doesn't come.

Leigh is taking seriously Thesiger's caution about sparing the camels. Not only did the man tell us in person, but he wrote of it in his book as well: "When all was ready we set off on foot. We always walked for the first two or three hours. While we were in the mountains each of us lead his camel, or tied her by her head-rope to the tail of the one in front." The discussion whether we should ride or walk ends when Musallim couches his camel and rides off without a word, forcing us to do the same.

Bruce takes some photos and I shoot video footage from camel back, the first such effort since our last fiasco in training. The terrain is arrestingly beautiful. Confused, wispy clouds of mist roll up from the valley and swirl back down, tumbling along the valley side we had hiked up the night before. Nature's artistry rolls by in my lens in the wave-like rhythm of a camel's walk. Beyond the great sculpted stonework, Jabalie grass huts occupy what little flat ground there is. One of the vanishingly few women we have seen since Masqat stands silhouetted against the sky—she is still, in the shade of a magnificent tree near her herd of cows. The sunburnt upland grasses here offer her animals little.

The woman stops to watch us pass. Her *kohl*-outlined eyes peer from behind the dark cloth of her veil. She carries a cane to herd her cattle, and a long black *abayah* drapes her frame, a frame I cannot see, must not be allowed to see, even in outline. I wonder about this woman, whom I shall never meet, whom I shall never be *allowed* to meet. I wonder about all the Bedu women I shall never meet. Grateful as I am for the encounters we're granted with the Bedu, and for the insights we're given, I cannot escape awareness that the door opens to only half their culture. The other half is ever hidden behind walls or kept away, high on hills, tending flocks. The female half of Bedu culture is constantly, powerfully present through the very absence, the very hiddenness, of these women.

But it is not only upon us westerners, us ethnic outsiders, that the female absence weighs. Undeniably, Bedu women and men lead separate and unequal lives. There is no denying the force of this judgement or its implicit cultural prejudice. And it's easy, of course, for a glib Canadian to pass this judgement. Year after year, the United Nations rates our country among the most desirable to live in, not the least for the relative ethnic gender equality people enjoy. But who would deny our own culture's sexism? Whether the symbolic sexism of bikini-based advertising or the practised sexism of the corporate "glass ceiling," we display willingly our own sins and the thin justifications our culture offers in defence. Sexism here is made more pungent by the physical separation of men and women. The veil of that separation is pierced, it seems, for limited and obvious purpose. The sexism of the Bedu—if *sexism* even be a fair term—may be more obvious than my culture's own, but it may also be more honest.

The woman whistles to her cattle and swings her cane, directing them down the slope. She turns and follows her herd. The trailing fabric of her dress, designed for this, drags behind her, erasing her footprints and leaving no trace of her presence. She is gone.

We have passed the Qara divide, and are now heading down the north slope. We are rapidly leaving behind the misty sea air drawn up our valley by the desert heat. There are no signs of the true desert here yet—just another range of rocky hills. To spare the camel's padded feet, we all dismount and walk the rocky ground. The slope is gentle but the stone is like fractured coral—sharp and complex, slanting northward with the slope of the mountains. The group splits as the terrain opens up to us. Although I am supposed to be concentrating on leading T, I keep looking up, expecting to see the desert, but it is not there. We drop steeply down into a 300 yard-wide depression. The camels protest and need to be pulled along. I forget about the desert with this new complication, until I hear someone shout from the other side. They have seen it. In a few more paces I look up, and there before us, quivering in rising heat, looms a wall of sand.

We stop in our tracks. The sand, in a startling flesh tone, stretches from left to right until it meets the mountain shoulders we stand upon. I thought these crags were huge yesterday. Now, seeing them suddenly engulfed in the sand, they appear small and insignificant. A new ocean of limitless brown and ochre hues presents itself, uninterrupted for more than 600 miles. At this moment it might as well be deeper than space, a place of unquenchable thirst for those who dare to enter. This is a place of hyperbole, and my mind turns it into a collection of melodramatic clichés. Silent awe is my best option.

The last of the valley's cool air rushes past into the vacuum created by the rising heated air over the desert sand. It pulls the cooler air out of the lower valley, which now blows wonderfully against my back, chilling the sweat gathered in the cotton and silk of my *dishdashah*. If I open my sleeves just right, the breeze swirls luxuriously around my ribs.

We come off the Qara's north slope, and find that the difficult jagged rock gives way not to sand but to pavement. Just when I thought we might leave behind the intrusions of civilization, a road cuts across our path. The Bedu are happy to use it. Still in the Salalah hinterland, we can actually make our way from one asphalt road to another. The hard pavement only accentuates the camel's stabbing gate and each lurching step sends shooting pain through my seat into my lower back. I can only hope that the sands will offer something better.

Children peer at us from behind rock piles in the surrounding fields, and huge acacia trees drift in and out of view as patches of fog mark the wind's speed and direction. We stop for water offered by the local tribe at an elaborate system of troughs used for their cattle. The camels refuse to drink from it. They could be offended by the scent of the cattle and quite happy to be high-minded and thirsty. We thank the tribesmen and carry on.

With Mr. T roped in tandem with Ali's camel, we move ahead of the group. I work on my Arabic, Ali on his English. When we can't find words for something a game of charades breaks out, and between bouts of laughter some meaning is exchanged. I learn that bin Ashara's camel is named Hamarah and Ali's is named Horaya. We have been calling her Kicker for obvious reasons.

Ali likes to stay ahead of the main group, moving fast, which regularly forces us to pull up and wait for the others. This suits me well. I like the time up front with him, seeing new terrain and then watching the group catch up. Each time we stop, we chat a while, then I shoot some stills or video footage and record my thoughts. Ali watches closely as I work, keeping quiet, deep in thought. He is quite focused on what I'm doing, and whenever I reveal a new piece of camera equipment he asks after it. I have no Arabic term for *digital camera*, and have to resort to hand signs and some ludicrous sound effects. He shows the most interest in my equipment and is quick to point out the gear he has. From his pocket he pulls a small pipe. Attached to it by a thin cord is a plastic bottle of dried tobacco. While I make notes he puts a match to the tiny bowl, breathes in and then exhales a cloud of smoke.

Ali is immensely likeable. I knew this the day he jumped from the jeep to greet us in Thamarit. He is the youngest member of our team and the best rider. At the age of six, he began racing camels, winning many events until he became too heavy at the age of twelve. Now Ali makes his living travelling across Arabia buying camels, which he trains with his brother and sells. Ali shows little fear of anything but lizards, which he despises. He is most helpful, and teaches us tricks to ride better and how to manage the camels. He has often come to our rescue, which he does generously and without recrimination.

Ali does everything at two speeds—extremely fast, as when riding, and extremely slow, as when doing everything else. It is frustrating that I can't communicate better with him. I wonder what he thinks of us. I certainly sense that he thinks we are all a little odd, though something short of outright crazy. This desire to do things in the old way, to test ourselves against this desert the way Thesiger had, as the Bedu have for hundreds of years, makes no sense to our companions. Even Ali, with his own spirited sense of adventure, can see little reason in it all. Why would we want to ride camels across the desert when others have been far more sensible and used air-conditioned Hummers to complete the journey in less time and greater comfort? My Sherpa friend Ang Temba was nearly as perplexed with our obsession to climb Everest. He wondered why I was actually looking to put struggle into my life. Climbing was different for the Sherpas, because it had never been a part of their heritage. I thought that the Bedu might have more understanding, as it is very much in the spirit of their heritage that we are crossing the desert by camel.

While we wait for the others to catch up, I watch an army of ants shuttle supplies across the road, making a little red highway across the asphalt. On either side of the blacktop they are well camouflaged in the iron-rich soil. The organized chaos of the ant line is a stark contrast to our frenetic departure this morning and each morning before. Here our departures are anything but silent and organized. Instead they are punctuated with shouts and disarray. What seem like heated arguments break out constantly over what load goes on which camel, what rope ties which bag. In fact the Bedu display a talent for conducting two or three of these "discussions" simultaneously with any number of people. One argument may be suspended briefly for the introduction of a new one, but it is never dropped and will be resurrected even hours later, everyone picking up where they left off.

Arabic is a situational language. Bedu speakers invest enormous meaning in their intonation and pacing, their arm gestures and volume. Arabic requires the speaker to engage in broad hand gestures and fluctuating tones of voice to be conveyed clearly. For a Bedu, much of a statement's meaning is conveyed through non-verbal clues. Listening to Bedu communication with a North American ear, one might assume a bloody brawl was about to erupt at any moment. We become gradually more familiar with this characteristic. With the stress of dehydration and heat exhaustion awaiting us, this linguistic difference may become intolerable to all. For the moment, the difference is interesting but entirely intimidating to witness.

Leigh's mood was not good this morning. He is still concerned for his camel after yesterday's hard march. Labian showed signs of fatigue last night and refused to go at times. Today the camel is slow and Leigh unhappy. There is tension in every adventure worthy of the name, and we must view moods and events in perspective. I stare back down at the red column of ants and admire their apparent affability.

Our transition from the north slope of the Qara Mountains toward the gravel steppes is made at the constant gait of our mounts—four miles an hour. It leaves us time to observe the passing world and to watch the more subtle gradations of terrain and vegetation. In the distance, distorted by the heat radiating from the surface, we can again see the sands of the Empty Quarter.

Ali stops at my request. Although I would just like to enjoy this moment, I feel I must film it for our *National Geographic* project. I frame the far-off beauty in the camera. Panning through 180 degrees, I catch my last glimpse of the lush pastoral land we have left behind. As I complete my shot I find a woman in long robes, beautifully silhouetted against the blue sky. She herds her cows with shouts and, like the woman I had seen earlier, rests in the shade of an old acacia canopy. I frame her and the tree against the bright sky behind. As I pack the camera away I am struck by how filming a scene removes me from it—feeling like an observer rather than a participant.

A cloud tumbles over the divide and washes over us. It's fresh and humid with the feel of the ocean and the scent of chlorophyll. The rest of the group catches up. A group of local men stick their heads out of a Land Rover and wave as they speed past on the asphalt. In the distance they pull over and unload. Six of them stand at roadside, shoulder to shoulder, waiting to greet us as we pass through their turf. When we get closer, I recognize them from among the group that gathered at our camp last night. Now they have come to wish us well. "*Salaam Alaykum,*" they shout as we pass. "*Alaykum as Salaam,*" we shout back. Musallim shouts at me, "*Sura! Sura!*" He wants a photo taken of these people. This happens every time we encounter someone. Most of the people in the region are familiar with Thesiger, who is known as Umbarak bin London. His book *Arabian Sands* is well known here, and since we are the first to travel through the region in this fashion since Thesiger, the locals assume we, too, will write a book. Every man wants his picture included with the text.

Musallim prompts me with aggressive gestures to take more photos. "*Sheikh! Sheikh!*" he tells me again and again and assures me they should be in the book. We stop to take photos while the rest of the group continues. Of the three Bedu, Musallim is the least affable at times. As he shouts at me to get my camera, I wonder whether he has any liking for us. Much is lost in cultural differences and formidable language barriers. I gather our largest challenge will not be the environment but, as Bruce predicted, communication with the Bedu. The stress of negotiating with our Arabic companions begins to reveal some cracks in our unity. Leigh slept alone away from the fire last night. He says our lack of organization and planning with the Bedu is dangerous. At best, he says, our efforts are inefficient, since the plans we make are rarely executed. We all know that we can afford the odd mistake here at the edge of the desert, but 200 miles north, in the midst of the desert with no help at hand, some mistakes could be deadly. My mind elsewhere, I finish up the photo session and ride on.

The transition between the two climatic zones is now sharper than ever, and I can see an impressive cut between the Qara Mountains and the desert. Before us, the ground stretches baked and lifeless out to the horizon. From camel-back I take some long shots of our group, which is now a couple of miles ahead. On the ground I suddenly have to struggle with the heat. We are now well beyond the reach of the cool valley mist.

A few more hours roll by, along with intermittent gaps in the terrain that offer views of what lies ahead. They kindle both anxiety and excitement. At the bottom of a *wadi* that runs incongruously east to west, I catch up to the group as it encounters more jagged edges of the eroded drainage basin. More gravel roads criss-cross our path. We tuck our party underneath one of these routes, crawling inside a concrete drainage tunnel, where we find shade, a funnelled breeze, and a place for lunch. The camels, unable to fit into the tunnel, stay out in the heat. Their capacity for enduring heat is far greater than our own. The camel's body temperature can fluctuate up to 13 degrees Fahrenheit, from 91 to 104. Able to withstand greater heat ranges, camels don't perspire as quickly in order to cool, as do most other mammals. Thick hair on the apex of their back and neck insulates from the sun. Their bellies are thin-skinned and fine-haired to dissipate heat. All of this allows the camels to sweat less, which preserves water.

Ali and I happily ride together the ten miles we cover after lunch before ending our day. Bruce rides all day with Musallim and Leigh with bin Ashara. I am not certain how the pairings have been selected, but it may be our ages, as Ali and I are the youngest and Leigh and bin Ashara the eldest. Regardless, Ali is such easy company I'd be happy to ride the entire journey to the coast with him.

We are at the edge of the interior plateau, 2400 feet above sea level. This plateau will lead us to the gravel steppes south of the Quarter's inner sands. The terrain is comprised of grey and lifeless rock. In a hollow, sand has gathered and here we camp, giving the team and the animals a soft place to sleep.

Engines roaring, a few jeeps struggle over the uneven ground into our little camp. One is driven by the local *sheikh*, who brings a gift. He offers a traditional leather milk bowl, colourfully decorated in wool. His son wants his photo taken sitting on the back of a camel. The boy's enthusiasm gives way to tears when the camel refuses to cooperate, and he returns to his father's Land Rover. A fire heats tea and dinner. Over conversation, Ali, always the first to break into song around the campfire, begins to sing about camels while the others talk. The day's light cloud cover has kept us from the blistering heat until it burned off. Now, more clouds drift in from the south and will keep the night warm.

Chapter Eight

١٧ شوال ١٤١٩
February 4, 1999
Visit Pool of Ayun, Wadi Ghadun

Day 3 — 17 17' N 53 48' E

Ali walks about camp with a tiny bottle of thick glass, containing a brown liquid. He doles out a drop to each of us, which we rub on the back of our hands. This is *oad*, the aromatic perfume Bedu men wear, and Ali says we should rub it on our beards and necks. A derivative of frankincense, *oad* is thick as molasses and brown as bark. It gives off a wonderfully woody earthen smell. There are many types of *oad*, and many exude a very sweet odour I find almost sickening. This is the authentic form, and the Bedu ration it carefully. A two-ounce bottle of mid-grade *oad* can cost over a hundred dollars.

Oad was just a part of the use for frankincense, which is the resin of hardened sap of the Olibanum tree (*Boswellia sacra*). Frankincense was used for numerous other purposes, from religious ceremonies to cosmetics and medicines. Ali's ancestors harvested the finest grades right here in the Dhofar region, with its perfect climate for growing Olibanum. Frankincense was the single most precious commodity in the world four thousand years ago. Its price rose six hundred percent from producer to consumer and became the foundation of wealth in the region. Kings and emperors paid handsomely for it and Christians believe the magi, who travelled to Bethlehem to pay homage to the Christ child, brought frankincense as one of their gifts.

The Queen of Sheba, whose kingdom encompassed much of Ethiopia and Yemen, travelled to this region around 1000 BCE and kept a summer palace in Salalah, harvested frankincense, and built an empire on the revenue. In a gesture of amorous (or at least ambassadorial) friendship, she offered frankincense to King Solomon, one of the Middle East's wealthiest kings. Today, Omanis still use frankincense often, burning it to welcome guests at feasts. As I start to sweat, the *oad* on my neck warms and fills my nostrils with each breath, linking me to the ancient history entwined with its origins.

After breakfast we ride along Wadi Ghadun, which angles sixty miles northwest and then northeast. Today is our third day out and I'm already wondering when our first rest day will come. Like Sherpas in the first weeks of a climb, Ali, bin Ashara and Musallim betray no signs of difficulty. But even the Sherpas, famous for their strength and endurance at high altitudes, begin to falter late in an expedition, and I wonder whether the Bedu will do the same.

Our current route was part of Thesiger's route as well. At its head is the anomalous Pool of Ayun, the only one of its kind in the area and the last surface water we will see before the coast at Abu Dhabi. Early in the day we crest a lip of rock and look 500 feet down into its inviting green waters. Like Thesiger before us and a myriad of Bedu before him, we will water our camels here after descending the crumbling east wall of the canyon.

The pool covers an area of two football fields, encircled by dense reeds and stunted palms. The water's darkness and the steep walls imply the pool's considerable depth. I think it may be sixty feet or more in the middle. An underground spring feeds the pool, constantly replenishing the loss that occurs through evaporation. As we walk down the worn animal path our shouts echo about us flushing out birds which have been enjoying the cool tranquillity. Two wild camels drink at the pool's edge, until our approach frightens them away.

The rocks are slippery at the water's edge, and the water surface teams with little creatures urgently swimming about. Many of these are beetles. The camels pay little attention to any of this or to the green scum floating at the pool's edge. They thrust their mouths into the water, sucking up a long throatful before lifting their heads to pour the contents toward their stomach. Bin Ashara begins singing the drinking song, which precipitates the flight of a family of sparrows from the waxy reeds in which they nest. Bruce, Leigh and I join in:

> My camel has a big hump, *Ya hye bye, Ya hye bye*
> Drink much water my friend, *Ya hye bye, Ya hye bye*
> Because you have travelled far, *Ya hye bye, Ya hye bye*
> Now we have unloaded you, *Ya hye bye, Ya hye bye*
> Under the shady bushes, *Ya hye bye, Ya hye bye...*

The camels' stomachs distend noticeably after they drink, and when we remount I can feel the difference in Mr. T's diameter. Camels can drink over twenty-five gallons of water—a small bathtub full—in a matter of minutes. Camels are slow to dehydrate for several reasons, including kidneys that are able to concentrate urine to reduce water loss, turning it as thick as syrup. Still, a camel can lose more than a quarter of its weight to water loss. A horse would die if it lost half that. Mr. T weighs about 1500 pounds, so he has the capacity to lose about 375 pounds or 45 gallons of water.

We leave this last moment of abundance and ride deeper into the valley. Above us, amber cliffs stretch to the canyon's rim. The *wadi* floor winds and bends like any aged riverbed, making our progress quite circuitous. Reeds and palms grow along the outside bank of each twist and turn, adding a touch of green to the picture. They bend lazily with each breath of wind.

Bin Ashara has fallen behind the group, and when we stop to fix a saddle, he catches up. With a kick and a tap of his camel stick he urges Hamra into a run over the worn rocks. His pack camel, loaded with two water-swollen *gerbers*, reluctantly runs along as well. In the silence of the canyon the sound of slapping hooves and sloshing water echoes off the valley walls. Waving his stick above his head, bin Ashara breaks into song. The camel's trot adds a staccato beat to his voice and the sloshing water adds a second syncopation. He is momentarily framed in the green reeds against the dramatic rocky ramparts. Bin Ashara's *dishdashah*, damp with sweat, lifts from his skin and flows in the wind. His legs are tucked up tight while his heels dig into the camel's dark coat. It is a majestic vision of the Bedu people whom Thesiger so admired yet warned were gone. In this man, Thesiger's desert wolf endures. Bin Ashara smiles and stabs his stick into the air as he sweeps past our astonished group.

We ride on north and west along the *wadi's* course. The sheer walls dictate our path and we eventually happen upon some forage where the camels can graze. Musallim decides this vegetation will also provide a place to have lunch. An acacia tree stands scenically at the confluence with a dry tributary. We unload our camels after hobbling their front legs with three-foot lengths of braided rope. This way they are free to move, but their shortened stride keeps them in reach. Within moments they disperse. Some are eating, while others follow Ali's camel to the other gully and sprawl out under the acacia to rest.

Musallim and bin Ashara build a fire and place about thirty small rocks among the coals. A canvas bag of raw meat from last night's meal is opened, releasing a cloud of flies. Ali cuts the meat into strips using a long knife. Bruce leans comfortably against a tree and writes in his diary while Leigh sleeps. I pull our sleeping bags from the loads, still wet from last night's dew, and lay them out to dry. For the first time since its purchase I examine my new rifle—as yet unfired and probably never loaded.

After thirty minutes Musallim takes up two sticks and works the hot stones to the surface of the fire, creating a bed. Bin Ashara then lays the strips of red goat meat on the rocks, and they sizzle loudly like strips of Canadian bacon. Soon we're eating succulent goat from the Bedu barbecue, chasing it down with tea. The others follow it all with a nap, while I make notes in my journal about the pools of Ayun and clean my rifle. I wait for everyone to wake before I set up some targets to practice marksmanship. Bruce takes a moment alone, but Musallim, not one to miss a chance to shoot something, joins Leigh and me and gives us a clinic. He helps us set our sights and demonstrates his preferred loading technique, one shell at a time. Musallim shows Leigh how to shoot from a seated position, using his knees for stability. When we begin to fire, Musallim groups his shots tighter by far then either of us. From a hundred feet his three-shot clusters are within a dime's circumference. Our shots are lucky to be caught in a silver dollar. My American shooting instructor would not have been impressed. While Musallim helps Leigh with the sights on his rifle, I try to recall what I was taught about weapons only five months ago.

Anticipating the Bedu desire that we all carry rifles, I had gone for training in the U.S., as firearms in Canada are more restrictively regulated. I wanted a hands-on, practical approach that I thought a shooting range couldn't offer, and presumed this to be more readily available in the States, where gun shops once outnumbered gas stations in some parts. Having completed the basic training, I'm not so much scared of guns as I am lacking simple marksmanship. I feel reasonably able to function in the weapons-oriented Bedu society, but wish I could better hit the bloody target.

Bin Ashara shouts to end our game and signals it's time to move on. By now the camels are a few hundred yards up the valley, eating their way along. I find T with his eyes tightly closed and his head in the heavily thorned branches of an acacia. His long neck is extremely dexterous and powerful enough to pull down thick branches to access food. We've heard stories that a camel's neck is strong enough to rip a man's arm from his shoulder. T's prehensile lips are equally dexterous. Split like a rabbit's, they enable him to manoeuvre among the nasty thorns and brambles in search of succulent leaves. Like that of a rhinoceros, the back of T's mouth is lined with hundreds of papilla, small fleshy fingers that protect the mouth wall by guiding those thorns he does eat to the rear teeth for mastication. T reluctantly leaves his meal. The rest of the camels are rounded up and quickly loaded, so we can press on toward a celebration the Bedu have been talking about. It is 111 degrees here in the valley bottom. As I sweat, the oad warms and lifts a pleasant smell to my nose, quite different from the fetid smells of the overworked bodies on Everest.

After a few hours' riding, the *wadi* suddenly widens, opening up to a width of three hundred feet. After the confinement of the canyon, we can now pick our way as we please among the boulders and the thorny trees the Bedu call *ghaf*. Ali and I ride together and talk about music. He mentions Michael Jackson, but isn't a fan. Ali doesn't like any of Jackson's songs, he says, because none of them are about camels.

Ali and I, the two youngest on this expedition, have begun to develop a friendship. I only wish that I could talk with him more profoundly. My greatest failing is my inability to speak better Arabic. Despite their efforts, Leigh and Bruce also have an insufficient command of the language. English-speaking travellers move about the world relying on the universality of their language. But the Bedu lexicon is wonderfully devoid of English. When we arrived in Thamarit, the Bedu frowned when we spoke English even among ourselves. Thesiger became fluently bilingual, which enabled him to better connect with his teammates. "Without my Bedu companions, my journeys in Arabia would have been a meaningless penance," he wrote, making me wonder what the journey will mean for us if we *don't* connect well.

With his command of the language, Thesiger could make plans, and though he too saw the plans change constantly, he was able to anticipate and modify the changes. Thesiger built a cohesive team that had no ties with outside parties. They started each day with the urgency of defining their own destiny moment by moment, and they enjoyed the rewards of that process. Due in large measure to the language barrier, we do not have this same cohesiveness, and in the end it is no one's fault but our own. I look forward to learning more Arabic in the weeks to come so I can develop my friendship with Ali and the others.

It's not long before we come upon the encampment of Sheikh Musallim bin Ayhouda. Before we dismount, a group of ten men gather in a circle before us and shout their welcome. "*Marhabah!*"

"*Salaam alaykum,*" we shout back and jump from our camels.

"*Alaykum as salaam,*" they respond as we come together shoulder to shoulder, facing them in a similar formation. The eldest in their group asks, "*Alume?*" *What is your news?* It is the tradition that the elders exchange the news on behalf of their group, so when

Musallim turns to me to answer, I offer the honour to Leigh, who gives it over to Bin Ashara. *"Mafi Alume,"* he replies, and asks the same of them. *"Mafi Alume."* As we expect, there is invariably no news offered at this point in the introductions—even if there really is news. Thesiger encountered the same and wrote, "No matter what had really happened, [the answers] never changed. [The Bedu] might have fought with raiders; half their party might have been killed and be lying still unburied; their camels might have been looted; any affliction might have befallen them—starvation, drought or sickness, and still at this first formal questioning they would answer, 'The news is good'."

We walk the receiving line shaking hands, extending our good wishes to their families. But we do not offer nose kisses like the Bedu, for fear of offending. The real news will be shared later over coffee around the fire. As we are about to unload, five of our hosts strip to their waists. A young male camel is brought closer and the men descend upon it, pushing it about until it stumbles on the rocks and falls to the ground. Once down, it is allowed to get up, only to be knocked down again. This time, four of the men take positions around it and hold the camel down, properly positioned, facing Mecca. Behind, I hear the sound of metal sliding on rock against the loud crying of the pinned beast. A fifth man grabs the lips and mouth and bends its head back, exposing the neck and immobilizing the panicking camel.

Sheikh Ayhouda walks past me, pulling his ten-inch knife blade across the stone one more time before tossing the sharpener to the ground. I want to look away, but hold my gaze. We are supposedly becoming inured to this but still, I am at once stunned by the harshness of what is unfolding, yet fascinated. With ballet-like grace and not a hint of hesitation, the *sheikh* kneels beside the creature and, offering a prayer, draws the blade forcefully across the camel's throat. A fountain of blood sprays above the head of a young boy watching. Another arch of blood leaps from the incision, propelled by the last heartbeats. A third comes, smaller than the first, which paints the white rocks in a ten-foot red fan. The lungs collapse and the screams of the camel drown in a gurgle of blood. The man at the head pulls further back, exposing more neck. The thick throat requires more than one cut. The tone in the camel's muscle fades. The men loosen their grips and stand back. Silence and the rich smell of blood hang in the air.

Everyone stands frozen. Heads are bent forward, shoulders droop, and a moment of heaviness takes us over. Regardless of how often the Bedu have experienced this, it seems to me that we are all acknowledging the intimacy of a life's passing. It seems fitting to recognize that a moment ago this 300-pound creature stood breathing and ready for another day of life. Now this great being lies crumpled at our feet. As with the dead I've seen frozen against a mountainside, the spark of life has vanished here, leaving only a heap of organic material. Dust to dust.

Our host breaks the silence with a baritone chant. The others gather with their knives and take up the chorus while they begin the work of butchering. A long slice is made from the neck to the tail. Pulling heavily on both sides four men tear the hide away as two others skilfully flense the skin from the meat, which is pink with oxygen and jewelled with fat. The exposed fleshy hump takes some work, but is cut free and tossed to wobble on the hide. Ribs are broken and a machete-like knife is used to split the hip and knee joints. Once the sides are opened, the visceral cavity lets go of its contents. Stomach, heart, kidneys and intestines spill onto the waiting hide. A boy of seven sits among the viscera searching out the edible parts, including the heart and liver. The small intestine is unravelled, squeezed clean of its contents and collected in a pile like spaghetti.

Flies descend on the scene but are ignored till they land on a sweaty brow. The men swipe at them, leaving streaks of blood across their faces. I have not moved in the half hour that has elapsed since the first drawing of the knife. I have neither been invited to help, nor do I wish to. I watch what once was a camel, now beyond recognition except for the head that lies untouched where Musallim placed it before starting his song. Its eyes are open. Its tongue droops out over its teeth and lies curled on a rock dyed crimson.

The chant beats incessantly with the work of cutting meat into forearm-sized strips. Orders are shouted back and forth across the pile. Bloodstains creep past elbows, over feet and up ankles. More brow-wiping, more cutting and hacking. And always, the chanting. They sing a prayer to bless the food, giving thanks to Allah for the gift. I move closer and lean down to examine the head. A fly crawls from its nose and I look into the camel's left eye. Bruce leans over my shoulder and points to what might be a small tear.

While the men continue working, I unpack and help around camp before gathering my jacket, camera, and rifle. Needing to get some space, I don Leigh's boots with extra socks and head out for a hike. I've been staring up at Wadi Ghadun's walls for two days and I want to see what's up on top. It's a bit of a scramble, including a search for snakes in the pocketed rocky face, and I'm on top in an hour to catch the sunset. There are more walls beyond the one I have scaled and I can see little of the surrounding area. I do have a wonderful view of our *wadi* as it serpentines back the way we have come. Word of our arrival has spread, and on the far side I see numerous vehicles using a gravel road to snake their way down into camp.

I'm still perched four hundred feet above the valley floor when darkness falls. I lie on the rock, hands behind my head, and watch the stars slowly illuminate the sky. Leigh, concerned, wakes me with a call on the walkie talkie. Uneasy that I'm not in camp, he wonders when I am coming back and reminds that dinner will be ready soon. After trying some low-light photography, I pack up, hoping the moon will rise and light my path. But this time I've misjudged its cycle. I would have to wait for an hour or two for it to rise. I can see the fire burning down on the valley floor and hear the songs drift upward. More vehicles arrive and a second fire is lit. I pick my way down in the dark and return to find a large gathering of thirty or more men underway. Back in camp, I learn our hosts have also been concerned for my safety. Despite learning from Musallim that I'm a mountaineer, they are satisfied only when they learn that I've taken my rifle. Leigh has saved me some camel meat, which I wolf down—my first food in ten hours.

This party is impressive. Rifles of all makes and vintages hang from many of the men's shoulders, as do bandoleers bristling with cartridges. When the men are not singing or eating, they dance with their rifles, which they dramatically swing overhead in rhythm with the song. Many men show off their traditional curved knives or *khanjar*, which are trimmed in gold and silver. The knives appear awkward to sit with, since they are sheathed at the belt buckle. The men dance, sing and swing their rifles for hours. In the Muslim tradition, not a drop of alcohol has been served.

Any *sheikh* will take advantage of a guest's arrival to spread his reputation for generosity. Bin Ayhouda has made good use of our presence, and we are honoured. Well-worn four-wheel drives outnumber our camels two to one. I join the group and talk with many of the newcomers. Most of the guests are strangers to us, but there are also some familiar faces flickering in the firelight. Sheikh Salim—the man we nicknamed "Sheikh and Bake"—has come from Thamarit, with his son. He gives me a welcoming nose kiss when we meet in line.

As we sit on the sand and eat, twelve men take to their feet at one side of the fire, link hands and begin a new song. Soon another group of ten or so do the same on the other side, answering the songs of the others. Back and forth across the fire, rich male tones flow in songs of good fortune and tributes to our expedition. When a new group drives into camp, they gather in the dark and prepare to march to the fire in lines of five or more to sing their songs of good luck and prosperity. They talk excitedly among themselves about new lyrics to familiar melodies. Once they settle on the new lyrics the men approach the fire with arms linked, singing as they come forward. Voices swell as each new group replaces the last. Those at the fire fade out and let the new group take over in a seamless vocal and visual transition.

Each new group wants to make a good impression on the camp. Once they sing a couple of their invented songs, the hosts, then invent lyrics in response across the flames. The singing shifts between the groups five or more times before it stops suddenly and the elder from the new group shouts, "*Salaam alaykum!*" This prompts a round of greetings, always in a counter-clockwise direction.

In this most recent group are a number of old Bedu men, several of whom knew Sir Wilfred or his Bedu companions. One of the men rode with Sir Wilfred's party in 1945 until they split into two groups north of here at Mughshin. Another speaks of his journey with Thesiger, telling a little of what a fine man Thesiger was but mostly about the number of camels they took and the nature of the water at the wells they visited. The audience listens raptly.

I appreciate this glimpse into a unique part of Bedu culture, and the opportunity to participate. Everyone smiles, shakes our hands and motions for us to eat and dance. We see none of the stoic Arab stereotype, but easy smiles and open affection. I wonder whether our commitment to remain on schedule is keeping us from more thoroughly appreciating the beauty of the desert and its people. Our schedule be damned—this is why we came.

Thesiger struggled here as well: "I fretted at the constant delays, counting the wasted days instead of revelling in this leisurely travel." Some things have not changed: The Bedu in *Arabian Sands* cared little for schedules, but Thesiger was obsessed. Plus ça change, the more things remain the same—it is a waste of energy to be so preoccupied with time in a place that is clearly less concerned with its passing. The Bedu teach us indirectly about enjoying the journey more, being less focused on the destination—lessons I learned from Sherpa friends but seem to have forgotten.

Bin Ayhouda recites a poem he has written in honour of our journey, and he is given a hearty ovation before the group begins singing again. We finally reach our limits and leave the party to bed down. The rest carry on with their celebrations. Though one enters such a gathering with much ceremony and attention, leaving is less complicated. There are no good byes. You simply slip away to find a place in the sand to sleep among the shadows.

Chapter Nine

١٨ شوال ١٤١٩
February 5, 1999
Wadi Ghadun

Day 4 — 17 24′ N 53 41′ E

It is bin Ashara's turn to rouse us from our slumber at 5:40 a.m. by reciting the Muslim call to prayer. Most of the guests left last night, but many of those who stayed felt moved by a strong east wind to sleep in their trucks. The few exceptions are now curled tightly about the weak fire. Happy at this moment not to be Muslim, I stay in bed and watch them crawl into the cold to pray.

We eat a few sandy dates and gnaw on cold bits of meat picked out of the congealed fat from last night's dinner, washing it down with sweet tea. The camels are saddled and freed from their hobbles. Salim bin Mohammed al-Toof smiles as he hands me a bottle of water. Our hosts rub sleep from their eyes and form a line to send us off with their good wishes. I feel sheepishly heroic as we walk along the assembly to shake hands. This is reminiscent of leaving Everest Base Camp in 1997 with my team leader Jason Edwards on our summit push, when we said goodbye to Bruce, in Base Camp. As then, I am happy now to be moving on, but feel uneasy about what awaits us. Ahead lies the real heat of this desert, scarcely any water, and no more hosts to receive us. On Everest we faced the wind, the cold and the rarefied air. Here in the desert, as on Everest, I am filled with nervous anticipation.

Following Ali on foot, I replicate his route among the rocks, stepping in his footsteps. I did the same with Jason when we moved from Base Camp toward the Khumbu Icefall. On the mountain my pack was heavy with gear. Here I pull my camel through the tough terrain. The moon lit the rocks of the moraine pushed aside by the glacier and the glorious pillars of ice tumbling in slow motion into the lower Khumbu Valley. Night was the safest time to be in the icefall, because the snowy cliffs and icy seracs became unstable in the heat of the day. The mountain's cold morning air decreased the risk of encountering dangerous, unpredictable hazards, such as avalanches, serac falls, and snow-bridge collapses.

Within fifteen minutes out of camp, we were at the end of the moraine, where we stopped to attach our crampons. Holding the crampons made my fingers instantly cold and I then fumbled with the climbing harness to set it around my waist and legs. I swung my arms in big circles to propel the blood into my fingertips. They began to sting as feeling returned. We stepped into the icefall. A towering monster, the icefall is 2600 feet wide and two miles long. It was spawned from the glacier that passes along the Western Cwm and topples over a 2000-foot rock cliff, creating a frozen falls as spectacular as Angel, Niagara, or Victoria.

Pinched between the ramparts of Everest's West shoulder and Nuptse, its sister peak, the Khumbu Icefall was the first formidable obstacle en route to Everest's summit from the south side. The palpably immense physical tension of these combined physical forces became evident as we walked onto this stream of ice, which flows at a rate of about a yard each day. The glacier shatters as it descends, breaking into huge blocks or seracs, some the size of houses, others as big as apartment buildings. Each block sits precariously on its own until its foundation collapses and it crashes into the jumbled flow. Jason and I worked through this labyrinth of jumbled ice saying little to each other. The fearfulness of the place was exaggerated by the constant grind of the glacier's movement. It roars, groans, and crashes along day and night, an eerie reminder of its constant state of flux. The noise had kept me awake earlier that night.

If it were not for the prize of the summit that lies beyond, no one would suspend sound mountaineering judgement and enter this place—despite its breathtaking beauty. As we moved deeper into the icefall, it became strangely silent. Our crampons squeaked as they took hold of the snow and ice. A crystal world of infinite blues flashed in the beam of my headlight—an artful display by nature. Were the danger any less, I would have stopped and gazed. I felt as though I was venturing into a forbidden place, which was not to be experienced first hand. The darkness only served to intensify the mystery of the place. Jason stopped to attach himself to a safety line using a karabiner, a detachable D-ring. I stole a moment to catch my breath, and looked up to see how the light of my headlamp danced across the jagged shapes that mirrored the fear rising in my throat.

The taste of fear had become familiar and served as an important regulating device in my life, prompting thought before action. I have found, though, that this fear can also cause paralysis if I let it overwhelm me. Though more subtle, the heady expanse of the Arabian Desert with its rolling dunes stands in complete contrast to the towering seracs of the Khumbu Icefall, but is no less formidable.

Just as I climbed Everest one step at a time, so, too, we will cross this desert; finding some confidence, we trust in each small step. This morning I follow Ali's steps and carefully walk T through the snow-white rocks lining the *wadi* floor. A rock spins from under Ali's right foot, causing another to crash into his left. He shouts "*Irkab!*" as he rubs his ankle, revealing an anger in his pain. *Ride!* We find some sand to couch and mount the camels. A large black beetle with long, spider-like legs and a teardrop body skitters across in front of me. In the early light its shadow is long and a bit unnerving. We ride on.

Ali and I ride together and settle into a welcome silence that is punctuated occasionally with conversation—some confused and some not. Ali has detailed knowledge of local plant life. The young Bedu makes an effort to teach me about the vegetation we pass. In many ways Ali reminds me of Thesiger's desert companion bin Kabina, who taught Sir Wilfred so much about desert life:

> We sat there happily together, and he taught me
> the names of the plants which grow in the sands.

The tribulus was *zahra*; and the tasselled sedge was *quassis*...He knew them all. Later [the botanists] were working out my collection in the museum in London, they sometimes thought that bin Kabina had given different names for the same plant, but nearly always when they examined them carefully they found that bin Kabina was right.

Ali points out a plant growing on a shelf sixteen feet up the *wadi's* east wall, calling it a *basiel*, then deciding it must be a *tarthuth*. By any name it is exquisite. Beet-red, the stem is as thick as a small poplar and covered in dozens of flowers. The *tarthuth* plant is mentioned in the Bible as juniper and is recommended as an emergency food. Traditionally the Bedu didn't wait for an emergency, and ate it during long camel caravans across the Empty Quarter. The entire plant is only ten inches high and has an awkward appeal, much like a mushroom's. Ali explains that camels love to eat it and I gather this particular plant has been spared that fate by its lofty perch. In a tropical forest it would go unnoticed. Here, its vivid colour and unique character make it stand out against the starkly barren *wadi* cliff.

After five hard hours of travel, we arrive at the confluence of a tributary to Wadi Ghadun. It is impossible to say how many miles we have actually travelled northward as we meandered east and west along the dry riverbed. At the mouth of the tributary, we turn east into a semi-permanent Bedu camp, noting the well and two concrete storage structures, each the size of a single-car garage. A dirt road leads into the camp. Two men huddle around a heavy angular branch broken from the trunk of an acacia. In its branches they lay out what looks like strips of red cloth. Around the corner, several Bedu butcher a camel carcass. They look up as Ali and I ride by. There is a familiar fan of blood seeping toward the east, a head and neck no longer part of the body, men with feet and hands covered in blood, white *wasirs* stippled a pointillist red. A smaller boy sits at a flank of meat, cutting it into forearm-length finger strips. Someone takes an armful of the sliced meat and walks away.

Ali and I ride into camp and jump to the ground. My feet are swollen with blood after being inactive for several hours, and they ache with the impact. We unpack and I walk over to the butchering area. One of the men hands me a pot full of meat and directs me toward the acacia tree. The red strips hung there are not cloth but drying meat. The acacia looks the part of a Christmas tree, its scarlet decorations slung from every thorny branch. They are for our journey, a journey we thought would be largely meatless, like Thesiger's. Due in part to the drought, the water at the oases we plan to encounter might be too brackish even for making bread, so we will depend upon the meat instead.

Musallim also explains—though much is lost in my translation—that heavy irrigation of crops of vegetables and animal feed in the UAE has sufficiently depleted the water reserves, and what remains is often too concentrated with salts and other minerals to be potable. The Emirates has one of the heaviest per capita water-consumption rates in the world.

In the UAE, wells drilled a dozen years ago to 200 feet must now be dug to 2000 to reach the same water supply. Musallim tells me that the unusual strain on water reserves arising from this new farming is connected to the length and severity of the drought. Technologically advanced irrigation is new in this region, and it may be too soon to understand its environmental impact. Regardless of the cause, conditions are markedly different from when Thesiger passed through here, and so we will eat meat.

A gravel road leads east from the camp. Manaa rejoins the group via the road, and announces that we'll rest at the camp tomorrow to let the meat dry and the camels rest. The journey through the Qara Mountains has fatigued our mounts. I am happy the camels need to rest. I had prayed for rest earlier in the day, when the pain in my lower back and knees was so great I had taken to holding my breath and clenching my teeth at the discomfort. I had to shift constantly on my saddle and reposition my legs, but this only calmed the pain for a few seconds till it set in again. Now my seat bones hurt even when I walk.

There is plenty of potable water here at this man-made well and we take this opportunity to wash our bodies and *dishdashahs*. A fire is lit and another Bedu feast is readied. Soon, Manaa tells us the heated rocks are ready. Meat is pulled from the tree and cooked to perfection. We eat. And sleep.

١٩ شوال ١٤١٩
February 6, 1999 Wadi Ghadun
Day 5 — 17 24' N 53 41' E

The night was cool at 45 degrees. Despite the fatigue of yesterday's ride, for the first time I awaken before the dawn prayer. We spend the day in camp attending to our journals, equipment, and saddles. The computer is wiped clean of dust and sand, as are the lenses. A blanket is darned of its tears from the first day.

Photos of the *wadi* and our camp, taken from our digital camera, are sent home via the satellite phone to waiting students, along with a written update of our progress. We take time to answer a couple of dozen questions piling up from children around the world. *What is the most dangerous part of your journey?* and *What are the Bedu children like?* the students ask. Each of us has come to believe independently that the camels are both the best part and the worst part, perhaps even the most dangerous part of our trek. We send an e-mail back to the school children about our attempt to make friends with the camels, about the pain of travel, and about how the Bedu children are at first shy until their curiosity overwhelms caution and they talk with us.

٢٠ شوال ١٤١٩
February 7, 1999 Visit Well of Mashadid, Wadi Ghadun
Day 6 — 17 33' N 53 42' E

I'm thinking of Thesiger today as we ride along the *wadi* floor. When he rode through here, a constant watch would have been kept along the walls of the *wadi* for potential attackers. Each Bedu, rifle at the ready across his lap, would have searched the ridgeline for movement. We ride without this tension, and despite the kidnappings in nearby Yemen, we never give thought to our safety, feeling quite unthreatened by raiders or other attackers at this point in the journey.

Since pre-Islamic times, marauding had been very much a way of life for the southern Bedouin. It had tapered off in 1932 when Saudi Arabia became a nation and Abd al-Aziz ibn Sa'ud, then the ruler, strictly forbade the practice. Traditionally, raiding was a large part of the economy and formed many of the customs of the Bedu. Camels were rarely bought or traded between tribes. The best way for an individual to get a camel and increase his wealth was to become a successful raider, and this pursuit was a man's most important occupation. Raiders were passionate about their craft and considered heroes by the people. One renowned raider named Audah Abu Tayah of the Huwaytat, who participated with Lawrence in the Arab revolt against the Ottoman Empire in World War I, was reported to have eaten the hearts of fallen enemies "on several occasions." The danger and sport of the raid was obviously intoxicating for young and old alike. A boy would look forward to the day when he could join his father. The edges of this desert sixty years before had been the scene of countless raids and occasionally these raids would have developed into genuine warfare. Men travelling through the desert, especially in areas far from home, would have to be alert, ready to fight or flee.

Raiding was never randomly done, and there were rules of engagement. For example, the Bedu believed that a camel should only be captured from tribes of equal or greater status. They also saw raids as a reciprocal adventure—while one tribe might be the victim one season, it would be the aggressor the next. Members of the same tribe were never the subjects of a raid, and women and children were never harmed, regardless of their tribe. If a large raiding party attacked a small group of families, the men would usually flee on their fastest animals to protect themselves. They would leave the women behind knowing that they would come to no harm. Great dishonour would befall the raider who harmed a woman or stole her possessions. Because of this, the women became the family "bankers." Around their necks and wrists hung elaborate jewellery of gold and precious stones—all of them safe from theft.

Bedouin who knew the Empty Quarter benefited the most from raiding, enjoying the advantage of being specialists in the harsh desert. Tribes like the Rashid, who took Thesiger across the Empty Quarter, would attack other more sedentary tribes living at the edge of the sands. They would move in swiftly, snatch a few camels, then steal away into their harsh desert home. The victimized tribe would attempt to pursue, but, unaccustomed to surviving in the deep desert, they would soon abandon the chase.

Spring raids were the least dangerous and often yielded the most booty. Since raids were often carried out over long distances to minimize the possibilities of a counter raid, summer was a dangerous time to plunder other tribes and then escape into the Empty Quarter, even for the Rashid. But the advantage of a summer raid was the fact that the enemy was often encamped at a well, and the raiding group could seize the element of surprise. Tribes resting at a well were aware of their precarious position and they often erected lookout posts. Yesterday, Manaa pointed out five-foot piles of rock at the ridge tops, explaining they were lookout posts which had been used for generations to defend the camp when travellers stopped to water. Areas like this where water is accessible have been the scene of conflict from antiquity to the 20th century.

When Thesiger crossed the Empty Quarter, the threat of being attacked by raiders was still entirely real. In *Arabian Sands*, he describes his party's reaction to the possibility of such an encounter:

> Suddenly the sentinel on the slope above gave the alarm. We seized our rifles...and took up our position around the well. The camels were quickly collected behind the mound. In the distance we could see riders approaching. In this land all strangers are counted hostile until they declare themselves. We fired two shots over their heads. They came on steadily, waving their head cloths; one of them jumped off his camel and threw up sand into the air. We relaxed as they drew near, someone said, 'they are Rashid—I can see bin Shuas's camel.'

During his time in Arabia, Thesiger and his companions always travelled with the fear of being attacked. Crossing the

Wadi Ghadun seen from above.

The ramparts of
Wadi Ghadun.

The Pool of Ayun—a surreal apparition.

A bowl of camel's milk poured for the team.

Musallim bin Abdullah.

Leigh—Abdullah bin Kanada.

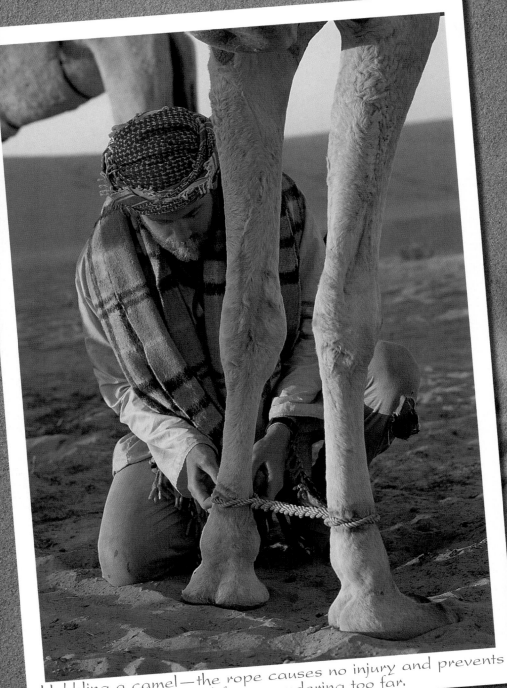

Hobbling a camel—the rope causes no injury and prevents the camel from wandering too far.

37

Sawad bares his teeth.

38

Leigh tracks progress with GPS.

39

A camel passes.

40

The lovely and talented Mr. T.

At the well's mouth—hanging from tattered ropes, squeezing deeper—Many snakes, many snakes!

The well of Mashadid—grooves cut into the rock through centuries of use.

46

Jamie chews at a cooked goat jaw.

A typical meal of **khobz**, **shaye**, and **gahwa**.

48

Camel meat drying on an acacia.

49

Musallim and bin Ashara study their countrymen in **Arabian Sands**.

Bin Ashara and Musallim load their couched camels.

A crescent moon marks the end of **Ramadan**.

After reading **Siddhartha**, Bruce sleeps.

53

Ali demonstrates his superlative riding skills in Wadi Rum.

54

Bin Ashara.

55

Bruce trying to persuade Lucy

56

Salalah—the ocean, and the journey's beginning.

Empty Quarter, Thesiger's group discovered that the Dahm, a Yemeni tribe, had been pursuing his tracks for days, planning to kill him and take his gold. Luckily for Thesiger, the Dahm were forced to turn back when their water ran out—only a day off his trail. By that time, raiding had already been strictly forbidden in Saudi Arabia for over a decade.

Suddenly we hear loud, aggressive shouts. In front of a rock outcrop stand a dozen men. Their waves and smiles make it clear at once that they are friendly. On the open *wadi* floor, a few jeeps are parked at odd angles on the uneven ground. Nearby, a white goat is tethered to the branch of a leafless *gadha* bush, struggling to escape. It will be our lunch feast. The men step away from their fire and shout greetings as we approach. To save the camels from the effort of couching, we jump down into a circle of smiling faces and stand awkwardly with bowed legs. Through word-of-mouth communication, word has spread about our route.

We exchange the news, and Bruce, assuming his leadership role, sets about explaining that we do not have time to share the goat because we are on a long journey, and must keep moving. I want to be free of deadlines and our other obligations, allowing us a longer stay in the generous care of these desert people. In the end we agree to share the fruit they offer, but not the goat. Our hosts are disappointed. I glance at the goat and wink.

We have arrived at the famous well of Mashadid. There is nothing to denote that this spot in the *wadi* is different from any other, but it is a remarkable place. Renowned for the sweetness of the water that runs in a stream at the bottom, this well has attracted countless Bedu over thousands of years. The "well" was not hewn through human effort, but cut through the rock by water over the aeons.

Geologically, Oman is predominantly limestone and other ocean sediments that were originally deep-seated mantle rocks. These rocks were thrust to the surface during the collision of the Arabian and Eurasian plates around 60 million years ago. Far under the surface of Arabia, extensive reservoirs of water are stored in the rock. These aquifers are the country's major source of potable water. The well of Mashadid is formed by a unique weakness in the surface of the limestone, which gives unusual access to an underground stream trickling northward.

Almost all the permanent wells of Arabia belong to particular tribes and have been owned within their family for generations. These men have come purposefully to host us at their well, which has probably been their tribe's for centuries. Each well usually carries the mark of a tribe or sub-tribe, cut into the rocky sides some way down the inside or engraved on one of the largest stones set around the well mouth. It is the same mark they would use to brand their camels. If ever there is a dispute over well ownership, the elders are consulted. By recalling stories from the past, the elders determine who has been the owner as far back as they can remember. That tribe is then given rights.

Having endured the foul water of the goatskins and the brackish mineral- and salt-laden water from other wells, I am thirsty for this sweet water. Extensive natural filtration leaves Mashadid's water as delicious as if it were bottled. Thesiger also visited this famous well and described his visit:

> The next day we reached the well of Mashadid...[The Bedu] reached it in the dark, clambering down seven shelves of rock with the help of ropes. The water flowed knee-deep and was said to have come from Ayun, for once a woman's wooden comb which had been lost there was recovered here.

Since reading Thesiger's book, I have been thinking about the well of Mashadid, especially during the last days, when good water has been hard to come by.

A couple of our water bags are low, so we take them to the well's mouth, hidden among the rocks and subtle enough to be easily missed. We survey the well closely. The entry is six feet in diameter. At its lip, cut into the rock, is a large, shallow bowl. I don't like small places, and the well is said to be filled with snakes. There is much discussion as the Bedu circle the dark hole almost reverently. The words are lost on me as I focus all my attention on getting mentally prepared for the descent. My heart races as I strap on my headlamp—the very headlamp I used to light my path into the Khumbu Icefall. The spiralling hole that descends into the earth—the well of Mashadid—is not unlike the gaping chasms that riddled our route across the icefall. Now, in an entirely different setting, the same fear sets in. A cat's cradle of synthetic and hemp ropes is anchored to a rock jammed in a crack at the well's mouth. One rope looks sturdy while others disintegrate when I grab them—they could be fifty years old or more.

The tools for negotiating the deep crevasses in the icefall are just as basic, though in better repair. On Everest we crossed numerous gaping holes, each dropping perhaps 200 feet below us—a little more than this well. A team of Sherpas had previously placed ten-foot lengths of aluminum ladder to form bridges across these broad fissures. Stepping into this well is frightening, like stepping onto the first ladder where the whole assembly bobbed and wobbled, creaked and twisted under my weight. I struggled to focus entirely on my boots as I placed each cramponned foot carefully on the metal rungs—metal to metal—and held the slack rope for equilibrium. I took a few more steps and the ladder bent deeply into the hole. I caught a tooth of my crampon on a rung and stumbled before catching myself with the other boot. I froze in the middle of the ladder, breathing more heavily. Fear of falling had paralyzed me.

"Focus on the rungs. Focus on the rungs," I said, trying to take my eye off the hole below. I took a step, and then took another, never forgetting about the hole below, but focusing on what I needed to do to get across. As long as my focus remained on the rungs and not the darkness, I was fine. I reached the other side, winning one of the small battles in the greater war. Climbing with Jason, we continued to another set of ladders—a group of five, strung in a vertical array, up an overhanging five-storey block of ice. The set was secured with sun-bleached ropes fanning out in several directions. The ladders and lines were tight because of the glacier's movement, which had pulled the anchoring points further apart. Jason and I had been in the icefall for two hours and the sun was painting the surrounding peaks orange, signalling the pending danger. Soon the frozen giant would awaken. Fear kept us moving. We stepped up, racing the sun. The ascent on these ladders passed in a blur of concentration and heavy breathing. At the top, Jason welcomed me into the safety of the open cwm plateau.

I enjoyed a certain freedom each time I climbed through the icefall, enjoying the surge of energy that came from overcoming my fears. Before we continued to Camp Two, Jason and I looked back into the confused icefall, bathed in sunlight. The ladders seemed to stand out more and more, the crevasses less and less, over the course of the expedition, but the fear of crossing them never left entirely. Here in the Arabian Desert I have encountered the same fear again, and must now accept that the war with my fear will never be won. I do know, though, that it will never be as hard again as it was when I first faced it.

With that little motivational thought, we descend into the dusty darkness that kills the light of our lamps. Neither Musallim, nor Ali, nor bin Ashara is interested in joining us, but Sheikh Musallim bin Said, whose family owns this well, will show us the way. As scary as this is, it's a joy to be experiencing it with Leigh and Bruce.

With a couple of *gerbers* in hand, we stand inside the first chamber, which could accommodate about five people huddled tightly in a circle. The tattered ropes hang past the rock lip at our feet leading us deep into the earth. We shall descend through a series of chambers connected to one another by tight passageways, to reach the water hidden below. I grip the ropes that connect us with the open air above and funnel down into the well. One by one, we follow the thinner of our two hosts, who has gingerly slipped beyond our view. I follow, then Leigh and Bruce. We climb down into another chamber half the size of the one before. The group above can no longer be heard, except when they shout. Before Bruce enters the second chamber, our thin Bedu friend moves down to make room. There is very little surface light in the next section, though I can still see a small patch of blue sky some thirty feet above. Our Bedu host has gone, and the only sign from below is the action of the ropes that support his weight, scraping across the rocks. The rope skips in and out of three notches worn in the rock, each about the size of a man's thumb. Then the rope holds steady and becomes less taut as the Bedu takes his weight off. It is my turn. I take the rope and work through the rock walls that are now tighter around me than before.

In the darkness, my feet search for a crack or a ledge. My hands drag against the polished rock. Thirty feet further down we enter another chamber. There is barely enough room for the two of us, and now no light reaches us. The air is thick with the dust of our struggle. We sit and wait for the others to catch up. Bin Said speaks to me but I don't understand. I tell him my Arabic is poor, and ask him to speak more slowly. He reverts to hand signs. In and out of the light, I catch glimpses of his hand and arm striking at me. He continues striking at my shoulder with two curved fingers while hissing at me to clarify his message that we are in snake territory. He points to holes in the walls and in the beam of my light I can see hundreds of small pockets where the snakes den—perfect vantage points for striking out at a passing warm body. I flip my head from one side to the other searching for a safer wall of smooth rock. Only two feet from my face and everywhere around us are curved walls thick with holes. A cold sweat breaks out on my skin, and the dust begins to run off my body in muddy rivulets. With every bead of sweat that trickles down my back, I reach behind, expecting to feel the cool skin of a serpent. A wave of panic rolls through my chest and my breathing becomes tight. I decide to leave and turn to climb out, but the hole above is blocked by Bruce's legs. The *sheikh* continues down and calls me to follow.

"*Khalee balak, haya!*" he cautions from below. "Be careful—snakes. Many snakes, many snakes!" Most of Arabia's snakes are venomous, and many inhabit the shaded cliff walls of a *wadi*. I wonder whether the saw-scaled viper, known to sun itself in this area, also likes cool dark holes. This is a snake that can grow to two feet from head to tail and sports two-inch fangs. I shiver with the thought despite the heat. Perhaps the gecko-loving carpet viper or the less venomous sand snake waits in the dark. I know I could choose not to continue down. I could let Bruce pass and then climb back out. But above him are Leigh and the other Bedu, who wait for their turn to descend. I would have to sit in this small cavern and wait for them to pass. Yet, at the bottom of this well, some untold distance below, runs a stream legendary for its freshness. I give in to my thirst—and my pride—and direct Bruce's foot placement before sliding even further downward into the bowel of the pit.

My body muffles the directions coming from below. Leigh and Bruce are silent above me. I wonder how they are handling this, or whether they're even scared. The deeper we go, the higher my heart climbs into my throat. The walls are now rough and uneven—and riddled with holes. Each successive chamber allows us ten feet of descent. I finally drop into a larger opening, where I am reunited with our guide. His eyes are wide with excitement as he tells me to flash my light about. "Sing! Sing!" he tells me in Arabic. I sing the camel watering song, which he likes. He joins in. During the pauses between breaths he searches the walls, explaining that snakes don't like either light or song. In my current state this makes utter sense to me, so I up the volume. He tells me to keep my hands and arms close to my body and away from the rock. This of course is impossible. We wait for the others and look into the dens for obvious nests. This chamber is nicely curved compared to the others. We sit back to back in the very middle of its pear-shape, keeping maximum distance from the walls. I can see no other passageway and think we must be at the bottom. There is no water here, but the air is more humid than before.

I think I see a flash of scaled skin slithering in the beam of my light, but see nothing when I inspect the little hole. A two-inch ledge, draped in dust, links this hole with others at the same level. My Bedu friend points to the slender track of a snake cutting through the dust. "*Wayn maya*?" I ask where the water is and he shifts, pointing to a hole behind him not much larger than a basketball. The panic is complete. I want to race out of the cave, to push the walls away and breathe from the blue sky, but Bruce is working his way through the last hole and again corks my exit. I cup my hands over my mouth and nose and try to breathe some carbon dioxide to calm myself. When I look again, my 120-pound

Bedu friend is wriggling down through the next hole. He descends into the last chamber, shouting at me to follow—and to be careful!

I put my legs through the hole but get hung up at my chest. I can feel no footholds, nor can I hear the directions being offered from below. The others are coming down. Sweat pours down my brow, stinging my eyes. I am certain I can feel the cool slide of a snake on my inner thigh. Unable to see or grab at my leg, the only way to prevent what I feel is a certain poisonous bite to my groin is to push the air from my lungs and slip downward. I drop four feet to the last floor and search my legs for the snake. There is none. Then I notice the cool water now running over my feet.

Though the flow is small—about a quart a minute—the gurgling echoes in the chamber as if it were a rushing brook. The multi-coloured rocks beneath its surface sparkle in the light. There is nothing of the smell of sulphur, nor any green algae growing on the rocks. The water is free of bugs—as pure as one could dream. We are the latest in a long history of people who have come here to drink in this cherished well. I cup my hands at the stream's entry and watch it pool in my palm before drinking it. This water is sweet as any I have tasted—cool and light in my mouth, and soothing to my throat. I can feel it tracing its way to my empty stomach, where its coolness tickles. I splash more on my face, a luxury in this arid land, just as Bruce drops into the hole and fills the chamber. Forgetting the snakes and the narrow passages that lead back to the surface, we laugh and drink together till my stomach bulges like a camel's.

We open the neck of the *gerber* and fill it till swollen. We attach it to a rope and call Leigh to pull it up. The rope slides across the rock lip and then slips into one of the grooves. They are at least two inches deep and are the most deeply cut in the cave. How many goatskins full of sweet water have been pulled over this rock to carve these grooves? The mute history of this stream is written in the stone.

Bruce climbs out of the lower chamber and now it is Leigh's turn to slide through. I am grateful to be able to share the uniqueness of this place with him, and we thank our Bedu companion for guiding us here. Leigh drinks deep and long, then retreats. As he disappears through the smallest opening I start after him when my Bedu friend speaks, slowly and clearly so that I understand:

"My grandfather lived and died in this *wadi*."

"How did he die?"

"Snake bite," he says. "Here in the well."

My belly, now full of water, makes the exit through the small passages more of a challenge, and the smallest one forces the water back up into my throat before I squeeze through. The story of the grandfather's demise is enough to keep me moving. I follow my guide upward and marvel at his sense of hospitality, a hospitality transcending even the dangers of the well.

Once we are back on the surface, water is poured into the stone bowl as a demonstration. I can imagine this scene in years past, a steady train of Bedu cycling up and down the well, discharging their *gerbers* into the great stone bowl around which their camels circle to drink.

In our absence, the Bedu have already slaughtered the goat I thought we spared and have it cooking. We ring the fire with our enthusiastic hosts, then eat heartily. It is after five before we resume the ride. The sun sets within the hour. Though the Bedu team was happy to stay and eat the goat, they are now becoming tense about all the delays in our schedule, so we ride on into darkness.

Chapter Ten

۲۰ شوال ۱٤۱۹

February 7, 1999
Well of Mashadid, Wadi Ghadun

Day 6 — 17 33' N 53 42' E

We encamp in the dark amid a healthy collection of *gadha* shrubs, with their numerous leafless branches. T chews on one while I stow his saddle. Soon everyone is tucked in to sleep. I record my thoughts on a dictaphone, curled up in my sleeping bag to avoid bothering the others. It was after our adventure down the well at Mashadid that I started to feel ill. The dust has penetrated my sinuses and now I can't breathe through my nose. My lower back aches, as do all my joints. Energy eludes me, and I begin to wonder what I might have picked up in the well's stale air.

Depression stalks me when I start feeling ill and begin thinking, *This shouldn't happen to me.* Sickness has visited more than one of my adventures, dating back to a nasty bout of dysentery in Kenya in 1990. Three Everest expeditions brought me sickness, including the last in 1997, when a chest infection overtook me on the trek into Base Camp through the Khumbu Valley. The most frightening of these illnesses happened in Tibet in 1994, when I had an anaphylactic reaction to penicillin.

Poor health on Everest made climbing a near-impossible undertaking. Here in the desert, minor health disorders are less debilitating, since the camels do most of the physical work—we humans need only endure. Still, I don't want to feel ill like this deep in the sands, where I'll be more susceptible to sunstroke and dehydration. Lessons learned in the high Nepalese village of Namche Bazaar come to mind. Days lying prone in my tent saw me playing out desperate scenarios of failure. Thick fog floated in over the rock walls of our campground, adding to the gloom. I felt certain that once again my chances for the summit were dashed—that I would stand at the edge of realizing my dream and that a virus would rob me of it.

I pushed myself hard before I went to Everest, and pushed myself too hard before coming to the desert. This time, doing the work of securing sponsorship and managing day-to-day business, along with physical training, have taken their toll, and now I'm sick again.

On Everest, extended time at altitude and lack of rest drained our failing resources. Immune systems were also failing us in the thin air. Everyone suffered. We reeled under the flu, sinus infections, gastrointestinal disorders, wracking coughs, and there was nothing we could do about any of it. Though mountain and desert are dramatically different, the total impact on the body seems similar. Here I already suffer blisters that refuse to heal, chronic back pain from being jolted on camel back, and the aftermath of food poisoning. Only days before my summit push on Everest, I ate unwittingly from a tin of spoiled corned beef. Few lesions heal on the mountain, muscles knot up and tear, and illness is commonplace. It's a race against time in either venue, and the winner is the one still standing at the end. In the stuffy darkness of my sleeping bag, here in the desert, I should remember that on Everest, debilitation forced me to rest and that rest brought healing.

I need to relax and let the illness take its course, relying on the knowledge that it will work itself out. It's half past midnight, and I am sweaty but cold even with two extra camel blankets over my sleeping bag. We will ride 54 miles to Shisur in the next three days—16 miles tomorrow, 19 for each of the next two days. Regardless of how I feel, I will endure.

February 8, 1999 Mutafah
Day 7 — 17 40′ N 53 43′ E

Fever has kept me awake most of the night. When sleep did come, it brought dreams of a pulsating iridescent sky and imaginary balloon people attacking me in technicolor. My sleeping bag and *dishdashah* were sweat-soaked when I awakened.

We are still within sixty miles of the coast, where it is not uncommon to see the occasional group of camels left by their owners to wander along the *wadi* in search of food. Travelling in groups of five to ten, they come within yards of us and often spook our camels, keeping us at attention in the saddle. There are periodic breaks in the walls of the *wadi* where the lower cliffs have allowed the construction of a road cut, which gives both camels and vehicles access to the *wadi* floor. At such places we might also encounter a local *sheikh* who has heard of our passing caravan and wants to wish us well and offers to slaughter a camel on our behalf. We tell the *sheikhs* that, though their generous offers are respectfully appreciated, we cannot accept. We settle on the gift of a bag of dates or a bowl of camel's milk instead. In his *Arabian Sands*, Thesiger also wrote of the esteem in which a generous person is held. He recalled an instance when an old man joined his group at a fire while they were camped in Oman at the edge of the sands, as we are now. The man was clad in only a loincloth and looked the part of a beggar. Thesiger was surprised at the respect paid this man when everyone rose to greet him. Later, while questioning bin Kabina, he learned the reason for their respect:

> 'He hasn't got a single camel. He hasn't even got a wife. His son, a fine boy, was killed two years ago by the Dahm. Once he was one of the richest men in the tribe, now he has nothing except a few goats.' I asked, 'What happened to his camels? Did raiders take them, or did they die of disease?' and

bin Kabina answered, 'No. His generosity ruined him. No one ever came to his tents but he killed a camel to feed them. By God, he is generous!'

We ride on a few hours. I still feel poorly, but changes in the terrain offer some distraction. Wadi Ghadun begins to fade to desert plain. The walls widen and become lower. Over the last two miles the distinctive *wadi* has fanned out. Numerous smaller dry waterways wind among islands of rubble. We are stepping into another world. The smooth polished rocks of the *wadi* floor are dispersed. We are no longer confined by walls. Over what remains of the ridge, I can glimpse periodically the sand and gravel flat beyond. The terrain looks suddenly harsh, compared with the hospitable confines of the *wadi*. Patches of windblown sand wash the *wadi* floor. The camels move well across this ground, but no more smoothly than in the *wadi*, and my hopes for a better ride in the sands are unfounded. Mr. T still jerks, bounces, and rocks—roll, pitch, and yaw. The camels pay careful attention to the change of terrain, remaining calm as we leave the sheltered riverbed. There is little life here. Few trees. No birds. Only lizards inhabit this area in any numbers, as proven by the tracks in the sand that Musallim points out to us. Ali hates lizards, but won't say why.

Bin Ashara is suddenly sombre. We take a break to adjust a saddle and he shows me a nickel-sized flower with four delicate yellow petals, growing six inches from the ground. He tells us the blooming of the *zahar* flower marks the coming of the hot season. "*Hare, hare, hare!*" he says, looking north and shaking his head at the coming heat, forecasting our fate. This pretty little flower is the first to bloom and marks the arrival of summer, which comes to the Empty Quarter with hellish 120-degree temperatures. This year it has come four weeks early, and our hope of getting through the desert in the last cool of spring is dashed. We still have six to seven weeks to go. "*Mafi zein, mafi zein*. No good, no good." Bin Ashara concludes and walks off talking to himself—or praying.

Now ahead of the group by 300 feet, Musallim has been leading us through the broken *wadi* since lunch. He has turned sharply west, then southwest—and now due south! We're heading into the mouth of a tributary *wadi* feeding into Ghadun. Each mile we gain is hard-won, the ride grinding, painful. By the time we catch up, we've lost over a mile of northerly progress. Bruce and I are surprised, and Leigh is almost beside himself as we try to find out why we've turned around. As if the reason will reveal itself, Musallim points ahead and says nothing.

A single rifle shot cracks the air. Everyone instinctively crouches in their saddles as the crack echoes off the rock walls, making it hard to locate its origin. Musallim jumps from his camel with the second shot. The rest of us follow. With a third shot comes the shouts of a man whose voice we trace to find him standing on the rim to our left. *"Marhabah, Marhabah!"* he shouts. *Welcome.* He fires two more shots. Musallim works his rifle free and returns two rounds into the sky, unaimed. I look at the faces of Ali and bin Ashara to get context of this situation. All I can gather is that they are a little tense, but nothing more.

Bin Ashara yells, *"Salaam alaykum,"* and *"Alaykum as salaam"* is returned. We all yell greetings back and forth to the stranger, sharing in this exciting if hazardous welcoming ritual without actually discharging more rounds. Off the camels, we walk another few hundred yards below the ridgeline until we round a corner and the village of Mutafah reveals itself. A dozen structures make up the town set at the *wadi's* edge. We stop in the middle of the *wadi* below the village to make camp. A group of young boys and men have gathered at the village entrance and walk down to meet us. A village elder appears with his antiquated rifle and fires off a shot at close range, startling both the camels and us. Musallim returns fire again as does bin Ashara but the old man now struggles with his jammed weapon. He tries a few blows with a small rock to the bolt, but to no avail, and he finally gives up. Musallim greets him with a nose kiss and a handshake. Unhappy with his gun's performance and the embarrassment caused him, the old man walks off to sit on a boulder, where he continues his struggle alone. I keep an eye on him, concerned he will return to redeem himself and his antique weapon or accidentally discharge a shot.

No sooner have saddles and bedrolls hit the gravel than two goats are dragged from the village by six of the boys. We learn that the party has been planned for days, though no one's told us. We are grateful but concerned that we will be even further behind schedule with an extra two miles added to our journey. This is an aspect of Bedu culture we wish we'd known about before. Then we could have built these social gatherings into the plans, and have relished them as we came to know these compelling people. I am here to experience and learn from the journey, to celebrate the distinctive elements of Bedu culture that separate it from my own. If we are to truly live among the Bedu, we have to be prepared to adopt their ways.

The three of us discuss back and forth this need for adapting, taking out on each other some of the stress that comes from having little or no control over the adventure we have planned, funded and organized. We are concerned about the planned dates of our arrival at the Saudi border—the most tenuous of our political permissions. We are to provide the Kingdom of Saudi Arabia with the date we intended to enter the country, as well as an estimated departure schedule. If we don't make better progress, this window will pass. And, with it, our precious entry permission.

While the meal is cooking, a young man brings a female camel from town. She is couched beside our gathering. Then, without a word to any of our team members, he takes the bull camel from our herd and facilitates a mating. None of our team is consulted, nor would consultation be expected. Bull camels are rare, because most males are killed for food shortly after birth. Females are always kept for their offspring and their milk. Females eat less, and while they display less brute strength than the males, they have better endurance and are easier to handle. Most males, if not eaten, are castrated. So, it is accepted that if a bull is available to mate, permission is unnecessary. This tradition became a cause of concern for Thesiger during his journey, as it occurred numerous times when he passed through villages or encountered nomadic families. Thesiger wrote:

> We were continuously pursued by tribesmen with females to be served. We had a long journey in front of us and this constant exercise was visibly exhausting my companion's mount, but he could not protest. Custom demanded that this camel

should be allowed to service as many females as were produced. No one even asked the owner's permission. They just brought up a camel, had it served and took it away.

In about fifteen minutes, with much aid from the young man, who helps the camels position themselves properly, the mating is complete. It is less than a graceful interaction, but this is always the case, as Thesiger discovered: "Clumsily [the bull] straddled the yellow camel, a comic figure of ill-directed lust, while Khuatim, kneeling beside it, tried to assist. Bin Kabina observed to me, 'camels would never manage to mate without human help'."

Thesiger crossed the Empty Quarter in late winter. Camel courtship and mating generally occurs from December to March. It is not surprising then that all of our camels are in an amorous state. To show their affection for their female counterparts, the male camels often blow a large reddish skin bladder or *dulaa* out of their mouths. The blowing of the *dulaa*, accompanied by a *blubblubblubblubblubblub* sound, makes for quite a dramatic courting display.

Mr. T has taken a liking to Lucy, and he never misses a chance to nuzzle her when we ride by during the day. While we camp at night, he always moves to get closer to her. Regardless of his efforts, she seems to not notice. Labian has an eye for Rosie, who goes berserk and kicks and yells whenever he approaches. He usually backs off.

The camels soon finish mating and the camp settles down in anticipation of the coming meal. As always, dinner is about more than just eating. It is about sharing the gifts of God. We gather at meals for equal measures of physical and social nourishment, sharing songs and poetry, stories and laughter with friends about the fire. Young boys of five and six, along with their older brothers, sit scattered among the group, with one eye to the goings on of the elders and the other to signals from their friends to break from the group. The youngest boy aged three or so, curls up beside his grandfather and rests his thick mat of hair upon the elder's lap. A sinewy hand lovingly strokes the boy's hair and face, settling him to sleep. A few stand and sing softly. Others dance to the new song, and always the conversation flows. Leigh, who needs a little distance, gathers his sleeping kit and moves some twenty yards from the group. The rest of us circle around the fire to sleep. We are careful to keep our feet away from one another's heads, as this is both offensive and unlucky, according to the Bedu.

٢٢ شوال ١٤١٩

February 9, 1999 Gravel Steppes
Day 8 — 18 00' N 53 38' E

Eleven a.m. We have been riding four hours and twenty minutes, and have covered fourteen miles. Although the pain of the ride is constant, I have been quite distracted from it by the sight of the last of Wadi Ghadun fading as we enter this gravel and sand plain. Nothing impedes our northerly progress now. Save for the odd saltbush, the featureless terrain is unnervingly empty. There is nothing for the eyes to rest upon. Since our departure from Salalah eight days ago, Leigh, Bruce, and I have ridden with our camels roped to the three Bedu. The uneven and unforgiving *wadi* floor was not the right place to complete our solo riding apprenticeship, since falling would be dangerous here. This morning the Bedu have decided that we three Canadians should all ride together in one line, tied to bin Ashara. Leigh is second aboard Labian, and Labian is roped to bin Ashara's saddle. I am attached to Leigh in the same fashion, as is Bruce to me.

It is a terrible bore, but am I ready to ride alone? Suddenly Bruce calls to me, "Cut me loose." He must be thinking the same thing. Are we ready to face this risk? Is my fear a healthy warning sign or do I just lack some requisite courage? Bruce calls again, "Untie me," and so I lean back in my saddle and pull the knot loose.

"Do you want me to untie you?" Leigh says, noticing the action. Without a thought I tell him to turn me loose. Bruce's boldness has spurred me on. As Leigh struggles with the knot pulled tight by Mr. T's lunges at passing saltbushes, I look back to check on Bruce; he has drifted back to the others without incident.

160

Leigh tosses me the second rein and we are free. T turns sharply to the left. A tap to his neck with my *yad* and he comes back to the right. Sweat stings my eyes. Ali gives me a thumbs-up and smiles broadly. Leigh shouts up to bin Ashara and signals that he would like to be freed. I am heartened by his encouragement and our triumph.

The next few hours pass easily. Each of us works on maintaining control of the camels. The *yad* and the reins work with leg and foot pressure to guide the camel's speed and direction. At first we fall behind the others as the camels test our authority, but we land a couple of hard taps with our camel sticks and catch them up for lunch. I stop T with a firm tug on the reins. Instead of couching him in the saddle, I save him the effort, leaning forward and swinging my right leg back and over his hindquarters, dropping seven feet to the ground. I share a quick and silent moment of celebration with Bruce and Leigh. We say nothing to each other but understand everything in our broadly grinning faces. A wonderful moment with my big brother and friend.

After lunch we cover twelve miles in three and a half hours, for a record daily total of 26 miles in seven and a quarter hours. Throughout the afternoon Bruce, Leigh and I focus on our camels while the Bedu navigate with impressive precision. Though there is nothing to guide them northward except the position of the sun, they lead us in an almost perfectly straight line—quite without GPS, compass, or map. We are well served by their sense of direction, their knowledge of the desert landscape, and their ability to interpret the subtle clues the land affords. Ironically, Bedu we've met seem unable to navigate the busy streets of Salalah, yet here in the open desert with no street signs or paved roads, they are remarkably accurate. Stunningly, even the GPS would have permitted a greater deviation.

It is the end of seven days' riding. We are camped 102 miles north of Salalah. As planned, Tuarish and Salim Ali arrive in the supply jeep with grass and water for the camels. Dinner conversation turns to the need for vehicle support past Shisur where we will arrive tomorrow. Bruce is angry about the Bedu not sticking to the plan, and reminds them we had agreed that the trucks would follow us only to Shisur.

The call to prayer rings out and breaks up what is becoming a tense conversation. I sit back and watch. It's a fitting end to a wonderful day. Though there is tension in the group regarding the frequency of re-supply, I am thrilled to have conquered my fear of riding solo and to have rediscovered a marvellous sense of freedom. It is a moment to let go of the sponsorship deals, the *National Geographic* film, and the distant worries of business.

٢٣ شوال ١٤١٩

February 10, 1999 Shisur
Day 9 — 18 18' N 53 43' E

Bruce leaps out of bed as soon as bin Ashara calls everyone to morning prayer. As usual, Ali is the last to rise, though he never misses his prayers. I'd like to sleep more, but Bruce's example gets me out in the cold, pulling on a damp *dishdashah* I'd forgotten in the sand next to my sleeping bag. Uncomfortable as they be, these desert mornings are nothing like the misery high on Everest. Above 23,000 feet I rarely slept well, and the 3:00 a.m. starts brought headaches and nausea. Despite the chilly desert nights, mornings here are much warmer. There is plenty of air to breathe in the desert, and I feel little real strain in comparison. In the desert I wake up with a fierce appetite, unlike the mountain, where nausea usually replaces hunger.

Something has happened through the night, and bin Ashara yells at Tuarish to get the truck. Some of the camels are missing. I'm only able to count four of the herd in the growing light. Labian is among them, as well as Rosie and two other pack camels. All the others are gone. The truck speeds off with Tuarish and bin Ashara. Meanwhile, I attempt to dry my *dishdashah* at the fire. Bruce is making tea and hunting for the sugar when Musallim arrives. He grabs the pot from Bruce and takes over the process with rumblings about Bruce making the tea too strong. Bruce angrily tosses the bag of sugar near Musallim's feet, but Musallim pays him no mind. This is the first time I've seen Bruce lose control of his calm. Musallim finishes brewing the tea beside me. He is not at all friendly this morning, and I wonder whether he is angry about Bruce's discussion on vehicle support last night, wanting as he does to have trucks with us at all times, not just intermittently. We still want to try the journey in the old way, unsupported from outside if at all possible.

I drink my tea, wondering how far the camels have gone. Their front legs were hobbled, so they could not have gone too far, although, if they walked all night, they could be over ten miles away. It's unusual for the camels to stray, since they normally tend to stick together. Bruce packs Crazy Dancer's saddle. I pass by him to get T's and ask him whether he's okay.

"That stuff is tiring," he says. "There seems to be no *Please* and no concept of instruction here, it's just *Give, give, give, here, here, here!*" I have rarely seen Bruce so angry, priding himself as he does on his patience. "So that's wearing me down, on top of the planning, and the fact that Leigh seems to be so unhappy. It's a tough situation just now."

Leigh has taken to sleeping away from the group at night. Beyond coping with the challenge of living in the desert, he is becoming increasingly frustrated with what he sees as our inability to make plans with the Bedu and follow them through. Leigh tells me he is still perplexed about why Bruce didn't more accurately share the lack of progress with the trip's organization months ago. I suggest he talk to Bruce about it, but Leigh says it's too late.

The missing camels add yet another layer of stress. I don't ask the question, but it must be on everyone's mind—What if the camels run off like this, deep in the desert?

We have been ready for half an hour when bin Ashara and Tuarish come back and report the camels are not far away. We jump in the supply truck while Leigh gets aboard Labian. As he is wont to do most mornings, Labian races off and starts to buck and spin. Leigh holds on despite Labian's best efforts, and Musallim, who will bring up the other camels, rides in to lend a hand. The rest of the herd has moved northeast and not south, for which I am grateful. In a couple of minutes of driving we come upon a dilapidated concrete water well. All of the missing camels are pulling at the grass growing at the well's edge. They had smelled the moisture from our camp two miles away. We make short work of rounding them up and by the time we are ready to go, Leigh arrives on Labian.

I ask Ali what we'll do if the camels run away in the desert. He tells me that this will not happen because we will tie their hobbles much tighter.

The truck races off toward Shisur some nineteen miles away and we resume our ride. We will stop for tea in a few hours if we find any branches of old trees to burn. The morning's trouble disappears as I concentrate on the ride and on building a connection with my camel.

Without any warning, T suddenly jumps forward and starts bucking. When T calms down I can hear Bruce, behind me laughing. He explains that his camel had lunged forward unexpectedly and had bitten T on the rump. I am too impressed with how well I've managed to stay on to be angry.

I have begun to notice a strengthening of my thighs and back, allowing me to stay on board during our recent camel frenzies. What surprises me is the pain in my knees. Without stirrups, my legs hang free. The combination of unsupported weight and the rocking sway of the camel swings my legs and puts a stress on the knee joint that I can not seem to relieve. We have been riding for hours without a break and I can't stand the discomfort any longer. I get off and walk for a while. Instantly, the pain stops.

The team rides past, checking to see that I am all right. Now T starts to act up, pulling at the reins and stomping his feet. The further the others progress the more distressed he becomes. T doesn't want to be separated from the group. I try to get T to the sand to mount so we can catch up, but he refuses to couch and bites my arm in protest. I shout at the others to wait but they are already beyond earshot, so I vent my wrath on T in a string of colourful epithets.

I have little choice but to run after the group, along with the camel. Once we are closer, T calms down enough for me to couch him. My body overheats as my head begins to pound, my pulse quickening. I move to the saddle and swing my leg over his back, when suddenly he leaps, flipping me to the ground and pushing my temper past the restraining point. I pull on his rein, jerking his head down hard, all the while bashing my camel stick on the ground, remembering that I must not strike the camel. I can use this anger and this energy to chase the group once again. This time I run ahead of them, couch T and successfully mount up. It takes me a few minutes to calm down, realizing I've probably never been this angry before, grateful I've managed to direct this new anger beyond the animal. The desert has begun to reveal weaknesses and there is little out here to hide them.

While training in Texas last year with desert survival expert David Alloway, we learned the heat does strange things to one's mind. Dehydration dementia is common in desert settings. Similar to hypoxia at altitude, it affects the mind and makes even easy thought processes difficult. Like altitude sickness, dehydration dementia strikes without real warning, but leaves the affected individual feeling angry and irritable rather than drunk and lethargic. All three of us have seen this in recent days.

Once I feel able to speak without spitting out all my frustration, I ride up to Bruce, who has been quiet since the tea incident. He says he's doing better, but clearly worries about our relationship with the Bedu. "I think the fundamental thing," he says, "is that when we ask something, it's easy for them to just say '*Inshallah*,' and then refuse to deal with us. What upsets me more now is Leigh's negative attitude."

During the trip's planning there was concern about the dynamics of Leigh and me as brothers—that we might feud, leaving Bruce in the middle. So far this has not happened and what tension there is exists between Leigh and Bruce.

While I can empathize with Leigh's concerns, sleeping apart from the group is no way to deal with them. And while I know Bruce did his best to do his organizing job, much of this could have been avoided had he more accurately shared with us his lack of progress with the Bedu months ago.

It is now one in the afternoon, and I think I can see an oasis. But I have thought this before and am reluctant to get my hopes up that it is really Shisur. As far as the eye can see, we are surrounded by desolation. Not a single feature breaks the horizon encircling us. We have not come upon a single stick of wood, and thus will not stop for lunch. Other than the high sun, there is nothing to help discern direction, and with the sun at its apogee, north might as well be south and east could easily be west. A little overwhelmed by the emptiness, I drop my head to hide from it and retreat into myself. No use—I can't hide. The desert is lifting its great mirror.

Shisur will bring welcome rest. We should be able to find plenty of water to drink and even to wash. We might be hosted to meat and fruit and, best of all, we will not have to endure riding an entire day. But I begin to wonder whether we will ever find the Lost City of Ubar, as Shisur is also known. Lost for good reason I speculate. Then, at two in the afternoon, we see it. The buildings look to be about six miles away, boiling in the heat rippling up from the gravel.

Shisur is thought by many historians to have been an important stop on the Incense Road, which crosses the Arabian Peninsula. As important as the Silk Road to the East, the Incense Road carried frankincense to be traded at great profit—often six times the local rate, once it reached distant markets. We are now riding on the track of the great camel caravans that transported the precious resin to Iraq and Egypt, from where it was then taken to Europe. I can still smell the oad Ali gave us near the Pool of Ayun, and imagine the men who drove those caravans smelled the same.

The dot on the horizon is growing in size and I'm certain we're finally approaching Shisur. The ground rises ten feet, affording a new perspective. What I'd thought was the entire village is only the treetops of the Shisur Oasis about three miles away. Lush trees stand five hundred yards out. Two structures stand out on the small hill where the village was built—a large water tower, and a mosque, blue-topped and whitewashed. Omani flags fly at half-mast. Excavated ruins can also be seen, under which the well is located. The camels need little encouragement to speed up—they can smell the water.

Up close, the collection of date palms is impressive—there must be more than a hundred mature trees. Their long waxy fronds shimmer in the sun. The sound of the place strikes me as much as its physical beauty. The wind makes a lovely rattle in the leaves. "Friendly sound, isn't it?" Bruce offers, thinking the same thought.

It is a friendly sound, a welcome break from the wind's scouring hiss across the scorching sand. Above us, large green fronds reach out from thick trunks and veil the sun's glare. On cue, a dozen birds, bee-eaters and wagtail, leave their branches and fly singing into the sky. They fly with the sense of urgency and determination that battling with desert winds has instilled in them over the centuries. At the Pool of Ayun I didn't fully appreciate the sounds of their echoing calls, of the wind in the poolside reeds, and of the gentle lapping of water at the cliff's rocky face.

As have many travellers before us, we stop and take water at Shisur. It is the only water in the central steppes that can be counted on, as other wells are susceptible to drying up. Its water is neither sweet nor plentiful, but its flow is consistent. Past generations of raiders escaping into the desert and thirsty caravan leaders have come here for water. I can easily imagine the sand stained in blood spilled in the frequent battles such a precious water supply would surely have caused.

Fifty years ago and more, travellers would have been forced to dig out this well, searching in the cave under the mound that now shoulders the ruins of a stone fort. Thirty-six feet down in the cave, a tiny bead of water flows. In the past this would be patiently directed into leather bags and carried out for thirsty camels. Those of the Bedu, not involved in gathering the water would be posted as guards or to help the camels cycle through. It was here Thesiger watered his camels and met again with his Rashid companions before heading off to Mughshin on his crossing. Unlike Thesiger's party and many before him, we do not have to dig out the well. Water is now pumped from much deeper up to the permanent settlement above. Diesel generators enclosed in a hut outside the village power the pump.

While I am inspecting the well opening, a young local boy draws near and tells me that King Hussein of Jordan passed away February 7th. This is why flags all across Oman are at half-mast, out of respect for one of the Middle East's most notable leaders.

The wind is now blowing at 25 miles per hour, so I return to camp to cover the gear. Bruce is napping among the palms, and I wonder why we are not camping there. The Bedu have often passed attractive camp spots such as this for basic gravel and sand patches. They seem not to care about the aesthetics as much as we do. Leigh is reading *War and Peace*. Bin Ashara, our wily desert veteran, tells me we are being buffeted by a lucky wind. From his rapid stream of Arabic I learn that the east wind is normally cooler, and thus "lucky" for us. So far, I can't tell the difference.

We unload in a dusty nursery of date trees, on the village's east side, which is protected with barbed wire. Manaa, Tuarish and Salim Ali arrive to help. An old female camel trots by. Seconds later comes a truck in pursuit, five locals stand in the truck's bed yelling at the camel. The wind is picking up, changing direction. Instead of coming from the south as it has since our arrival, it now blows from the east. Bin Ashara says again that this wind is lucky, that we are blessed by Allah for it. I find the wind frustrating, since everything is becoming bathed in sand.

Ali and Musallim walk the last hundred yards into the village. I walk around, exploring the area. On top of the hill sits a museum of sorts. On the walls are photographs and newspaper clippings that headline the discovery of the lost city of Ubar—lost owing to God's wrath when, legend has it, He destroyed the city for its sins. The ruins of Ubar were first detected by NASA satellites, which picked up the traces of the old frankincense caravan routes, all converging in one place. In 1990 the ruins were excavated and the Atlantis of the Sands, as T.E. Lawrence called it, was revealed.

We receive an invitation to a feast. At dinner and close to midnight we sit about the village square with men from the twenty or so local families. The rice is fatty and flavourful, but the meat is tough. We are now eating the old female we'd seen earlier being chased down by the lads in the truck.

Chapter Eleven

٢٤ شوال ١٤١٩

February 11, 1999
Rest day, Shisur

Day 10 — 18 18' N 53 43' E

The Bedu reveal themselves slowly. I have sat with Musallim, Ali and bin Ashara, hearing them talk about their lives. They are reluctant to talk about their families—such talk attracts bad luck, they believe. Nor will they disclose the number of camels or any other possessions they own—this might be seen as boasting. It is clear the Bedu are keen observers. They miss little. They forget less.

Ali catches me searching for my diary. Having seen me place it in my saddlebag earlier this morning, he reminds me of its whereabouts. He did the same the other day when I misplaced my pen.

I send out an update for the students, including six digital photographs. One is a shot of a dead lizard we have found at the base of an acacia. Bin Ashara thought it a bad sign. "Lizards eat anything, and when they die there is nothing," he tells us in Arabic. He believes that the lizard, like the early bloom of the *zahar* flower is a warning of danger. "*Mafi maya, mafi ackle, ye muth,*" he adds, pointing to the lizard. *No water, no food—you die.*

On that cheery note, we repack our gear trying to lighten it for the next phase of the journey. By agreement, from here to Mughshin, a week's trek away, we will not see the supply truck and will carry all that we need.

A local man invites us to take a shower in his home. Bruce decides to sleep instead. Leigh takes advantage of the water to wash all of our *dishdashahs*. After the shower we are invited to dinner. A dozen men gather in a room of the *wali's* home. The houses here are not as numerous as the houses of Thamarit. They are the same as Manaa's house, save for one noticeable difference. Instead of sitting on carpet, we take to large couches, which line all four walls. Though we insist they shouldn't, the men make space for us by taking to the floor. Intricately carved double wooden doors close behind us. Among the faces here we see our Bedu team, showered and dressed in fresh *dishdashahs*, everyone smiling brightly.

Bruce's absence is questioned. We explain he is sleeping. They are offended that he hasn't come and ask whether he is sick. At the time, we didn't realize the invitation to a shower came with an invitation to dinner. Feeling awkward, Leigh and I sit looking about the room. The concrete walls are bare, and a single light bulb hangs by its wire from the ceiling. Its light lands harshly on the gathered faces, and heavy shadows distort their features.

Everyone is still standing. Even the elders, who had to call on Allah for help in getting up. We walk around the circle of men and greet everyone. My Arabic soon fails me, but I continue to try to make contact through my eyes and a firm handshake. When we try again to sit on the floor, the men insist that Leigh and I sit on a couch at the head of the room. They ask questions of bin Ashara and Musallim. I listen to the questions flying through the room.

"Do they pray?"

"No, never. They're Christians," bin Ashara says.

"Do they tire of camel riding quickly?" I don't grasp the answer.

A boy of eight serves coffee to Leigh and me. Another offers a bowl of dates.

Too tired to listen to the real questions, I start to imagine them:

"Why are they crossing the sands?"

"We don't know."

"Will they write a book like Umbarak?"

"We think so. Suhail is always making notes and talking into a machine."

"They all take photographs and shoot film, which slows our progress."

The talk shifts to news from Salalah. Someone responds to Ali's questions about the recent camel races in Thamarit.

We discover the meal has been ready for two hours. Because of our poor Arabic, we missed the details of the invitation—we were invited to dinner and asked whether we wanted a quick shower beforehand. We are embarrassed that we've held them up for so long, wondering what else we have missed and whom else we have offended.

Our remorse is buried under the weight of two huge plates that arrive, bearing mounds of scalding hot rice and steaming meat. Atop it all sits the head of a goat. Appetite suddenly overcomes our fatigue, and despite the goat's empty stare, we eat. My hands still are not conditioned to handling the hot food, and they sting with the heat. But I tear into the platter of food anyway, stopping only to pick the stringy meat from my teeth. Our hosts, quite accustomed to the heat, reach into the piles of food without hesitation, pulling out great chunks, which they offer to us. In the Middle East, it is customary to eat what has been put before you, and we are now at least savvy enough not to offend. The entire goat has been cooked, save a few glands. At most meals, the Bedu honour us by popping from the skull the highly favoured eyeballs and placing them before us as gifts. At this meal, the tongue is drawn out of the head and divided in two—half for each of us. After this, we are offered a piece of liver, some stomach, then a chunk of something unidentifiable—a testicle, I suspect. We down it all with grateful smiles.

Though feasts are always social occasions, all talk ceases once the food is served. I try to finish a conversation while eating, but an elder gives me a dark look and signals to the food. His message is clear: *Shut up and eat.* Though there is a huge quantity of food, eating lasts for only minutes and so to talk is to miss one's share. The Bedu do not linger over meals. As with the Sherpas, quantity supersedes variety. It makes sense to eat quickly in the desert. Any gust of wind deposits sand in the food, and that sand is so fine it cannot be removed without discarding the whole meal. Though the Bedu now live a largely settled life indoors, the tradition of eating quickly continues.

We rise from the plates on the floor and return to the couches. I work a hand-fashioned wooden toothpick about my teeth and observe the men in conversation. A metal bowl heaped with glowing charcoal arrives when the plates are taken out. A pinch of frankincense is added, producing a cloud of perfumed smoke. Each man passes the bowl to the next after wafting the smoke into his beard. I remove my head wrap to scent my hair as well as my beard, knowing it will be some time before we shower again.

The room's light has softened in the lingering smoke. I catch the stare of an elder while rewrapping my head, but I am proud of my new proficiency with the *masar*. Though variations are subtle, each man displays a distinctive tie to his wrap, such as the way he tucks in the end or the number and tightness of the coils. Leigh admires Ali's style with its loose coil, and practises tying his *masar* in the same way each day. It looks as if Ali's headwrap could fall from his head at any moment, though it never does. I tie my *masar* tightly, preferring not to worry about it during my daily struggles with Mr. T.

The elder holds his stare. His well-groomed snowy beard illuminates a dark and wrinkled face. His beard is highly stylized and must require regular maintenance. The sideburns are cut tight to his temples and shaped along his jaw to a point. There is a bare patch shaved below the bottom lip, and the moustache is trimmed below the nose to form a perfect frame for the upper lip. He speaks to the others but keeps his eyes on me. His voice is powerful, surprisingly deep, and quite lacks the rasp of age. Though his body has begun to atrophy, his hands are still large and strong, agile enough to spin his camel stick with considerable skill. He is 85 or more. His eyes are clear and penetrating, and everyone listens when he speaks. On his forehead, a dime-sized callus has formed, evidence of his years of prayer and reverential prostration before Allah. I finish tying my head wrap, leaving a corner of the fabric to hang down by my left ear as my own little signature. The old man surveys the wrap, then nods with an approving smile. He turns back to the group and pays no further attention to me. I am glad I have come.

٢٥ شوال ١٤١٩
February 12, 1999
Day 11 — 18 32' N 53 45' E

All twelve camels loaded and ready, we say goodbye to Manaa, who is reluctant to see us go. His concern for us is apparent in the expression on his face. The way he stands and waves goodbye reminds me of Sir Wilfred when we left him more than a month ago at his retirement home.

The twenty mile per hour wind that has blown throughout the night continues today. The excitement of being entirely self-sufficient makes the wind of little consequence. All six of us now command two camels each—one for riding and the other for packing. The pack camel is linked to the saddle of our riding camel by a five-foot rope. The pack camels are loaded with *gerbers* of water, bags of food for us and the camels, the satellite phone, solar battery charger and filming gear.

After yesterday's rest, the camels are energetic, and skittish about the new arrangement. Having just mustered the courage to ride alone, I find managing two camels is challenging. Bruce takes his third fall when his ride, Crazy Dancer and his pack camel become caught up in each other's ropes. Ali, demonstrating his riding magic again, swings around to gain control of the panicking pair.

By noon the wind gusts at over twenty-five miles an hour. We stop for lunch only long enough to couch the camels for ten minutes. Bin Ashara digs into his saddlebag and pulls out a handful of dried camel meat. He picks out bits of grass, dirt, and insects, and distributes six finger-size sticks of dark meat, one for each of us. We sit in the lee of the camels, backs to the wind, and chew heavily. We finish with swallows of brown water from one of the goatskin *gerbers* and ride on.

At four we arrive at a cluster of rocky outcrops and trees—the only prominent points we have seen for days. To the west, a clutch of three *ghaf* trees is the sole vegetation. Sand and fine gravel make up everything else. Leigh talks to bin Ashara about how far we have come. The two are an interesting mix of old and new—Leigh with his maps and GPS, bin Ashara with his hard-won desert sense. Each appears to be gaining respect for the other's knowledge. They estimate we have covered twenty-one miles today, point to point, by taking a twenty-three mile route. This deviation is small overall, but large by the exacting standards our Bedu companions have set. Hour by hour, the wind consistently nudges us subtly off course.

We stockpile our gear, careful to leave nothing lying about, lest it be covered by blowing sand and never seen again. The *gerbers* are hung by their ropes on the rocks. Great care is taken not to puncture them. All we have done today is sit and ride, but everyone is abnormally tired from exposure to the constant wind. I have to force myself to shoot some videotape. Musallim makes a fire in the shelter of the rocks, using wood brought from Shisur, and brews some tea. The tea is poured, Ali breaks bread and dips the chunks deeply into his cup, past the fine layer of grit collected on the surface, into the sweet tea below. Someone has an orange from Shisur, which the six of us share. Bin Ashara canvasses the group about coffee. No one will join him but he makes a batch anyway. Not wanting him to drink alone, I have a cup.

There is a legend that coffee drinking first began here some twelve hundred years ago. While resting in the afternoon sun, the legend goes, a Bedu goat herder named Khalid noticed that, though the hot sun made him tired, his animals were energetic and vigorous after eating the berries of a particular bush. Eager to enjoy the same vigour as his goats, Khalid ground and boiled the berries to produce Arabia's first cup of coffee. Since Khalid's discovery, coffee drinking has been an important element of Bedu culture and the attendant rituals have little changed over the centuries.

To get my attention, bin Ashara taps my knee with his camel stick, then digs in the pocket of his *dishdashah* to retrieve three dry, flattened dates. He pulls one apart, and asks me to pick my portion. He chews the dates and sips his coffee and I follow suit. *"Suhail"* he says. *"Tamar ma gahwa zein. Tamar ma shaye mafi zein."* *Dates with coffee is good. Dates with tea is not good.*

Dates and coffee have always gone together. The sugar contained within the date complements the bitter coffee flavour. Tea is always served with sugar and, along with being overly sweet, its flavour is too similar to that of the dates. Bin Ashara explains that drinking tea and eating dates at the same time threatens stomach trouble.

As the little fire burns out, bin Ashara and I finish our coffee perched as we are above the wind and flying sand. A dust devil sweeps over, forcing us to finish our coffee. The wind now carries so much sand that the sun is obscured even before it passes the horizon. Bin Ashara takes my empty cup and wipes it clean of the grounds with his finger.

The meal is simple—dried meat and bread. That it is cut short by the wind seems of little consequence. We arrange our sleeping bags and camel blankets atop a flat rock. Though it is exposed to the wind, the rock is away from the scorpions and spiders that scuttle about the desert floor. By eight o'clock we are all bedded down. Once again I pull my sleeping bag over my head trying to keep out the sand while writing in my journal. Beside me in the bag for the first time is my rifle. Moments ago, Musallim showed me two positions for sleeping with it. The first is lying on my back with my hands crossed at my chest. The barrel of the rifle rests inside my arm at my elbow, the muzzle jutting past my ear. The butt rests beside my thigh. The second position is lying on my stomach, the rifle under my left shoulder, my left hand on the barrel. Bin Ashara showed his favourite sleeping position—lying on his side with his rifle cradled in front. He rests the stock between his knees and places the barrel in his hand next to his head, cuddling it. Bin Ashara gives us a demonstration.

"Mushkilla?" he asks rhetorically. *Problem?* Then he crawls under his camel blankets with his weapon and pretended to sleep. In an instant he jumps to his knees with his gun at the ready. *"Mafi Mushkilla!"* *No Problem!* he concludes to everyone's laughter, while

mock-firing at raiders. It was this concern for speed that had the Bedu initially uninterested in the sleeping bags. Thesiger was warned that camel blankets were better than a bag: "I crawled into my sleeping bag. Bin Kabina said, 'God help you if you are caught in that. You will be knifed before you can get out of it'."

Over the wind Ali shouts, "*Kanadi, al yowm zein?*" Good day, Canadians?

"*Aiwa, colla zein! Shokran.*" It has been a good day. We are grateful.

٢٦ شوال ١٤١٩
February 13, 1999
Day 12 — 18 44′ N 53 58′ E

Up by six, we're on the move by eight. The wind, which blew all night, is still with us. The camels' eyes water constantly, dripping sandy tears into the soft hair of their cheeks. They are well adapted to this sandy wind, with thick double rows of eyelashes, which catch most of the sand. Most interestingly, the camels have two eyelids—a second, transparent eyelid protects the surface of their eye leaving the camel sighted even in blowing sand.

By mid-morning, the dunes begin taking shape along the horizon. By midday, ten miles further along, the Empty Quarter's inner dunes are just visible beyond the gravel steppes. Mughshin lies to the northeast, and so we ride parallel to them, too far away to see clearly, close enough to feel their magnetic pull. Pink dunes line the northern horizon and roll like Himalayan ranges, constantly tumbling into another without ever changing place.

After covering another twenty-two miles, we make camp. Down in the flats, the sun has left us, but the dunes catch its final light. The distant glow beckons me toward them, now that I have an idea of their true mass.

February 14, 1999
Day 13 — 19 01' N 54 14' E

One in the afternoon. We have stopped for lunch under the shade of the only tree to be found between the horizons. It is larger than most others we have seen. We have been moving steadily since dawn, and have already covered sixteen miles.

Leigh turns on his GPS system and delivers a report. "We are currently at 18 57' N 54 08' E," he explains. "That's over sixty miles from Shisur. We have nineteen more miles to Wadi Qitbit, then fifty more to Mughshin." Even though we took a full day off at Shisur only two and a half days ago, the thought of three more days before another rest worries me. Our hopes that we would become hardened enough from our training in Thamarit to make the riding tolerable have been dashed. Beyond the pain in the saddle, the temperature is 113 degrees Fahrenheit, and the heat is not improving my ability to cope. The entire team is lethargic by midday. Even the thought of leaving the shade is too much. Little appetite, allows a couple of sticks of meat from the bag to satisfy me. We have all found a place on the ground under the tree, and nap with our head wraps over our faces to keep the flies from the drops of sweat. We rest a while, then we get up and ride on. The day is without wind, and is the hottest we have encountered so far.

We cover another twenty-two miles before dismounting for the evening. There is nothing here save another stunted acacia. It is Sunday, February 14th. Valentine's Day. The solo acacia symbolizes something of tonight's loneliness. The temptation to call home is irresistible, but the satellite phone is reserved for reports to the school kids and for emergencies—not to call my wife, Barbara. The phone rings half a world away. It's nine in the morning back home.

"Hello."

"Happy Valentine's Day," I whisper in the phone, my heart in my throat.

"Oh, Jamie. Thank you." Her words melt me.

This is our second year of marriage, and distance and time apart take a toll on our relationship. When away, I am fully engaged in the task at hand and have no time to muse about home. I never felt homesick on Everest. Something always distracted me there—some vital task to accomplish, some immediate danger to manage. Here in the desert, there is much more time to think, to remember how I have been blessed with Barbara's support. Limited battery power cuts our chat short.

Using the light of my headlamp to make the call and write more journal entries has been a huge mistake. Insects, crawling and flying, suddenly inundate the area. They swarm about my head and face, bombarding my journal, and sneak into the sleeves and neck of my *dishdashah*. I continue with my dictaphone and kill the light, hoping the bugs will lose interest. In a darkness unlit even by the moon, I can lie on my back and gaze up to stars so clear and so bright that the night sky seems three-dimensional.

A meteor flashes across the sky. It burns in the atmosphere like a stunning display of fireworks. The night sky on Everest was also stunning, with jagged mountains jutting up to frame the stars. At Camp Three on the Lhotse Face in 1997 with climber Jeff Rhodes, we watched Comet Hale-Bopp on its headlong dive into Mount Pumori's summit, the comet's twin tails easily visible to the naked eye. Unfortunately, the temperature was colder than the comet was beautiful and after a few minutes we were driven back into our tent.

٢٨ شوال ١٤١٩

February 15, 1999 Qitbit
Day 14 — 19 18' N 54 30' E

We awake to the call to prayer. Musallim takes a turn today. Musallim's prayer call is more melodic than bin Ashara's, which befits his vocation. His intonations are complex, like those of a

songbird, rising and falling. This is all so incongruous, as Musallim rarely smiles before nine in the morning. Though he is sometimes sharp with us and usually barks orders, he sings and prays in dulcet tones: *Allahu Akbar*
God is most great.
Ash hadu ahn la Ilaha Illallah
I testify that there is no god but God.
Wa ahn Mohamed Rassoul Allah
I testify that Muhammad is the Prophet of God.
Haya Ala El Salat
Come to Prayer!
Haya Ala El Falah
Come to salvation!
El salat kheir min el nohm
Prayer is better than sleep.
Allahu Akbar
God is most great.
La Illaha Illallah
There is no god but God.

After prayer and another of our hurried dried meat breakfasts, we ride again. Time easily passes in studying the footprints of the other camels, searching for the clues that bin Ashara uses so successfully to differentiate them. The art of tracking has largely been lost among the Bedu, and bin Ashara is one of the last of the skilled trackers. During the first days of our trip, passers by often asked him, "Bin Ashara, have you seen my camel?" After one inquiry, he paused and then replied: "Yes. It was in Wadi Qitbit, heading south with two of Sheikh Said's camels. They will be south of Thamarit by now as they were moving fast and that was one and a half months ago."

The prints look all the same to me; their subtleties are not yet apparent to my untrained eye. Bin Ashara answers my questions and seems happy to teach. There is much to learn. Every camel makes a distinct print. When one is proficient, the depth of the footprints will tell whether the camel was being ridden or whether it was pregnant. A camel from the gravel plains has smooth pads, while one from the sands will have loose strips of skin. Each leaves distinctive marks. We are learning from one of the best—some say bin Ashara is among the best ever.

A baby lizard sprints into the path of our small camel caravan. Too far from its den now, it panics, darts left and right in the confusion of the hooves. It's under us now. T steps on it. I look behind, expecting to see it crushed, but the little lizard is still alive as he pops first his head and then his body free of the sand into which he was pressed by T's footpad. The stunned lizard staggers for a few feet, regains its bearings and scrambles away, lucky to have survived the only traffic it will likely see in its lifetime.

"*Qitbit!*" Ali shouts, pointing to a building of some sort, lying beyond a small rise. The *wadi* by the same name that runs its course to the east is Ali's birth place. Because Leigh is lagging behind on Labian, who shows a consistent inability to keep up, we all stop and wait. While he catches up, we guess at the distance to the building. All except Musallim guess that it is more than three miles away. But Musallim's dead reckoning is perfect. We ride for two miles then reach the Police outpost at Wadi Qitbit. A green, white and red Omani flag wafts lazily from a pole, marking Oman's reserve near the Saudi Arabian border just to the north. Four mobile trailers square up to form the post. The courtyard between the trailers boasts a clothesline from which hang some towels. Some oil barrels, a large, leaky propane tank, and a bicycle lie about in the courtyard. Two old bed mattresses lean against a wall, giving shade to a few chickens. Three Land Rovers of varying vintages and states of repair stand outside the square next to a 5000-gallon water tank. A single gravel road emerges from this place past a makeshift corral, heading southwest to Highway 31, the route we had driven from Masqat to Thamarit a month before. We are now 201 miles from Salalah.

We unload the camels, then tie them to the rusty fence posts forming the corral and go off for tea, rifles slung on shoulders. Musallim stops to help me button the collar of my *dishdashah*, similar to the caring way in which a father might adjust his son's attire. Now, in the afternoon, Musallim seems a different man. He smiles often, with a warm grin that makes up for all the usual discontent of the morning. I am moved by this friendly attention.

Three middle-aged men occupy this camp—two Omani nationals and a Sudanese worker. We share tea and chat. Bruce slips away with the NEC laptop, the satellite phone and the keys to one of the Land Rovers. Using the vehicle's battery power, he types a report for the kids. In the dispatch, Bruce shares intimate and painful memories about his father's death four years ago. Bruce's dad never did know of his son's prouder achievements, of his time on Everest, or his time in this desert. But there was a wonderfully mysterious bond created between a son and his father, a bond that Bruce might never have found, had he not also found Thesiger. Bruce writes:

> One of the hardest things for me as time has passed has been the inability to share with my father my joys, achievements, and failures. The summer after he passed away I began guiding twelve-day river trips on the beautiful Tatshenshini River in northern Canada. After four summers and over 200 days on her banks, the river became an important part of me. I always wish that I could have described her course to my father, show him my photos, and share with him my tales.
>
> Later I had the good fortune to spend six months guiding sea kayaks in the Caribbean, join a Canadian Expedition to Mt. Everest, and climb to the summit of Mt. McKinley in Alaska. All these things would have been of such great interest to Dad, and yet they remained unknown to him in his lifetime.
>
> ...While I was at home over Thanksgiving, my mother mentioned that Dad had his own copy of *Arabian Sands* in his bedside table! I was shocked. Mom further told me that it had been one of his favourite books. He had been given it in 1959 as a present from my grandparents; the inscription still visible yet slightly faded on the inside jacket. That it was still there, forty years later, among the small

collection of books Dad had kept by the bed, was astounding.

An interesting link, back and forward—not only Bruce reaching back to his past, but Bruce's past reaching forward to us in the here and now. Though the readings had been separated by miles and years, it was easy to make the connection, as if father and son were reading together, each having happened on Thesiger in his own fortuitous way. Now Bruce is living a part of an adventure his father had read about long ago, passing the same features, treading the same ground beneath the shifting sands, pausing at the same pools to be refreshed, resting perhaps beneath the same acacia.

Chapter Twelve

۲۸ شوال ۱٤۱۹
February 15, 1999

Day 14 — 19 18' N 54 30' E

Wanting to get to Mughshin in the evening's cool, the Bedu urge us on, past our intended camp here at Qitbit. In four hours we cover another twelve miles, stopping momentarily for prayer. It is now quite dark, another moonless night, but the temperature is accommodating. Despite the brilliance of the starry sky, nothing can be seen of the ground passing beneath. A sharp rock, a dead shrub, a dip in the ground, or the steep incline of a miniature *wadi* rim—all entirely unpredictable for us, but not for the camels, whose eyesight is superb. They can recognize familiar humans at great distance. Like many mammals, other than humans, camels have behind their retina a membrane called the *tapedum lucidum*, which enhances their night vision. This membrane is what causes the unsettling glow of an animal's eyes under bright light, like that of an automobile's headlights.

Musallim, Ali, and bin Ashara, fifteen feet ahead, start singing the riding song to pace the camels. This gives me more confidence, and T speeds up at my request. The air feels wonderfully cool. The ground is softer than usual, the ride much less painful. Each of T's steps sounds as if we are walking in mud. We must be sinking into the sand a few inches at each step. Bruce and I join the chorus when we can, and a lump gathers in my throat. For some reason—perhaps the stress of these last days in the team, my happiness at simply being here—tears flow down my dusty cheeks into my beard. I am thankful for darkness.

Thirty minutes later, bin Ashara yells *"Irkab aw nahm?" Ride or sleep?*

"Whatever you want," Bruce and I answer. Three miles on, he asks again. We give the same answer. Leigh points to the danger of riding in the dark on uncertain ground and votes to stop. Knowing the Bedu have a history of riding in the dark during raids, we want our companions to know we are willing to ride as long as is necessary.

Eight-thirty. We've been riding an hour and a half in utter darkness. We stop again. Leigh says he wants to camp. Bruce says nothing. Everyone sits waiting for bin Ashara to speak... *"Nahm!"* he yells at last. *Sleep.*

We eat just a little dried meat, too tired to face the effort of cooking bread. While the others settle in to sleep, I ready the video camera for an early morning shoot. I set my alarm for four, wanting to film the group waking to the new day. To be sure of hearing the alarm, I put my watch near my ear under my balaclava—a trick learned from my friend Alan Hobson on Everest. The others are asleep when I'm finally done.

٢٩ شوال ١٤١٩
February 16, 1999 Pass through Montassar
Day 15 — 19 31' N 54 43' E

My alarm assaults my ear and jars me awake. My body aches. A rush of cold air infiltrates my sleeping bag. This is enough to kill all resolve and convinces me I can film the group tomorrow morning. I wrap myself back in my sleeping bag. Bin Ashara rises at 5:20 for prayer, and I finally get on the move, getting good shots of the team crawling out of bed, drinking tea and eating dates. While they saddle up, I jog a half mile north to film their advance.

The men walk toward me, five abreast, ahead of their camels. Behind them the sky begins to glow—an impressive scene. Their sand-hued *dishdashahs* blend with the sandy landscape. Head wraps add red and gold into the frame. The men swing their *yads* in time with their strides, while the camels, gear loaded with colourful blankets, peer over the men's shoulders. They pass through the frame and disappear northward.

When I rejoin the group, bin Ashara and Ali are having trouble with their camels. The camels, unaccustomed to continuous desert travel, are rebelling. Rosie, her name a reflection not of her temperament but the colour of her hump, is carrying *gerbers* with half of our water supply. She is jumping about and we worry she might fall and burst the skins. Thesiger and others who travelled this desert routinely lost camels to starvation and fatigue. Rosie tries to bite bin Ashara's forearm, receiving several handfuls of sand in her mouth for the offence. Ali takes a kick in the shoulder from Lucy. Fine red powdery sand flies everywhere. Musallim stops to help and tells us to carry on.

It is more than an hour before we see the Bedu again, this time a half mile to the west. Unsuspecting, we have been drifting east, without the Bedu to keep us on the correct heading. In just a few miles we have lost our route. I was certain we were on track. Leigh, leaning on his new desert navigation skills, leads us northwest in order to intercept them. Reunited as a group, we ride on for another couple of hours to the small oasis of Montassar.

The well sits in a subtle depression in the sand, ringed with rocks stained black by sulphur, which fouls the air. Bright green grass grows among the rocks. It is a startling and welcome break from the brown monotones that have dominated our world. The ground is covered with the dung of birds and animals that have come here to drink. Our camels do the same, but not deeply.

North of the well, the terrain changes. We have crossed the thirsty gravel plains that absorb the entire runoff from the north slope of the Qaras. Broken intermittently with sand dunes, the gravel flats stretch back beyond Shisur all the way to the mountains, then on to Salalah and the coast. Ahead, bleak gravel gives way suddenly to five-foot dunes of orange and yellow sand—a sign of things to come. Once we reach Mughshin, we will turn north and enter the red sea of rolling dunes and ride to the heart of the Empty Quarter.

We stop under a *ghaf* tree for a drink and some meat. We take a short nap and ride on. The dunes greet us like red-stained ocean surf. They provide welcome visual relief, but slow our progress by forcing us to meander through them. A few more stunted trees come into view as we travel northeast. To our left, we begin to see quite clearly the monstrous dunes of the Rub al Khali. They get closer with each mile, and hour by hour look more intimidating.

This is our fifth straight day of hard riding. We end it among some larger dunes at the edge of a sprawling *wadi* that divides them. The dunes are now all of thirty feet high. We stop at six, just as the sun is about to leave us, and according to Leigh's calculations, twenty miles closer to Mughshin. With only eleven miles to go, we should arrive there tomorrow by midday. We will rest for two days while replenishing our food and water. Then we will press on into the hardest part of the journey, travelling through the Uruq al Shaybah.

This area is riddled with the largest dunes in all of the Empty Quarter. It is a place of mythic proportions, and some of the dunes are thought to be more than 2000 feet high. It is our misfortune that we now intend to cross these legendary dunes in the heat of a summer come early. This part of the crossing was also the source of Thesiger's greatest concern. The great dunes of the Uruq al Shaybah are bordered on the east by the Umm as Samim, or "Mother of Poison." Hundreds of square miles in size, the Umm as Samim stretches from the Uruq al Shaybah in the west to the mountains near Masqat in the east. The water throughout is so brackish that not even a dying camel would drink it. Passage through the area is said to be foolhardy at best, owing to the great tracts of quicksand and unfriendly salt flats.

٣٠ شوال ١٤١٩
February 17, 1999 Mughshin
Day 16 — 19 33' N 54 53' E

There is little for breakfast this morning—food is low. The *gerbers*, too, are low, and what water remains now resembles a greasy chocolate milk. The bits of goat fat and clumps of hair floating in it are unavoidable. Although I've had a half a gallon in the past two days, I can't bring myself to drink this nasty brew. As a result, dehydration has made me edgy. I'm not in the mood for much of anything this morning—food or drink. Or aggravation.

We start off in an unusual fog bank that keeps the temperature from climbing, though the sun's rays are still able to penetrate and burn the skin. The dunes force us into a twisting *wadi*, where trees grow larger and more plentifully, furnishing homes for great spiders to hang webs in hope of future meals. A few birds fly overhead, while some take to a tree limb to watch us pass. One tree stands in the path of a creeping dune that slowly engulfs it in sand. Beneath the surface there must be dead branches and withered leaves now choked from the sun. Among these there may be a smothered bird nest. The mother might have returned after a sandstorm unable to find it. Blowing sand would have quickly sealed the fate of the shrivelled chicks.

The perched birds add their cries to this eerie morning start. The *wadi* floor is hardpan and T's jolting steps have brought back all the searing pain the soft sands had relieved me of the day before. Through my aching haze, Mughshin finally comes into view at the top of a distant rise. It is the largest settlement we have come across since leaving Salalah. Numerous buildings become visible—a water tower, a mosque's minaret, all surrounded by a concrete wall.

Though progress is slow, Leigh is again lagging behind the group on Labian. We are riding in the great Wadi Mughshin, which was formed by the convergence of numerous smaller waterways that spill out from the coastal mountains. This is the lingering terminus where the last of the water fans out and disappears into the ground. Smaller dunes blown from their parents to the north now trap us in the uneven ground of the water channels. Below the surface, the water table is constant and gives life to trees with penetrating roots. Dunes and trees render a straight route to Mughshin impossible, so we wind our way through the maze while the village seems never to get any closer.

Beyond our arrival point, a healthy stand of trees rings a tiny pool of salty water. This is the only surface water we have seen since Ayun. We pause at the village entrance, at the end of a low incline. In 1942 Sultan Said bin Taymoor, the father of Oman's current leader, Sultan Qaboos, ordered a fort built here to mark the northern reaches of his southern kingdom. At the time, the British government was overseeing the attempted delineation of national boundaries in Arabia, and the Sultan wanted Omani flags to be seen flying here.

In 1987, Qaboos ordered further development and built a government outpost along with condominium-like living quarters. A new mosque was added and a face-lift given the old one, which now sports a stunning teal-coloured tile dome. The government subsidized the work, and gave many of the houses to Bedu families who were unable to find their place in one of Oman's booming coastal cities. Today, soaring temperatures have driven the villagers into their homes. The place appears deserted. Around the perimeter of houses, Bedu families have built corrals at their back doors. Fashioned from sheets of wood, lengths of wire, empty barrels and bits of corrugated aluminum, they are alive with faces watching our approach. From one pen peer goats, from another a few chickens, and from still another a couple of curious camels. A little boy spots us through a glassless window and runs away. Village elders materialize to greet us. In their midst we see Manaa, Tuarish and Salim Ali. We circle up for the customary greeting, and are invited to unsaddle our camels, water them, and put them in a corral on the edge of town. Bruce, Leigh and I are led off and the Bedu disappear elsewhere. The *wali* generously offers us a two-bedroom furnished condominium and we gladly take it, feeling suddenly strange amid all the comfort.

After we unpack, a young boy arrives to invite us to have dinner at the home of Ghanim bin Mohammed, whom we had met in Thamarit. After eating heavily with our host and our Bedu team, we retire for the night, agreeing to meet at eight in the morning to review our plan for the next stage of the trip. Back at our lodging, a steady stream of local citizens parade by our front door, perhaps curious about us and our equipment, perhaps wanting to socialize. Some just look in from the outside, while others come in to examine our gear. It reminds me of the yak herders in Tibet, who were also fascinated by our technical equipment. A few engage us in conversation. We regret that we have no tea or other sustenance to offer them. The guests handle our cameras, our computer, and our rifles. They take aim at a spider ascending the wall. The assembled townsmen seem to approve of everything, especially the .22s, though, like everyone else, they tell us the calibre is too small. One man points out places on our maps to his friend, while another flips through the pages of my diary. He finds the odd English word that looks familiar and asks for my help pronouncing it.

١ ذو القعدة ١٤١٩

February 18, 1999 Rest in Mughshin
Day 17 – 19 33' N 54 53' E

Musallim, bin Ashara and Ali arrive, just as planned. Manaa is with them as well, looking at his phone and complaining about the lack of cell site coverage in Mughshin—some materials were to arrive at his construction site in Thamarit and he wants to confirm.

Leigh, as navigator, is piecing together the huge topographical maps of the Arabian Peninsula on the floor of our two-bedroom suite. Manaa starts by outlining the route from Mughshin through the big dunes to Liwa and on to the coast at Abu Dhabi. He wants to establish the points of re-supply before we continue.

"The supply truck can meet you once or twice a day. Whatever you like."

This is a shock to all three of us. The plan had been reworked for re-supply only at major villages such as Shisur, Mughshin, Butabol, and Liwa. We had wanted to approximate Thesiger's crossing as closely as possible. Under pressure, we had agreed to have extensive truck support from Salalah to Shisur. After that, we had agreed that we would be on our own between re-supply depots. This had been the case for the last five days and it had gone well. Now we sit on the floor examining the maps with Manaa. Bruce restates the previously arranged plan emphatically in his best Arabic. Bin Ashara, Musallim and Ali, looking crisp and clean in their newly washed *dishdashahs*, shake their heads but say nothing. Their faces are darkened from the sun and their beards longer than when we started. They sit on the couches and twirl their camel sticks while looking down at us.

Bruce swallows a couple of times and tries again in English. "Manaa, we all agreed to the vehicle support to Shisur. We rode alone here to Mughshin, and that went well. Now we want to do the same to Abu Dhabi."

Three more local men join the meeting. Musallim and bin Ashara get up to welcome the men, and invite them to sit on the couches. With little notice to the newcomers, Manaa gets back to the issue at hand. He says that without extensive support the crossing is not possible. Bruce presses him for the reason, but Manaa won't give it. Finally, he explains: "The Bedu are not coming for adventure; they do not want life dangerous for them. They want comfort and relaxation, not hard times."

One of the visitors speaks up in excellent English. "From here into the sands there is no shadow, no wood to make meal, and no people. Very impossible to cross. These people [our Bedu companions] want no part in that hardship." The Bedu are clearly not interested in the challenges that we are almost guaranteed to suffer in this crossing. And who are we to ask these men to suffer in the name of our own personal adventure?

Beyond this, however, why have we asked these people to undertake this? We could go without them, but we know this is foolish. And for me it would undermine one of the very reasons I have come here. It was the Sherpas who brought the cold Himalayas to life with their remarkable character. It is the Bedu who give great life to this place. To travel without them would be to lose much of our journey's value.

Everyone is talking among themselves. Three more locals arrive and squeeze onto the couches and join the discussion. Though they are not formally part of the riding team, they are all connected to it, symbolically and by tribal association. All share the culturally mandated responsibility to join in the discussion and lend what advice they can. Thesiger encountered this, too:

Among the Bedu, anyone, however young, can always express his opinion, and will probably do so even if the argument has got nothing to do with him. No Bedu would ever think of saying 'For God's sake mind your own business,' as he would accept that anything that concerned him concerned everyone else in the community.

The three of us quietly sit while the debate heats up. Bin Ashara kneels beside the map and draws our route from Salalah. Two of the strangers kneel as well, nudging Bruce and me out of the way to have their input.

I sit back, lost in thought while a few more people arrive. The room warms with all the bodies. It had been our goal to head into the desert and to see no one until the end. But in the face of the extensive drought that has left the desert bereft of grazing sites, this is clearly impossible. Even Thesiger relied on chance encounters with others in the desert, for milk, for food, and for the news of grazing locations for his camels. He offered supplies to others, and the favour was often returned. This is the nomadic code of the desert, once critical to the survival of these desert people.

The discovery of oil and the settling of these wild territories have changed all that. The nomadic life is all but gone, and we can't count on chance encounters with others to bolster our supplies. There will likely be no one else in the desert. With grazing destroyed by ten years of drought, uncommon even in the Empty Quarter, Thesiger's grazing stops will be denied us. We will need water and food supplied to us every few days for the camels. Trucks will be essential.

A couple of the strangers tire of the discussion. They are replaced by others who immediately jump in with their opinions. One man offers this compromise: "You can take small water and little dates, and you can have adventure this way. The Bedu will take their own meals and eat okay. This will be no danger." Apparently the Bedu think adventure and danger are one and the same. We try to explain the difference, but make no progress. The steady flow of people coming and going continues. Each brings new ideas and opinions.

Suddenly Musallim speaks and one of the men translates. "If you want to go in old Bedu way for adventure, Musallim says you must not have so many equipments. No more camera. Only water and food and then you go."

The idea is immediately appealing and not surprising, coming from him. We could lose all the gear save one video camera and one 60-minute tape and two batteries—just what I carried to the summit of Everest. We could file a report to the children advising them of our plan and then make one big push. We could abandon the sat-phone and solar power equipment. Here we are, pushing to go unsupported in the nomadic tradition—but at the same time, making that impossible by the need to carry so much gear. I'm ready to take this idea seriously. But before we can, Manaa tells Musallim that, even without all the gear, we will still need water and food for the camels. And that the desert can't offer. Musallim nods and the idea dies as quickly as raised.

The room is still full. Some say the crossing is impossible. Others ask why we don't drive. We explain again that crossing the desert in a truck is of no interest. We want to travel in the traditional Bedu way, with just our camels and each other, close to the desert. We try to explain we have come for adventure. Manaa tells us to take the "soft side." Bruce counters by saying that we want the "hard side and the safe side" of adventure. "No! Too much dangerous!" Manaa says emphatically. We are getting nowhere. Bruce is upset and so are the Bedu.

Bruce and I sit back against the wall while the room fills with loud Arabic conversation. I look across at our Bedu teammates. I thought Bruce had determined with the Bedu team that we would all cross the desert in the traditional Bedu style. This meant, I assumed, that they were willing to undergo with us whatever hardship that might entail. The possibility that this agreement had not been reached—or that it had been reached and the Bedu no longer want to stick to it—is frustrating. Bruce had struggled with this very issue early on in the expedition preparations, but thought he had come to an agreement with the Bedu, as outlined in his December 18th report to the webpage:

57

58

A lizard—the last holdout in a ten-year drought.

59

Bruce aboard Crazy Dancer in Oman.

Precious shade—the oasis at Shisur.

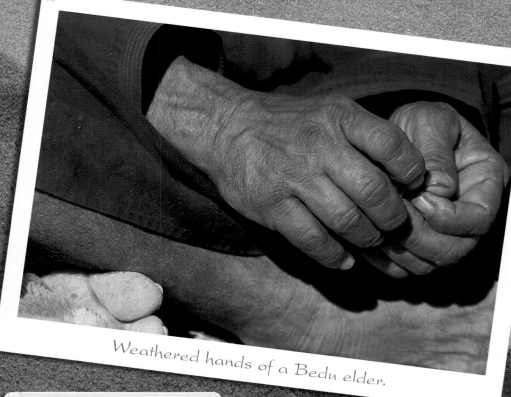

60

Weathered hands of a Bedu elder.

61

A long day ends with
dried meat and tea.

62

Sleep as you ride—bin Ashara
shows the way.

Approaching the first large dunes of the Empty Quarter.

Deliberating on the course —a daily event.

Water from a goatskin or **gerber**.

The heated route debate in Mughshin.

Celebrating the moment—Jamie and Leigh in Mughshin.

The caravan approaches Mughshin.

Manaa, Tuarish, and Salim Ali—note the **khanjars** sported in belts.

Facing Mecca in prayer.

Riding through the rippling heat of a **sabkha** flat.

A vain attempt to escape 125-degree heat.

Lunch under a lone **ghaf** tree.

74

Labian growls as
Ali helps Leigh.

75

Branding—ancient and
effective treatment.

76

Leigh and Labian
falling behind.

"This cruel land can cast a spell which no temperate clime can match." — W. Thesiger.

In Oman I spent four days meeting with our support staff and local Bedouin. Again our progress was astounding. Initially it had been difficult to convince the Bedu to undertake the journey in the traditional manner we proposed. They thought we were a little crazy, and suggested attempting the crossing in a few four wheel drive trucks would be much more comfortable! But the excitement and momentum surrounding the fast-approaching event have grown through Oman, and so has the Bedouin's devotion and dedication to the expedition. All our planning and strategizing went flawlessly.

When did things change so dramatically?

Manaa quiets the group and speaks again. "You must help the Bedu with the GPS because they do not know the way from here. Sometime they talking too much and lost the way."

This is news. Bruce had initially come to Oman in search of men who knew the sands from start to finish. Thesiger found such a man in Mohammed al Auf, and we understood we had found the same in Manaa's contacts. Leigh's anger grows in the frustration of the two fruitless hours we have been sitting here. He said before the meeting that we should resist changes to the plan, that we "must stand by our word and complete the journey as we claimed to Nat Geo, the kids and the sponsors we would." Leigh now raises his voice to get the attention of Manaa, who is now talking to a group on the couch: "Manaa. Manaa!" Leigh calls. "You said you knew the route!"

"We know the route," Manaa replies with equal force.

Leigh continues. "You represented to us that the Bedu knew the route. They either know the route or they don't."

"We don't know every tree, every rock, every dune," says Manaa, bending to the map. He presses hard with a pencil, which tears through the lamination. "We know the way, but not every rock. In the Dhofar, this is our home, we know every rock, every tree, all dunes. Not here. Not possible here!"

"I give up!" Leigh says, retreating to a chair. Bruce asks whether there is anyone here in Mughshin who knows the route and can join the team. Manaa responds, "We need no one, Mr. Salah. The Bedu will know the way. Trust me."

Our enthusiasm diminished, we start to work out a plan. It is agreed that water and food for the camels must be trucked in every few days. We agree on one drop from here to our next stop at Butabol, well over 120 miles away. The meeting ends and Bruce asks what time the Bedu want to get under way tomorrow.

Manaa's reply is curt. *"Bokrah, mafi zein. Yimkin baad bokrah.* Tomorrow no good. Maybe the day after tomorrow," he says, heading for the door. Bruce intercepts him on the porch and suggests we leave tomorrow since summer is coming. "Bin Ashara must take a truck to Salalah for Saudi stamp in passport. He come back *bokrah* and *baad bokrah* we go," Manaa replies in a medley of languages.

Though the others have proper paperwork, they will go along as well. Why bin Ashara does not have the stamp is a mystery to us, but we'll wait here until he gets it. Bruce tells Manaa there is little hope that they will be back tomorrow, since it is the weekend and the offices will be closed. Manaa tells him not to worry. He is told that we will start to ride again soon enough. Everyone leaves.

As we roll up the maps, I ask Leigh and Bruce what they think of Musallim's idea of a lightweight crossing. Leigh says nothing. Bruce only offers a passing comment. "It's an attractive idea. It would give us more of the romance of the expedition," he says. But ultimately he is not interested in more talk. Measured by his silence, neither is Leigh.

"I'm keen to explore any and all options at this point," I offer, fussing with my gear until Manaa bursts into our room, panicked and shouting at us to get ready. We have been invited by the *Wali* of Mughshin for a feast. People have come from Thamarit, Salalah, and across the Dhofar some two hundred miles to celebrate our expedition. We must hurry to meet them.

We continue to be held in thrall with last minute-by-minute information, never knowing what might happen next and with little chance to have an influence on any of it. Although this can be tiring, this is an exciting way to live, never knowing what may happen next, but it's become too stressful. Without complaint, we change into our clean *dishdashahs* and depart for the feast.

At the door of the *wali's* home, Manaa stops and cautions us about conducting ourselves properly. He tells us to sit on our knees and to ensure that our *dishdashahs* cover our legs. Nothing will go unnoticed, he says, and if we make a mistake our "faces will be darkened in shame." Manaa has never been this concerned about us before. Have we become something of an embarrassment? We learn that the room is filled with important elders of the Kathiri clan. He does not want shame brought upon himself and us.

Forty or more men are gathered at Sheikh Musallam's home. They sit covering most of the floor. With a swoosh of cotton, all of them rise to their feet to greet us. We are given honoured places in the room—we sit before a huge platter, piled knee-high with tempting fruit. Each man passes regards to our families and camels while we are served tea. As we answer their many questions, they look us over. I would love to have a piece of fruit, but Manaa has me so fretful about my potentially offensive behaviour that I just sit and sip my tea, trying to answer the odd question I can understand. Young boys arrive and depart continuously, bringing more fruit, taking away empty glasses and the peels of bananas and oranges—clearly *somebody* is eating, but it isn't I. A boy arrives with burning frankincense to perfume our beards. Another offers a glass bottle of Egyptian perfume, complete with spray pump. Its chemical scent clashes with the earthiness of frankincense. Before there's a chance to refuse, the youth blasts me three times. Then the plate of fruit is removed, and I regret having missed it. Once the fruit platter is gone, another appears with the main course. The two boys carrying it make twisted faces because of the strain on their arms and the hot rice now burning their thumbs. Perched atop the pyramid of food is another goat's head. Beneath the empty stare, its well-cooked dismembered body steams. Under this is saffron-flavoured rice saturated in fatty gravy. Behind the meal comes a parade of drinks. Armfuls of Pepsi and Coke, 7-Up and Fanta, as well as plastic cups of water, are all placed throughout the room. Though supplies are hard to come by and understandably expensive out here in the desert, no cost has been spared. In their generosity, the Bedu have offered us the very best they have. A goat such as the one we are now eating costs about $250, we're told. Our expedition has been féted at some fifteen of them so far. Three camels have been sacrificed for us, and they cost about $2000 apiece. I try to show my gratitude with smiles and a hearty appetite, but know at the same time that I shall never be able to return this generosity as the code of the desert dictates. Today we are guests, but if we lived here in the desert we would certainly become hosts tomorrow and join the circle of hospitality. In reality, though, "tomorrow" I will board a plane and break the circle.

At the banquet we eat more than our fill, and my stomach begins to ache with the thought of another mouthful. Bruce, Leigh, and I sit back against the wall trying to take some weight off our aching knees, now bent for an hour at this impossible angle. Sleep would be my next choice, but I know even the suggestion at this point would offend. Manaa, sitting on the other side of the room, looks at us and smiles. Everything seems to be going well. Despite the frustration left by this morning's meeting, I'm happy we are able to please him by doing well with the Bedu customs.

What's left of the food disappears, and another bowl of fruit arrives—oranges, bananas, plums, and grapes. Not having had fruit since Shisur, we make extra room to enjoy the sweet freshness. Bruce is called over to speak with the *wali* while I peel an orange. When he returns he explains what is happening.

"To make a long story short, he was asking me a lot of questions. *'Why are you here? Did your government send you?'* Then he asked me what I thought of the Bedu life. I told him we have a problem trying to do this journey in the old way, that the Bedu don't want to. I figured I'd stir the pot," Bruce says. "I told him I thought things must have changed a lot in the fifty years since Thesiger, and he got upset and said, 'No, no change! Now is just the same!'"

Things have indeed changed—oil revenue has increased wealth, and motorized vehicles have replaced camels, graded roads offer desert access, water is now pumped from wells, cell phones sometimes replace firelight as vehicles for conversation. While there is no denying these changes, much of the old ways has remained—hospitality and generosity, family-centred values, camel care as seen in the branding and feeding songs, tribal affinity, and desert navigation skills are just a few pieces of the past still evident.

Not sure what to think, we sit back. I survey the room, looking at the men who have gathered to feast with us. We are failing in our explanation of why we are here, of our interest in their old ways, or what even motivates us. And aren't we arrogant to think that they even want to know.

Bruce makes an extra effort today to speak his mind, to communicate with the Bedu. He says he's still frustrated at being unable to gain control. We talk about the concern that continuing to rely on major truck support could render the entire adventure into a farce. At the same time, we understand we are entirely out of our element. We all frame the same question: Who are we to push the Bedu into our adventure and the danger they have seen in it? Bruce says in a low voice. "I haven't said this yet—but looking at the map this morning, and knowing the pain I've endured to get here, it made me think that, support or no support, whether we make it or not, it's going to be *very* hard."

He is right, of course. Things are not turning out the way we'd hoped, the way we'd been led to believe they would, but as far as the trip's being a lark—well, I've been learning a tremendous amount, and suffering too, quite out of my comfort zone since our arrival in Thamarit. Whatever happens, we should be happy with what we've accomplished thus far.

We enjoy more of the fruit. Manaa signals it is time to leave. We meet him at the door, where he tells us an Omani TV crew of three has arrived from Salalah and wants to interview us. The day takes another strange twist. The film crew wants us to stage a mock arrival as background for their report. We ask whether it is really necessary to disturb the camels on their rest day. "Daily days you worry about the camels," Manaa says. "They are strong. *Mafi mushkilla.*"

The film crew attracts every male child and adult in the village. When we get to the corral, the crowd agitates the camels.

They need to be pulled forcibly from their rest. As we attach saddles, the cameras roll. One of the village boys jumps into the frame, T gets to his feet, and the shot is ruined. Manaa yells at Bruce to move Crazy Dancer to a better angle. Bruce ignores him. The crew tells us to move here, stop, start, untie this and tie that. The locals tell the crew what to shoot, what not to shoot. Arguments buzz through the crowd, while Leigh, Bruce and I sort through five sets of helping hands.

When everyone is ready, we are told to walk away, leading our camels on a mock departure. We are then to mount up and ride in a big circle to the front gates for the staged arrival. The village elders and guests line up and we say goodbye. The men shout *"Maa Salama, Maa Salama"* at each of us, making sure the microphone picks up their farewell wishes.

After a one-mile loop, we approach the gates, where the group has reconvened. Behind the men, a dozen or more sport utility vehicles are carefully packed together. Behind the vehicles is Mughshin's entrance gate. And behind that gate, from behind black veils, women stare at us. In between, children run about. We shout *"Salaam alaykum"* from our camels and jump to the ground. The village elders and guests answer us. They stand shoulder to shoulder in a semi circle before us. *"Aloume,"* Bin Ashara yells, and *"Mafi aloume,"* one elder replies. All this is played out with great seriousness with an eye to the camera crew zipping about, filming between the spaces.

A great debate breaks out with much shouting, then halts abruptly, when the men start to sing a song of welcome. Musallim gives guidance with a hand signal, telling me to stay where I am. Two boys appear with long unsheathed swords and begin to dance. They skip and step and jump in circles before the two groups, and periodically thrust their swords in the air. Thankfully the camels are calm. When the song builds, one boy throws his sword high into the air to the delight of the group, and to our relief catches it cleanly by its handle. The ceremony is wonderful. I only wish it had happened for real.

Three older men break from the line to retrieve their rifles and *khanjar* knives from their Land Rovers. Before re-joining the group they put on their belts, which now display their knives. Each struggles to buckle the belt. It has clearly been years since these men have worn their belts, and the straps are now not long enough to wrap comfortably around their expanding girths. One man sucks in his stomach with great effort. A second needs a little help from a friend, who pulls at the belt while pushing until the clasp is fastened. The last man has no hope of getting the belt hooked—it's about twelve inches too short. I can't stand the agony of it any more, and turn to the dancers, who are now kicking up considerable dust.

The welcome song done, we walk into the village. The *sheikhs* lead the way and we fall in among them. The camera crew jogs ahead. Everyone else jockeys for position next to the camels and the *sheikhs*. Teenagers run from behind, scrambling to get in front. A couple of them toss rocks at Mr. T and the other camels. Some of the younger children poke at the camels with sticks, and when one lifts a leg to kick, the kids scream and jump away. I silently hope that T might bowl one over to rid him—and us—of them.

Everyone pushes to get into the front to be photographed. I start to feel disgust for the whole exhibition, asking myself whether this tacky display is the legacy left by Thesiger's popular account of the region and its people. The author is well known here, as is his book *Arabian Sands*. The Bedu are certain that we, too, will write a book about our journey, and many people want to be photographed for it. What struggles of the Bedu will we write about? Today, it seems the only struggle is to the front of the crowd to be photographed. They carry guns, which they have never had to fire in battle, and camel sticks, which they rarely if ever use to guide a ridden camel. Only one generation removed from their nomadic ancestors, these people now live in concrete homes with air conditioning, TVs, VCRs, and a healthy supply of sweet water. They drive about in $45,000 vehicles, perched on plush leather seats in air-conditioned comfort. Their connection to the desert is a birthright, but for this generation, has it become an empty birthright? They are insulated by concrete and steel from the desert world their parents knew intimately. It is unsettling to witness their parade of traditional ways for the camera's sake.

In my mind, I leave the filming scene behind and consider a different perspective. Who would not want to change their ways if given the opportunity to have an easier life? Who would want to spend all day with their back bent pulling salty water in leather bags from a sandy well under the pounding sun? The water supply for this village is now pumped through plastic pipes from deep underground, where it is still sweet. Why would anyone want to live in darkness after the sun sets when a generator can turn night into day? Who would want to endure the 120-degree temperatures of this superheated slice of the planet? Yet just hours ago we were trying to force these men to do exactly that. We are the ones who find romance in the fabricated hardships that we refer to as adventure.

The contradictions in ourselves and in this society, and the ironies in our conflict with them, are perplexing, but if there is any fault or criticism to be assigned here, it is to us. I am concerned for these men, who are kind, generous and welcoming. They are a generation caught between two very different worlds. Their fathers lived the old life of the Bedu. Their children will live the ways of new Arabia. They are caught somewhere in between, unwilling to capitulate to the dramatic changes that have taken place in their culture. They whirl in the middle of it all, grasping at a romanticized past, while awkwardly approaching an utterly different future.

Chapter Thirteen

۱ ذو القعدة ۱٤۱۹
February 18, 1999
Mughshin

Day 17 — 19 33' N 54 53' E

The Bedu members of our team have gone to get bin Ashara's passport stamped. Manaa is racing to Thamarit to find a faster camel for Leigh, since Labian can't keep up. Meanwhile, we wait.

The extra time here in Mughshin is useful, since it offers a free moment to collect some photographs for our sponsors—promotional photographs of their banners here at the edge of the Empty Quarter. Bausch & Lomb, NEC Technologies, and Ingle Health will all get photos of their corporate and product logos in the field. These photographs can then be used for internal promotion and consumer advertising. Along with inspirational slide presentations, the photos form part of the sponsors' return on their investment in us.

Neither Leigh nor Bruce is keen on the photo session, given yesterday's dramatic, unanticipated changes to our plans. Photographing the banners is a time-consuming process that includes finding a suitable background, setting up cameras, then taking several exposures of each banner. Taking promotional photographs has always been an awkward part of expeditions.

After a few hours reading, Leigh takes his turn at filing a report on our internet site. I enjoy reading part before he sends it off along with photos. He is the best writer among us, and it will be interesting to learn what he is willing to share with the children. He writes:

We are pleased to have been able to make the push from Shisur to Mughshin without personal vehicle support. We have been forced to adjust some of our plans by providing food drops for the camels at predetermined points as there is no grazing for them due to a ten–year drought in the eastern Empty Quarter. We have spent the last two days resting and planning for the more difficult stretch north to Butabol and then into Saudi Arabia.

The Bedu are worried about the coming heat and the difficulty of the dunes and salt flats awaiting us. The route is said to be heavily duned all the way to Liwa oasis in the Emirates and the 21- to 28-mile a day pace we managed from Shisur is expected to drop significantly—perhaps as low as 9 to 12 miles a day. With more than 300 miles of this sort of terrain yet to cross, we are a little apprehensive about the coming days and their impact on our camels—and our spirits. We still plan to move north without vehicle support (except for camel food drops), but convincing the Bedu to continue this way has been a major challenge as they see our desire to be unsupported as quite impractical—which it is, of course. Nevertheless, we are still hoping to leave tomorrow.

The journey has been both a physical and mental challenge. I think our spirits all soar and sink day to day, hour to hour. Sometimes, riding along, barely able to move in the saddle because everything has gone numb, and with the sun pounding down, I find myself thinking *I love this—this is great.* Another time, same circumstances, I think to myself, *This is crazy. What could possibly have motivated me to leave home for this?* For me at least, there seems to be very little consistency in my feelings about the journey. Perhaps too much is happening moment by moment, every day, to have one consistent impression of it all.

Noon. As all three of us have feared, the Bedu haven't returned, and though no one says anything, a dark mood overtakes us. We share a sense of dread that they'll not be back soon. Leigh spends most of the day reading in his room—off somewhere in Moscow, or perhaps at the Battle of Borodino.

Later, I find a moment alone and take my .22 to the village dump. The noise attracts every teenage boy in the village. They all come to measure my marksmanship, giggling when I miss the target, cheering when I hit it. They even follow me back to the condo. The steady stream of curious passers-by hasn't ceased since our arrival. This intrusion didn't bother me at first, but now, after three days and the added stress of our delayed departure, it is difficult not to let frustration get the better of me. Ironically, this desert trip has provided almost no solo time, and this is especially true when we are in a settlement. The Bedu seem to need little solitude. Thesiger also wrestled with these critical differences:

> I knew that for me the hardest test would be to live with [the Bedu] in harmony, and not to let my impatience master me; neither to withdraw into myself, nor to become critical of standards and ways of life different from my own. I knew from experience that the conditions under which we lived would slowly wear me down, mentally if not physically, and that I should be often provoked and irritated by my companions. I also knew with equal certainty that when this happened, the fault would be mine, not theirs.

I steal away from the group to record some thoughts, finding a spot to sit near the central mosque with my back against a light pole, in a mounting breeze. The sun has nearly set. Like each sunset in this part of the world, we pass from slowly fading light to total darkness in only a few moments. This is quite alien from the lingering evenings of light that make summer such a wonderful time in Canada. Loudspeakers at the top of the minaret crackle to life with the voice of the *moazzin*— *"God is Great. Most Merciful"*—which draws people from their homes to the mosque. When the call ends, a diesel engine sputters to life on the other side of the village wall. Shortly, a buzz of electricity sweeps past my back and up the pole to the light above, which casts a yellow glow on the ground around me. The streetlights are spaced every thirty yards, but the circles of light never meet.

Beetles in astonishing variety converge from the surrounding darkness. They fly clumsily or crawl sluggishly into the artificial light. The winged beetles nose themselves into the wind and spread their wings for takeoff into the night. One creature stands tall waiting for the right gust, which finally comes, but his flight ends noisily as he crashes back to the ground somewhere beyond the light. Leigh is coming my way. For an instant he is illuminated in a circle two poles away. A few more beetles take off near my light, then crash and sit stunned at odd angles a few feet after take off. After a moment they are ready once again to spread their wings, find the wind, and try again. One of them finally catches a good breeze and soars up into the yellow glow, only to hit the glass of the light's mantle and tumble down again.

Leigh steps into my light and stands above me. "I'm thinking about going home," he says. Like the beetles, I need a moment to recover from the blow. Leigh has been struggling with the trip, but I never imagined he was reaching this point. All I can manage at the moment is a lame comment. "Wow—that's big news. Are you sure?"

"Yeah. I've been thinking about it a while."

For a moment it is easy to think that it might be better for all of us if he leaves, but in my heart I want him to stay.

"What's the main trouble?" I ask.

"Lots of stuff," he says, and shares an inventory of things that have eroded his confidence in the project. His greatest concern is that he thinks Bruce's leadership of the Bedu is ineffectual, citing the example of the camels having arrived late and untrained, despite Bruce's having come to oversee this months before. "Why didn't Bruce tell us he never actually saw the camels in Thamarit?" Leigh asks rhetorically. Leigh says that Bruce had not worked effectively with the Bedu before we came and this continues now that we are here. Leigh is frustrated with the arguments about ground support. He is willing to be regularly supplied by truck, but thinks miscommunication will continue to rule. "We made promises to Nat Geo and the kids about the trip—we have to stick to our original plan." Leigh's voice betrays no anger. He appears resigned to what he now views as the way of life among the Bedu. His voice is quiet, pensive. In fact, it might be better if he were angry—then we might be able to focus some of his angry energy toward another try. We sit silently for a while, watching the ongoing struggles of the beetles.

We return to the condo and are invited by the *wali's* two teenage sons for dinner. While we eat, the knowledge of Leigh's distress sits heavily with me. Bruce knows nothing of the conversation and it feels bad to know what he does not. For better or worse, I suggest a team meeting back at the condo. We sit at the table and listen to Leigh announce his plans to leave. He never articulates his exact concerns about Bruce's leadership, but does talk about the frustrations he has shared with me. Bruce says nothing. Bruce and Leigh are not looking at each other. Leigh's head is down and Bruce is looking about the room.

Finally, Bruce looks straight at Leigh and tells him, "I feel this black cloud hanging over my heart, knowing you aren't having a good time."

Leigh discloses more, saying he's lost confidence in the Bedu, as they don't know the way, and thinks we are all at risk. He is frustrated with the lack of consistency and the fact that we can't make plans that stick.

Bruce jumps in. "This is like when you're out on your first mountaineering trip and tied to the rope. You're so over your head you're just trying to keep going and not even thinking about reading the map or leading the way. You're just barely hanging on. That's how I feel with the Bedu."

Leigh then says, "If you don't want me to stay on, if you want to force my hand, I'll bow out now if you feel it's necessary."

"If staying any longer would make you stay till the end, I want you to be here," I tell him.

Bruce says nothing for a moment and then speaks: "Like James said, I'd want you to be here for as long as you want." But there is a hint of doubt in his voice when he says it.

Between silences, we table a plan to push to Butabol and see how it goes. Relieved to have an escape, everyone gets ready for bed. It is after midnight, and still the Bedu have not returned. Sleep won't come, so I write.

Maybe Leigh is discovering that the adventuresome life, which on the surface seems so romantic, is riddled with the mundane and the monotonous, and rife with compromised decision-making. This is precisely what he came here to escape.

Ironically, Leigh has rejoined the ranks of the adventurous, only to discover continuous discontent. At this moment Leigh is in no mood for further inner discovery, but he tells me he is painfully aware of how much he needs to be more reflective, personally. He says he is frustrated with the trip's progress, but even more upset by his inability to transcend this frustration. This failure, he says, merely compounds his anxiety and this loss of control depresses him, further souring his mood. He is depressed about being depressed, caught in a terrible downward spiral. While I try to empathize, I also have to tell him how difficult it is to be with him. "I'm my own worst enemy," Leigh says in a defeated tone. He goes to bed.

٤ ذو القعدة ١٤١٩
February 21, 1999 Mughshin
Day 20 — 19 33' N 54 53' E

Manaa and the Bedu still haven't returned. No one in town knows when they might come back, so we decide to act. We head to Thamarit in the Land Rover. We find Manaa at 12:30, two hours after leaving Mughshin. He meets us at a local cafe. Bruce's Arabic is the best among us, which puts him in the unenviable position of being our main communicator. Bruce does a good job sharing our concerns, saying we have a big problem on our hands, a *mushkilla kabira*, reciting the foul-ups we've encountered, beginning with the lack of trained camels, and the unstructured training sessions in the first weeks, with their late starts and their miscommunications about route selection. He cites the trouble in Salalah, with the late departure, the dead end routes, and the mess we got ourselves into, hiking into the night through the mountains. He talks about the struggle with the frequency of re-supply, decision-making without consultation, and finally this delay in Mughshin which makes no sense, considering that the Bedu have said the summer is coming soon and we can't afford to waste time. I interrupt once, but my comments are superfluous. Leigh says little.

While Bruce and Manaa continue back and forth, I begin to wonder what we are really doing meeting here. It is unrealistic for us to attempt to force the Bedu into some particular mode or style of crossing. What we should probably argue for is some chance for input, and a shared control of the expedition. We must not lose touch with the fact that, at the moment, we ourselves are still more liability than asset in this process. We can only barely manage our camels, and whenever one goes wild we have to stand aside and watch while the Bedu bring order out of chaos.

Bruce tries hard to get our position across to Manaa, who was at first a little surprised that we have come all the way to Thamarit just to seek him out, and has now fallen into stony silence. Bruce escalates his approach to break through Manaa's veneer.

"I'm *very* angry, Manaa!" he barks in English.

"We will get some food," Manaa replies curtly, calling to the waiter to bring menus.

Again, Bruce says he is angry, but when the menus arrive, Manaa gives one to Bruce and asks him what he wants. His anger seemingly ignored, Bruce pushes the menu back. "I'm fine. I just want to talk about these problems!"

We realize that Manaa thinks Bruce is saying *hungry*, not *angry*, and we all begin to laugh. When we explain to Manaa, he laughs as well, breaking the tension of the meeting. Manaa says,

"Angry, not hungry. I see. English very hard." Evidently we are both angry and hungry, so the three of us order masala chicken, fried rice, a cucumber platter with onions and lemon, and a bottle of water.

With something of a new perspective, and the map on the table, we work out the plan from Mughshin to the Saudi border at Butabol. Leigh seems happy with our progress.

After we agree to a couple of re-supply points, our food arrives and Manaa leaves to dine with his family. We are told to meet him, Ali, Musallim and bin Ashara, who now has his stamp, at the old training camp where we will pick up the new camel to replace Labian.

We eat quickly and go. "Jerry Purple Knees" is the only camel remaining in the old training camp, his name the product of the antibacterial salve that was applied to his knees. We didn't take him due to the infected cuts on his knees, which he sustained during his truck trip from the UAE. The truck box is lined with hay and further reinforced with cardboard boxes. The Bedu do not want to risk injuring him again.

The truck is backed up to the same embankment we used to load the others three weeks ago, and Jerry is just as reluctant to get in. The stress he'll be under during the ride to Mughshin is worrisome. The bed appears to be too small to accommodate Jerry's length, but he tries to step in anyway only to slip on the waxy cardboard. His shin scrapes down the tailgate, but there is no apparent damage.

Some local Bedu, herding their own camels, stop to help. At first we are grateful, but they soon confuse matters with ineffective ideas and conflicting instructions. Each man has his own loading technique, invariably different from all the others and always better. One man jumps on the roof of the cab with a rope tied around Jerry's nose and begins pulling. This procedure doesn't work, and is supplanted by the more straightforward whack on the rump with a camel stick. This fails, two others take up the challenge by adopting a rugby stance, putting their shoulders to the camel's meaty hindquarters. Less violent than other methods, it, too, fails to move the camel, who has finally had enough of the fuss. He noisily voids his bowels, spraying the result upon the backs and shoulders of the very men most dedicated to helping him. That done, Purple Knees jumps spryly into the truck box, quite unaided.

The struggle is over. I give Jerry's face a rub and pick a handful of large ticks from his hide. His knees look good and the scabs are all but gone. Pretending the ticks are grapes, I offer some to Ali. He pushes my hand away and the ticks bounce across the ground, all purple and bloated with blood.

The group splits up, boards the trucks and heads back to Mughshin to prepare for tomorrow's departure. Musallim rides with us. Before leaving town we stop for gas and food, buying oranges, apples, tomatoes, along with butter, jam and bread for tomorrow's breakfast. We can't resist the cold Fanta orange drinks sitting behind the fridge glass—it must stand for "fantasy" out here in the heat of Arabia.

This break in our journey into the sands is a complete departure from the epic trek Sir Wilfred made after he had left the south coast on his famous crossing. I would prefer not to have had this interaction with civilization. We were thirsty and hungry in the desert just days ago, and longed for these foods. Here they sit before us, and I wish I could resist. Something becomes painfully clear to me which makes our effort seem but a pale imitation of Thesiger's accomplishment. He had struggled on his journey as we do on ours, but he struggled with having too little. We struggle with having too much.

Fruit, candy and other snacks in hand, we head out for Mughshin with the sense that we've made some serious progress toward an understanding with the Bedu and toward holding our team together. A plan is in place and a new camel is en route for Leigh.

Musallim sits beside Leigh in the back seat, fidgeting with his pop can. He opens the window and pours it out, humorously spraying the side of the truck. He then starts to write what I vainly hope might be the official expedition poem. He is often commissioned throughout the region to write poetry for special occasions, such as weddings or other important family events.

Musallim's creative side gives him an endearing softness. I'll try to coax a poem from him when we're back in the desert. It's easy to picture his grey beard awash with firelight, his handsome smile enfolding his flowing words.

The strong Bedu oral tradition is a product of their traditionally nomadic lifestyle. Poetry found its value with the Bedu as a tool to prompt with rhyme, the memory of messages. Some of the cerebral cargo was conveyed over long distances, through many people with often serious topics. The details of a young man's death in a raid hundreds of miles from home might be lost in normal memory. His companions would lock the events in a poem while travelling back to his kin and share the tragic story of his death on their return.

Almost all that is known of the Bedu has been passed on verbally through every generation across the flames of many fires. Though much else has changed for the Bedu, this rich cultural inheritance has remained strong in some parts of the country. Today, it is not unusual for a man to find in poetry a place to share intimate thoughts and feelings normally inexpressible in this reserved society. Bedu poetry often addresses the love of women, an otherwise taboo subject. During this expedition, many of the poems we have heard have been love poems, but so far most have been addressed to camels.

Chapter Fourteen

We agreed last night to meet the Bedu at six this morning and depart at six-thirty. It's after seven now, and Bruce is off to find them. Leigh and I haul over to the camels the *gerbers* we filled with water last night, and the burlap food bags we loaded with sugar, coffee, tea, rice and flour. Bruce arrives at last with the Bedu team. A group of locals has gathered to see us off and Manaa talks to them. Ali takes Labian for a ride, then gallops back at full speed in front of Manaa and the local men, stopping sharply and leaping to the ground with a flourish, as only Ali can. He hands the reins to Manaa, who points out some of Labian's positive features in a vigorous sales pitch.

Instead of selling Labian, Manaa prefers to trade him for another camel owned by a local. The new camel is kept in a separate pen, owing to its wild disposition. It is being inspected by bin Ashara. The animal jumps, stomps, and kicks while bin Ashara speaks softly and pulls on a rope he's wrapped around the camel's front leg. We have enough difficulty handling the tamer camels in our caravan. What will be the impact on the herd of this crazed, unbroken beast? The new camel's name is Usayma, which means *Beautiful*. Her large and shapely hump implies she is very strong. When the other camels are long dead, we're told she will keep going. Probably because she will have killed the others, I suspect.

While packing, we remember a forgotten bag of meat at the condo. Bruce and I race back in Manaa's truck to look, deciding we'd better check for anything else left behind. As we race along the road, we pass an old man shuffling toward us, and I slow down to prevent kicking dust at him. On the way back, we pass him again and see he has made little progress. Worrying that he's come to see us off and will miss us, I stop to give him a ride, but instead of wanting to get to the corral, the man wants to be taken to his home a block away.

When we arrive, the old man's invitation for coffee can't decently be refused, though we've argued incessantly with the Bedu for on-time departures. Mr. T is ready to go and I doubt the Bedu will be geared up to leave for some time so, I jump out of the truck and send Bruce on ahead. His home is among the houses Manaa pointed out as belonging to the Rashid, the tribe upon whom Thesiger relied so heavily as he crossed the Empty Quarter. They became essential to his journey when his Bait Kathir companions refused to continue and left his party here in Mughshin. In Thesiger's time the Rashid, who roamed from the borders of the Hadhramaut to the Persian Gulf, numbered only three hundred men, while the Bait Kathir numbered twice that. The Rashid lived deeper in the desert than the Bait Kathir, and because of this Thesiger believed they knew it better. To him they were the most "pure" people in the world, "(living) under conditions where only the hardiest and best could possibly survive. They were as fine-drawn and high strung as thoroughbreds." The old man before me could have easily been one of the very men Thesiger so admired. My curiosity could not be satisfied without spending more time with him.

Oddly, four Rashid women and a clutch of children, all apparently related to the old man, gather around us at the vehicle. The women are speaking to me—the first female voices I have heard since leaving Masqat, and this so surprises me that my Arabic is gone for a moment—and offer coffee. Once through the gate of their yard, we sit under a black wool tent at the front of the house. The roof blocks the sun, and the space between the fabric and the ground allows for a pleasant breeze. The same wind fans a fire, which is now being lit in a metal box in the middle of the enclosure. An elderly woman works the ashes to life and adds new wood. A small plastic bowl filled with an unknown liquid arrives in the cupped hands of a young girl whose eyes remain fixed on me as she crosses the tent. She is five or six years old, with plump cheeks and arms. Her hair is long and black and falls on a flowered dress. Her feet are bare and her toenails richly painted. She wears bracelets tight around each ankle, matching those on her wrists. Her eyes are thickly framed in *kohl*, applied by her mother to help protect the eyes from the sun. Made of wood ashes and animal fat, *kohl* has become as stylish as it is functional. She is a lovely child, and her sweetness lifts my spirits. The girl delivers her bowl, which is filled with kerosene, then sits beside the old man who brought me here. The fuel is used to hurry the fire along.

There is a choice of tea or coffee. The coffee, a strong brew with a heavy dose of cardamom, is smooth. Dates are offered as well. Tea, with a faint saffron aftertaste, comes next. The tent fills with a dozen or more people. Unlike any of our other gatherings, here there are equal numbers of women and men. The men all look to be over sixty. Once the women enter the tent, they drop their black and indigo veils. Among our Kathiri companions we are not even allowed to speak of their wives, much less see them. I try to contain my enthusiasm about being welcomed into this intimacy, wanting not to offend. Their beauty is intoxicating, and prompts an exaggerated reaction, as it is generally forbidden for unfamiliar males to socialize with women in their culture. Protected from the sun, the women's olive skin looks smooth as satin. Their lovely mouths break into easy smiles. Their eyes are framed in thick lashes, some lined with *kohl* and others not. It is to me a wondrous blessing to sit among this family, around their fire. It's a struggle not to stare too long at the women and the little ones.

Someone begins to ask me questions in Arabic.

"Where are you going?"

"Abu Dhabi."

"How many days until you get there?"

"Maybe thirty."

"This is too little. It is a great distance."

"Drink your coffee. Eat more dates."

"Thank you, but I must go ride my camel."

I think I'm asked if I want to see (or perhaps buy) some weapons, including a rifle. Word has spread of my presence, as an old man and a small boy from another family arrive and add their advice. "You must take a good rifle. Mohammed, go get the other rifles. You must buy a rifle."

"No, no, thank you. I have one already."

"A knife, then. You must have a knife."

I answer more questions while my gaze is drawn to a lovely young woman sitting across the fire, who watches me intently with hazel eyes. Not wanting to look directly at her for too long for fear of being rude, I keep her fixed in my peripheral vision. An older woman brings a crying baby to her from inside the house, and without hesitation she begins to nurse. The baby's hand, small and delicate, kneads the soft flesh of its mother's breast. The tenderness of mother and child is an overwhelming reprieve from the desert's harshness.

We have been in this region a month now, and have only seen women from afar, as black spectres seeming to hide from us. Until now, we have not uttered a single word to a Bedu female. There are six or more of them here, completely dominating the conversation. What seems clear is that, while the outward visible life of the community is the domain of men, the inner, hidden life of the family is the province of women. This is symbolized by their ownership of the family tent that we now sit under.

An old Rashid man asks, "Why have you no Rashid with you?" and before there is time to answer, a woman asserts, "The Rashid know the sands." I explain that I don't know why we don't have Rashid with us. This does not satisfy them, and they continue to discuss it among themselves. I'm left to look about the tent and acknowledge with respect each glance I catch.

"A photo! You must take a photo!" one of the men shouts, pointing to my fanny pack. The nursing mother packs up to feed her baby elsewhere. I silently resent having to take the blasted photos and reluctantly snap shots of the men with their *khanjars* and rifles. Bruce returns, takes a few more photos, drinks a cup of coffee and signals to me that we must leave. Still in a daze, I express my thanks to all, and Bruce and I jog to the corral south of the town.

The others have loaded up and are on the move. Leigh raises his shoulders and arms as if to ask, Where the hell have you been? I shout my apologies and promise to explain later. Bin Ashara is up front with Mr. T and my pack camel. He's tied a short line on Usayma, the new camel, who jerks left and right. Bin Ashara refuses to stop, so I jog along beside him to untie my animals. We pass the village again and the house of the Rashid family. The women are sitting out front on the ground in a circle while the children run about. Old men lean on their canes, holding their unsold rifles. They point in our direction while talking to each other. I wave goodbye. They wave back.

Then, more strange and unwelcome news. Bruce and I stop with our camels when Manaa pulls up in his truck to talk. Before he drives off to Butabol, Manaa explains to Bruce and me that, after meetings last night with the Kathiri tribe elders about the route, it was decided we would not take the one we agreed to yesterday in Thamarit. Though we assume Manaa has the authority to make such decisions in regard to the journey, it is clear he cannot—at least not on his own. This is no reflection on his competence, but rather of Manaa's culture, a culture we wish we better understood. We have failed to grasp that any action by an individual in Bedu society reflects upon the entire tribe. All Bedu are members of one tribe or another, and all within a given tribe are related in greater or lesser degree of kinship, being descended from some common ancestor. As Thesiger observed, the nearer that relationship,

> ... the stronger is the loyalty which a man feels for his fellow tribesmen, and this loyalty overrides personal feelings, except in extreme cases. In time of need a man instinctively supports his fellow tribesmen, just as they in like case support him. There is no security in the desert for an individual outside the...tribe. This makes it possible for tribal law, which is based on consent, to work among the most individualistic people in the world, since in the last resort a man who refuses to accept a tribal decision can be ostracized.

Knowing this, I'm beginning to understand that Manaa must consult with the elders before making any decision as they have a stake in the success of the journey not to mention knowledge of the area.

No wonder Manaa, alone without his tribe, struggled with our decision-making in Thamarit yesterday. When we were done, it was for him a matter of course that he must seek his elders' counsel. It is easy to forget this, as on the surface Manaa appears so similar to ourselves in his business dealings. He races about in his vehicle checking off tasks on a list written in Arabic, talks on his cell phone, and manages details for his construction project. We left the meeting yesterday thinking the plan was set, having no appreciation of the awkward position into which we had forced Manaa.

Now, the requisite consultation having occurred, Manaa explains the route we'd decided on is too difficult and would take many days. Standing beside Manaa is a man who apparently knows a more direct route, and we are told this is the way we'll now go. Musallim and bin Ashara have been told as well. Manaa finishes by announcing, "Our way is long, but our time is short." He jumps in the cab of his truck and drives off.

Bruce and I look at one another and then to the rest of our group, which is becoming smaller in the distance. We shrug and walk on after the others, at ease with this new twist, knowing a bit more about Bedu ways and resigning ourselves to the shifting nature of this adventure. We are off to Butabol by some route or other, five to seven days from here.

When we catch the others I climb aboard T, but before Bruce is properly mounted in the saddle, Crazy Dancer leaps up and tosses Bruce to the ground. Reacting more like me, he angrily takes a few frustrated swings at a stone with his camel stick and swears at his camel. Then he mounts successfully and we ride on.

"What do you think of the differences between the Bait Kathir and the Rashid?" I ask Bruce. He says he doesn't know anything, but notes that months ago he had asked Chris Beal, our British contact in Oman, the same question. "Chris says there's little difference between the two tribes in terms of desert skill, and that there are really no more tribes. He said Bedu are Bedu."

Was Chris right about all the Bedu now being the same? What knowledge did the old Rashid man from this afternoon have to share with us that the Bait Kathir couldn't? There is no denying the Rashid of Thesiger's time held a superior knowledge of the Empty Quarter.

We are well behind the guys now, and in a twisted turn of fate, Leigh and Purple Knees are falling even further behind us. It is true that the Bedu are always faster, even when they ride our camels. This is due in part to our extra weight, but mostly to their skill.

We catch up some hours later, and stop for lunch. The Bedu are resting under a tree. My pack camel carries the teapot. The fire Musallim made burns unproductively beneath his scowl. We eat a little meat, careful not to bite down on the many little pebbles now mixed with it. Bruce offers me his water bottle and it's all I can do not to drink the last pint in one gulp.

After lunch we ride on, holding to our line directly north east of Mughshin. With each mile, the dunes creep toward us from the left. If we continue along this tangent we should intersect their rolling masses tomorrow. We can see them clearly, dune upon dune. The most mountainous ones, pyramidal in shape, would cover several city blocks. Arms of sand radiate from summits, flanks dappled in smaller dunes casting slight shadows. The dune shapes add the only texture to a landscape flattened by the midday sun. Beyond, we can just see some of the richer red sands deep in the interior, sharp contrast to the grey gravel plains we have been treading over these past two weeks. An apparent unbroken sea of beige, seen from a distance, the sands, viewed closely, are actually composed of a splendid array of subtle hues, each grain carrying its own shade. As with northern Canada's tundra, which looks bleak when viewed from afar, the true beauty of this place can only be fully revealed on close examination.

We are travelling in the last part of Wadi Mughshin's drainage basin. The eroded ground gives better access to the water table. Small trees, patches of grass, and thin brush bring a little relief to the gravel bottoms. The camels like to eat the bright green saltbushes which grow close to the ground in clumps. They lunge at them as we pass, but consuming the bushes would give the camels dehydrating diarrhoea, and some suffer from this already. T's neck is far more powerful than my arms, and he swallows mouthful after mouthful. It is possible to stop him only by anticipating his actions and tightening the reins before he ducks his head. T knows precisely when my attention wanders so that he can snatch another bite without being jerked up short.

After a few more miles, we are past the mouth of the basin. Above, the vegetation is thin and stunted. There are no more trees of any kind and only a few dwarfed saltbushes. To our left is nothing but sand, smaller dunes rolling like foothills to the base of the giants beyond.

The scene is remarkably similar to what we saw south of the Tibetan town of Xegar in the Himalayan foothills, at 14,100 feet atop the Pang La Pass. There was an unobstructed view of the snow-covered peaks that dominate the world's highest range. The Everest massif is so high that it splits weather patterns and deflects 130 mile-an-hour jet stream winds.

As intimidating as those mountains were to face for the first time, the range of dunes that stands before us now daunts us no less. At least in the Himalayas, I was in the kind of mountainous environment familiar from my youth in Canada. This desert is far more foreign. These mountains of sand are terra incognita. Though these sculpted dunes rise "only" 2000 feet above the desert floor, they are as physically imposing and every bit as implacable as their rocky 26,000-foot cousins half a continent northeast.

We skirt the southeastern face of a medium-sized dune, and make camp in a spot that has been used by others on the same route. Tire tracks leave this place heading eastward, forking not far from here, one fork toward Masqat, the other back to Mughshin. A pile of garbage sits near a concrete trough, filled with stale water provided by a gas-powered pump drawing water up through a plastic pipe sunk into the ground. An old mattress, a pair of shorts, a single sandal, and an assortment of plastic jugs and engine oil filters are among the recognizable bits of trash littering the landscape.

These surroundings remind me of the last camp on Everest's southern route. The South Col is the high mountain pass joining Everest to its sister peak, Lhotse, and is the launching point for summit climbs. On this wind-scoured saddle, discarded oxygen bottles litter the rocks and blown snow. We tried to leave nothing behind but footprints in the Everest snows and hoped to leave less here, but the desert expanse is treated by others as the ocean often is—as a repository for waste. In certain poorly managed areas, loose garbage is so common that the windblown plastic bag has been flippantly dubbed the Bedu national flag.

We find some clean sand and make camp as darkness nears. Using a metal bowl we've found at the bottom of the trough, we retrieve some wash water. Hundreds of ticks lie dead in the bottom, having unwittingly dropped off drinking camels at precisely the wrong moment in their life cycles. The size of grapes when swollen with the blood of our camels, these are no ordinary parasites. The camel is the preferred host of the world's biggest soft-bodied tick, *Hyalomma dromedarii*. Well adapted, these insects can lie dormant beneath the sand for years until they sense body heat or carbon dioxide, at which point they emerge and do their best to attach themselves to a host. Despite our efforts to pick these creatures off our camels, their hides are still peppered with them.

I try to care for my own personal hygiene, worried about the flesh of my seat and its susceptibility to ulceration and infection. It would be wonderful to be able to bathe like this each day, but this is beyond possibility. Leigh, who feels ill, joins me to wash. In an unanticipated gesture of aggression, Purple Knees head-butted Leigh when we arrived, and he can't sort out whether his headache is from the blow or from simple dehydration. We take the cue to fill our water bottles. Musallim helps us draw water from the tick-infested trough. When I get painkillers for Leigh, Ali asks quietly for one as well, showing the first signs of the desert's slow devastation.

While I finish washing, my eyes are drawn to the dunes, holding them warily at this safe distance. The dunes mesmerize—they are the wild, the unknown. Here they are: golden, flashing bright brass in the last light of sunset. There the dunes stand as dark, sombre shadows along the northern horizon.

We drink some tea and settle in for the night. In the dark, the presence of the dunes isn't lost. But night's dunes are defined negatively, in the undulating horizon they carve from the lower reaches of a sky stunningly filled with stars. *Big Sky Country* is the tourist motto of Montana, the American state just south of my Alberta home. But there may be no "bigger" sky than here in Arabia—certainly there could be no fuller. Gazing up, I am dwarfed by the third boundary of Arab land and Arab culture: As ocean and desert are the first two boundaries, this thousandfold splatter of stars is the third and, in its way, greatest.

Orion the hunter— "Gloomy Orion," T.S. Eliot once called this massive, rectangular constellation—dominates the sky. Western sky-lore is entirely Greek in origin—or so our culture's account of itself would prefer. Greek myth has it that Orion was a great hunter and, not incidentally, lover. He angered the gods with his thoughts of superiority over all creatures. This arrogance cost Orion his life when the gods sent a scorpion (itself a hint of underlying Arabic legend) to kill him for his boastfulness. The moon goddess Diana felt badly for Orion and asked that he be placed in the sky, as consolation, for all to admire. The Scorpion accompanied—now the constellation Scorpio on the opposite side of the heavens from Orion—as reminder that no one is infallible, everyone vulnerable.

The myth, as passed through western culture, arrives in Greek garment. But Orion's star names are Arabic. Though they invented an early version of the astrolabe, the Bedu and other desert people navigated largely without instrument. We carry not only compass and sextant but the revolutionary Global Positioning System. Bedu and other Arab forebears navigated by means of an acute science of astronomy, a science which flourished as Europe lay choked in its Dark Ages, and which pointed their way to water, to home, and—no less importantly—to Mecca. Indeed, says the Christian story, to Bethlehem.

The impossibly vivid sky, which holds my rapt attention even past the need to sleep, contains more stars than I have ever seen. Unsullied by cloud, pollution, or artificial light, this velvet sky is studded with stars whose names we have borrowed or taken wholesale from Arabic. In Orion, for example, *Rigel* is a latinate/anglicized form of the Arabic *Ar-Rijl*. *Betelgeuse* comes to us from *Yad al Jauza*. *Mintaka*, in Orion's belt. *Achernar, Aldebaran, Alphecca, Deneb, Fomalhaut, Jabbah, Murzim, Rasalased, Shaula, Shedir, Thuban, Vega,* and *Zubenelgenubi*—the sky's star-census is peopled with names handed down from a science devised by the Arabs before Europe awakened enough to receive it.

* * *

The sound of a roaring engine awakens me four hours later. It is well after midnight. The moon is now high, casting enough light that we can make out the features around our camp. Musallim is awake and quickly unzips his gun from its cover. Ali and bin Ashara do the same, so I follow suit. The snap and click of Musallim sliding a shell into the breach and working the bolt. We can now see the lights of a truck about fifty yards away. Musallim stands with his rifle in both hands. The muzzle points to the ground but his finger is on the trigger. Ali and bin Ashara are on bended knee, weapons ready.

Though marauding is something of the past on the Omani side of the peninsula, the desert is still far from safe. Smuggling continues a fruitful occupation for some. Goods move through the desert under the cover of night from the UAE into Saudi Arabia and the other Gulf States. I recall a conversation with a man in Salalah. He cautioned us to be careful in the desert, saying that many supplies from the UAE are not available in Saudi and that this results in smuggling. I had asked him what sort of supplies he was talking about.

"Oh, everything," he said.

"Electronics, clothes—what?" I pressed.

"Yes...and more." The "and more" had come with raised eyebrows. I left it there. I was more interested in understanding the kind of people we might encounter. The temperament of a man smuggling Levi jeans is likely to be quite different from one smuggling drugs or other serious contraband. The man in Salalah had added, "Be careful of everyone you meet in the desert. Maybe they are just smuggling sheep from Iran. Then again, maybe not."

The truck's lights blind us briefly as it approaches. I place my rifle on its case in the sand so I can free my legs from the sleeping bag. At the same time, I search through the grey light for cover, just in case, deciding on the water trough, and locate each of our team relative to the approaching vehicle. The truck pulls up ten yards away. The lights fall past me. In the dark I grab my rifle and pull the butt up to my armpit. I work the bolt and rest my finger on the trigger guard, remembering one of the four major rules about handling weapons: "Finger on the trigger only when the sights are on the target." I slip an extra box of .22 shells in the pocket of my *dishdashah* and feel altogether ready, a bit frightened, and quite silly.

Two men jump out of the truck. Musallim tightens in the light and raises his weapon a foot pointing it near the fender. "Why don't you say something!" I mutter at the intruders. If I were jumping out of a truck in the dark in the middle of nowhere, I would surely be saying something by now. What about a little *Salaam Alaykum*? Yards from Musallim, the friendly greeting comes at last. Bin Ashara and Musallim offer coffee to the newcomers while they prod the fire back to life. A couple of sticks are added and flames leap through the wood, casting light on the new faces. The men are middleaged and seem no different from any other Bedu we have met. Still, the exchange among the seated foursome is formal, polite. I keep an eye on Musallim for signs that everything is fine. He has relaxed some, but still holds his rifle in his lap. It's easy in the dark to listen to their questions.

Our guests open. "Where have you come from?"

"The Dhofar."

"Why are you here?"

"We are riding to Abu Dhabi. Are those your camels past the dune?"

"Yes. We're moving them south."

As quickly as they came, the strangers finish their coffee, jump back in their truck and head out. The friendly exchange moments ago with our Bedu means little, for a guest is always welcomed to a new group and is offered the safe keeping of the host for three days—the length of time the food requires to pass through the guest's body. We have been told of a man who hosted a guest at his fire. During the natural conversation, the man discovered that his guest had killed his son some years before. The host let on nothing was wrong until after the third day, when he slit the man's throat. If nothing else, the moral should be: Never wear out your welcome.

All this leaves me to wonder: Are these men actually smugglers whom we might see later under less friendly circumstances?

٦ ذو القعدة ١٤١٩

February 23, 1999

Day 22 — 19 49' N 55 15' E

After fitful sleep we awake in a thick fog that obscures the sun. The camels have had a rough night. Disturbed by the truck, they never calmed down. Although the morning is damp and heavy, the Bedu are moving about briskly, shouting orders. Bin Ashara chastises Bruce for having secured Crazy Dancer too close to Sawad, the bull camel. We are told that his camel could have been killed. In the late-night commotion, one of Sawad's girth hitches has slid back to his groin. Now it is pinching his genitals, making him unmanageable. The Bedu have Bruce hold his rein while they use a camel stick to slide the line forward as gently as they can. They tell Bruce to be careful and hold the rein tightly, but in mid-operation Bruce's attention wanders. Sawad spins his head and bites down on Bruce's forearm. In an instant, he has pulled his arm free. The camel's teeth bruise the arm but do not break the skin. Bruce is more fortunate than we realize. A camel's jaw and neck muscles possess the power to crush a man's arm and rip it from the shoulder socket. The shock of the moment breaks the creeping complacency that has overtaken us all. With renewed caution, we mount up and ride on.

Leigh, who has been working hard to achieve a comfortable saddle configuration, has recommended I try a new set-up. He promises it will be more comfortable, but it feels awkward being higher off T's back than usual. Within yards of setting out, T reaches for a saltbush. Not wanting him to set the precedent for the balance of the day, I whack him with my stick. He jumps with a start, then gallops off at full speed, pulling my pack camel along. With the combination of the new saddle configuration and my questionable riding skills, I start bouncing in the saddle. T senses my loss of control, plants his front legs and kicks out his back ones, launching me into the air, not frontward over his head, but backwards over his rump. Ali reacts immediately, races after my camels, cuts them off and grabs the reins. I gather my headgear and glasses, and re-mount T, who is now agitated at being separated from the rest of the group. Before my seat hits the saddle, he is up from the sand and galloping off to the others.

Sand now chokes off the gravel flats and its softness absorbs some of the jarring of the camel's steps. We climb up and stumble down each dune and weave among the larger ones. It takes much more effort to stay mounted and to keep the camels moving forward. The extra effort the camels must make in order to cover the same amount of ground as before is immediately obvious. We are not moving forward with nearly the same efficiency as we did on the hardpan flats. But camels in any event are the best kind of animal for these conditions. A camel's foot is a soft pad that acts like a snowshoe, splaying out in the sand and dispersing its weight. The deep sand makes it easy to understand the efficiency of their slow swaying gait. Unlike a horse which walks with alternating strides, the camel paces by moving the legs of one side simultaneously. This disturbs the sand less, giving the camel a better foundation for each stride. Though horses might offer a much more comfortable ride, the Bedu insist that a horse would last only a day or two at most in this sand.

Ali and I ride toward a lone tree, about five feet high. Ali jumps down beside it, and in its paltry shade begins to pray, wrapping his rein around his ankle and facing Mecca. His camels stand calmly taking the chance to search among the branches for any tender buds. I cut to the right to avoid coming between Ali and the *Kaaba*. Ali places his forehead on the sand. The stiffness in my neck and shoulders after my fall makes it painful to turn my head and watch him. There appears to be more than just spiritual value to Muslim prayer. We spend entire days cramped up on top of our camels, while the Bedu take regular breaks to rejuvenate their faith and their bodies.

To continue north, we now must penetrate the dunes. Ali is back up front after praying and turns us onto a sandy face. The incline is as steep as an intermediate downhill ski run, enough that we need to sit forward in our saddles to avoid slipping off. The camels fall in single file, like a string of climbers heading up a high mountain slope but here in the desert, there is no threat of avalanche, nor the painful effort of moving oneself up through deep snow and across hard ice in thin air. Here, the camels do the work.

The lee side of the dune affords no wind and the temperature soars. The Bedu yell ahead to Ali, but it is difficult to make out what they are saying. The slope is steeper than expected. The camels begin to protest and start cutting side to side. Ali stops to dismount just before he reaches the dune's crest, 400 feet above the desert floor. This is the first major gain in elevation we have made since leaving the Qara Mountains three weeks ago. We stop for lunch—a strange place to stop since it offers no flat ground or shade. It is also awkward for the camels to rest on the steep slope, and without the breeze, the temperature is debilitating. At two in the afternoon, we are in the maximum heat of the day at 121 degrees and some nine miles, as the crow flies, from camp, though we have ridden farther than that to get here. We eat a little meat and drink some tea while the camels hop down the slope with their hobbled front legs. I stomach a little dried fat with a piece of meat, for the sake of the extra calories.

After our rest the Bedu make no sign of being ready to move. Bruce asks Musallim when we are planning to go, and Musallim shakes his head. Bruce presses for a reason. Finally we are told that they want to wait to talk to Manaa about the route again because they are uncertain where to go from here. Leigh has the maps out and the route looks reasonable to us, though challenging. The Bedu are unfamiliar with topographical maps and take no comfort in them. There is no negotiation. We will wait. According to the previous arrangement, we're not to see Manaa again until Butabol. The Bedu say they are sure he will pass here before heading east to the road for Masqat. They are sure Manaa will pass. What they are not sure of is when. *"Allah Karim,"* says bin Ashara. *God is merciful.* Manaa may come today or maybe tomorrow. Till then, we wait.

Leigh, Bruce and I leave the Bedu and walk up to the top of the dune twenty yards away. The hot sand burns the sides of my feet above the callused skin. We stop at the top and wiggle our feet into cooler sand below. The crest offers a view as threatening as it is beautiful. I am awestruck by the landscape that stretches before us, and intimidated by the mere thought we intend to cross it. The horizon is ragged and meets the sky ambiguously with an endless depth of field. Salmon-coloured dunes rise and fall in rolls that stretch endlessly under the northern sky. Subtle shades of colour fade from one into the other. Where we can see to their base, salt flats boil grey in the sun. Nothing is hard-edged. Everything blends together in this painted canvas. Distances are baffling. If *hot* is something that can be seen, this it what it looks like. Beautiful, and at the same time frightening. The desert's apparent lifelessness tells us quite directly that we don't belong here. It appears that nothing belongs here, yet I am filled with an inexplicable urge to venture deeper into it.

Deep within are the secrets of this desert carried in whispers on the wind and heard only by those willing to go and listen. But will we have a chance to hear?

Struck by this amazing view, we say little to each other, then return quietly to the group. Leigh wisely suggests we fashion some shade by stringing his *wasir* between our camera tripods. We do this and try to nap in the shade, but it's still too hot. We are baking in the heat and wasting time, on the hope that Manaa will spot us up here. We are as helpless as a fish flopping on a beach, desperate to be kicked back into the water. Bruce gets up to brew tea.

Leigh asks how this compares to frustrations on Mount Everest. I explain the situation is similar to Everest with its weather delays and personnel conflicts, but that there's a different flavour here. "Maybe it's because we have so little control over our own destiny here, and there was some control, at least over my own life, on Everest."

From the maps and our GPS, we know there are 318 miles through Butabol and Shaybah on our variation of Thesiger's original route, remembering that he never did go all the way to Abu Dhabi. Our route, then, translates to well over 375 miles on the ground, winding through the dunes. In thirty days we would have to travel at least twelve miles a day, which would put us (with February a short month) at the coast by March 25th. This timing is about right, according to original plans. But can we consistently cover that much ground? With that staggering thought, Leigh wonders whether we should contemplate using more truck support and simply race to the coast. I ask Leigh whether the method we use to get to the Arabian Gulf is becoming less and less important. He pauses. "Time is passing," he says.

Bruce struggles in the heat with the tea, while I suggest to Leigh another possibility. We might run our water dangerously low by sitting here waiting. One option may be to pack our gear and head back to last night's camp to replenish.

"If we did that, I'd keep going backwards till I got to Mughshin and get on the first bus out," says Leigh.

Everyone is on edge. We should measure the stress of dehydration dementia that we studied in our training sessions. I have been exhibiting some strange behaviour—fatigue, headaches and irritability, uncommon fits of anger and frustration with my camels followed by intense sadness. Bruce is no exception. He told me some days ago about breaking into tears for no particular reason while riding his camel, and about regular bouts of anger. Changing the subject, Leigh tells Bruce he should wash his scrapes from Sawad's teeth. "Yeah, I normally would, but not in the desert. Water's too precious."

Musallim heads down the dune to herd the camels and I join him. The camels have made little progress, but are instinctively heading back to the trough of water they drank from last night, water they may even be able to smell. The footprints of our own camels are becoming easier to follow now. I am still trying to understand the differences in the prints from camel to camel, and it's a challenge to distinguish T's prints from the others. Bin Ashara showed me that T has a thick scar on his left rear pad and particular flaps of skin on both front pads that leave distinct markings in the sand.

With each passing day, my appreciation grows dramatically for what Wilfred Thesiger did in this desert. His journey will never be replicated. Like Tenzing and Hillary, first to stand on the summit of Mount Everest in 1953, Thesiger was able to complete the first crossing of the desert in a unique fashion now no longer possible. Thesiger travelled through here at a time when he could depend upon the generosity of nomadic groups that are now long since gone. His guide Al Auf had twice been through the sands. His loyal friend bin Kabina stayed with him every step of the way, and was as committed to the journey as Thesiger himself. His camels—the kind that could endure long marches—are now also long since gone. Thesiger and his guides were also willing to sacrifice their mounts, and they lost many to exhaustion or starvation. Even so, it is astonishing to think that he came out here without support, no one knowing where he was—no GPS, no satellite phone, and no emergency beacons. He relied solely on his compass, his considerable abilities in these desert lands, and the knowledge of his companions. His achievement, like Hillary's and Tenzing's, is untouchable.

But why did he do it? He was the last of a long line of names in exploration linked to the prestigious Royal Geographical Society, and certainly he wanted to be the first to cross this, the most difficult sector of the Rub al Khali, citing that "the Empty Quarter offered me the chance to win distinction as a traveller."

After being hounded by the media for a reason to climb Mt. Everest, George Mallory, a British climber, hastily said in a now-iconized pronouncement that he wanted to climb it "because it's there." Sir Wilfred crossed the Rub al Khali to make a name for himself as an explorer, to number himself with Scott, Shipton, Shackleton. I climbed Everest, and now cross this desert for little more than the pure adventure of it. I simply enjoy the struggles and the triumphs of fully engaging in an adventure—the more challenging the better. For me this has nothing to do with "firsts." Reinhold Messner, one of the greatest living mountaineers, wrote that whether you are the first or the ten thousandth to climb a mountain, the reward is the same.

I agree with Messner, and believe that adventure is measured individually, not comparatively. And so I have chosen adventure as my vehicle for inward and outward exploration. It is my guide to freedom. Freedom beyond fear and weaknesses—beyond all that holds me back. The pursuit and attainment of this freedom in the spirit of adventure is, for me, the very purpose of life.

Chapter Fifteen

٦ ذو القعدة ١٤١٩
February 23, 1999
(continued)

We walk the camels back up the hill, Musallim and I. Trudging the sand steals our strength. We have walked only a mile and already thirst is thick in my mouth. Luckily, Bruce is brewing tea, while Musallim and I set about tying the camels for the night. Bruce moves quickly about the fire. A flow of curses springs from him, unlike any we have let slip within earshot of the Bedu.

"I've made thousands of gallons of tea and coffee on the river and it's been perfect every time," he shouts when I ask him what's wrong. As a river guide in northern Canada, Bruce is familiar with using fire to cook, but try as he might he cannot get it right here. Under the watchful eye of Musallim, who's very particular about his tea, Bruce keeps making mistakes. This batch is too strong, and Musallim throws away half. The remaining half will be cut with water. Bruce disappears with his camera to shoot some photos and cool his temper.

Just after sunset, we hear jeeps in the distance. We flash our portable headlamps. Manaa and Tuarish spot us and drive up the dune. Leigh, Bruce, and I drift over to where everyone has congregated.

"Before we join the group, I think it's key for us to know what's more important—completing the journey or the style in which we do," I say.

"Let's just go see what the plan is," says Bruce.

I ask Leigh his opinion. "I just want to get to the end, however that looks," he says.

I stop and pull out some of our camera equipment to videotape the planning session. The sand is now much warmer than the air, so I work my feet down into its comforting heat.

At the fire, Manaa presents the new plan. Maps are drawn in the sand with half-charred sticks pulled from the blaze. The fire's yellow light draws a few moths, and at its flickering edge a spider lurks. The size of my thumbnail, its skin translucent, the leggy little creature spins circles in the sand. I put it under the camera's light and film the spider enshrouding a maggot. The victim desperately burrows downward headfirst, a quarter of its body flailing above the surface while the spider spins a tube of silk to encase it. Ten or twelve spins completed, the spider sets its mandibles into the grub, pulls it farther out of the sand, then wraps it anew. The process will be repeated until the maggot is completely a meal encased, and preserved for another day.

The small-scale struggle for life and death carries on while Manaa wearily talks on about our travelling to Butabol alone. Because the grazing is almost non-existent, several bales of hay will be dropped at predetermined locales. Bin Ashara and the others agree. Bruce argues a little more, and then we decide to stop forcing our will. It seems we are in no position to argue, anyway. We know nothing about the sands ahead, beyond the little revealed by our maps. We talk for more than an hour when the spider finally plucks out its prey. The spider tugs on a line attached to the casing and the dying insect twitches and curls, then lies still as it's dragged across the sand.

Our group adjourns and the Bedu ready themselves for sleep. Bruce suggests we top up the *gerbers*. Now that we have thirteen camels, including the new and crazed pack camel, we can fill the goatskins to their maximum. We have eight in all, each holding about four gallons. At the moment we are consuming roughly one and a half goatskins every day or just over a gallon per person, though it is impossible to tell with any precision, as no two *gerbers* are equal in volume.

Leigh manages to connect the satellite phone as Bruce and I finish with the water. Even the Bedu come to help and everyone in camp feels a new energy. The day's frustrations and short tempers have been exaggerated by the 120-degree heat. In the cool of night we work well together. Using a length of hose, Ali siphons water from one of two 55-gallon barrels for the camels. The water in the supply truck comes from Qitbit.

The watering done, Bruce walks toward his trough in the sand. His broad shoulders are heavy with the stress of the trip. His *dishdashah* is grey with dirt, stiff with dried sweat. I turn to Leigh, whose face is aglow in the blue light of the computer screen. He connects with his law firm and learns he has been passed over for partnership—a result of the time away in the desert, he guesses. We have received a dozen questions from students, but no news on the job front for him. An e-mail from an adult is among the correspondence, from someone who views our trip as nothing more than a "lark," because we could have driven in a Hummer. There is a note from someone who attended a Tom Cochrane concert in Calgary last night. A renowned Canadian rock star, Cochrane apparently stood on stage before 30,000 local fans in our hometown and dedicated a song to us. "This is for Jamie Clarke and the boys in the desert!" he shouted before playing his classic *White Hot*—a tune quite fitting the day we have just endured. I had seen Cochrane play up close and personal at the University of Toronto's Convocation Hall, one of the best concerts I have ever attended. This is exactly what I need to lift my spirits.

We pack up the satellite gear and go to bed. Thirst pulls at my throat, unquenched by the salty fluid in my bottle. This is the re-supply water and, though it is far better than that from the *gerbers*, it is still heavily mineralized. I add my last ration of flavour crystals to kill the taste and crawl into bed, the last in camp to do so. Bruce is already sleeping—snoring loudly. Propping my head up on a saddlebag, I can look comfortably at the sky and contemplate the days ahead.

Everest presented its share of sickness and personal conflict, but we always worked through things. I have to believe we can achieve that sense of success here. That lovely moment between consciousness and sleep, where dreams and reality pleasantly blend, washes over me. The moon is only half full, but it shines brightly enough to blot out half the stars.

٧ ذو القعدة ١٤١٩
February 24, 1999 57 miles NNE of Mughshin
Day 23 — 20 07′ N 55 19′ E

One moment I am watching the heavens, and the next Musallim is calling us to prayer. We are up quickly. I roll up my sleeping bag and notice a curious collection of tracks around it in the fine sand. A dung beetle has searched my perimeter for morsels, but there are also two new tracks. The larger one is light and all legs. The other is heavier, with a dragging torso. I shake out my bag to ensure no unwanted visitors have taken up residence. Our early start is a blessing in the cool air, and the sand has lost the heat that burned our feet yesterday. Now cold from the night, we are numb as we climb back to the summit of the dune on which we had camped. We drop down its steep face and Mr. T hesitates with every step even though the other camels are moving well. Something is bothering him.

At the bottom of the dune we couch the camels to mount. Out of character, Mr. T rises slowly once I am in the saddle. He normally jumps up the instant he feels my weight on his back, if not before. We are at the edge of the first substantial salt flat. The grey-white surface reflects the sun and heats the air above the ground more quickly than the sand. Only minutes into the ride, T begins to lag behind. His gait has changed. It is uneven, the result of an injured hoof, a sore knee, or a damaged shoulder joint. Leigh and Bruce watch as we ride along, but they see nothing. After all the hours on T's back, I know there is a problem, even if its precise nature isn't obvious. That I've become this attached to Mr. T is unexpected. I have picked ticks from his hide and brushed sandy tears from his cheeks, fed him half my date rations and broken my sleep to check on him. I never thought I would think of my camel as a companion. He has endured my

234

singing and our mindless chats, and he has been unusually patient with my poor riding skills and my increasingly bad temper. He has also bucked me off too often, kicked me numerous times, and is not above biting and vomiting. But he's *my* camel and I'm starting to hold him in great affection—bad breath, bad attitude, and all.

Bin Ashara examines the camel at my request. After ten minutes, he announces something I cannot understand and calls up to Musallim, who drifts back to look. They chat back and forth and then ride on without a word. We have 94 miles left to Butabol. There will be no rest for five days. Will T make it?

The terrain is complex, with chains of dunes running perpendicular to our route. According to the map, some of the chains run more than sixty miles east to west and straddle our route till we near the coast. Too steep and too high to climb, we must weave around the dunes to make northerly progress. Perfectly horizontal tracts of baked mud, salts, and gravel separate the massive 750-foot dunes. We ride at the dunes' edges, where the sand overlaps the salt flats, and by 11:30 we've made twelve miles. Mr. T is struggling at the back of the group. Leigh is working better with Jerry, and on the one day I could have been back keeping him company he is up with the others.

We head due east among smaller dunes that give texture to the ground like chop does on the open ocean. In some of the dune troughs we find pools of mud. Mr. T is wary of the thick grey soup and hesitates as I steer us along the dry sand. He is labouring. While the others are moving at the normal four miles an hour, T is struggling to do half that. The main group is out of site but Bruce is waiting for me. After a quick greeting he rides off. I decide to dismount and walk the balance of today's distance. Only seven feet below my perch on T's back, the air temperature at ground level is markedly hotter. The salt mixed with the sand reflects the sun and heats the air. Walking is difficult, and the soft ground quickly saps our energy. Worse, though, are the scattered troughs through which we must walk. The muddy ones are not an option, but many are dry and offer the best alternative to walking up and down the choppy dunes, though the dried salt is cracked, uneven, and sharp. After a mile, the soles of my shoes are starting to shred. The rubber could not survive more than a day or two of this.

The ground is even worse for the padded hooves of the camels. The heavier camels are breaking through up to their fetlocks. Bloodstains now mark the salt under Mr. T's two front feet, and he is not the only camel to suffer. Many of the other hoof prints are stained red as well. There is no other way through this short section. Above these waves of sand, the great dunes surround us tightly in all directions. On their flanks some vegetation grows freely, but down here shrubs cling to life only where the salt beds allow.

Mr. T's limp worsens and he stops more than once in protest. We round a dune ridge and see the others sitting in the sand, their camels tied to some of the scrubby bushes. Without a word, bin Ashara takes T from me and couches him. Though Musallim is the team's camel doctor, it is bin Ashara who prods T's shoulder. Everyone looks on to see whether one pressure point irritates the camel more than another. T is walked in a circle followed by more pressing just above the shoulder joint, causing him to squirm and step away. There are no outward signs of this injury.

A fire is started. The teapot is filled, making me think a hot water compress might be the remedy. But instead of salt, I'm asked to find the tea and sugar. While we drink and watch Mr. T, the conversation among the Bedu continues in serious tones. 119.4 degrees. Sitting around a fire in this heat is cruel punishment. Bin Ashara looks at me, then waves a hand toward his saddle.

"Hat el bunduk. Hat el bunduk!"

I pull his 7.62 mm rifle from his saddle, worrying that T is about to be shot, but bin Ashara unscrews the cleaning rod from under the rifle's barrel and thrusts its end into the coals of the fire. Mr. T is going to be branded.

Branding, or *wasm*, is a traditional Bedu technique for treating ill health caused by evil spirits. It is commonly used for both animals and humans. Many Bedu carry scars on their bodies. A brand between the eyes or on the cheek will drive away the demons that inflict headaches and toothaches, a technique that would seem more apt to prevent complaints than actually cure the ailment. I wonder at the cure for chronic bowel trouble.

Musallim and I pull T's head away from his sore right shoulder. Bruce and Leigh film and look on. I stare into his eyes past his angry growls and spurts of green mucous. Bin Ashara grabs the rod with his *masar* and moves quickly from the fire to kneel beside T, then presses the red-hot metal into the camel's thick tan hair. Smoke streams straight up without a breath of wind to stir it. Once through the hair, the rod is spun and the crackling of burning flesh hisses between T's screams of protest. Bin Ashara's hand shakes with the force, and T pulls away hard. The smell of burning hair and flesh is foul. My eyes fill with tears for the animal. Within forty seconds the first branding is done. T twists his head around to lick the wound and calms quickly. I have grave doubts that this branding will do any good, except that one pain might serve to mask another—for a while.

Instead of letting the rod cool, bin Ashara stabs it into the fire, searching for the hottest coals. Musallim and I are soon back at T's head. The event is troubling. T is not the first camel to see a brand in the sands of Arabia and will not be the last. Will there ever be enough time to harden to this desert life? Will there be any peace to find about the effect of our presence here?

Bin Ashara works three more vertical brands below the horizontal one and is done. T recovers and we shuffle loads to free him of my gear. Lucy is saddled for me to ride. Taynoonah, the crazed camel that kicked Manaa in Thamarit, is my new pack camel. Her aggression unnerves me. Lucy kicks back at her as we start moving. T is tied to his pal Crazy Dancer and does not look any better.

Lucy's gait is much different from Mr. T's. Being smaller, with a shorter stride, she almost trots to keep up with the others. In a faster gait she jerks less from side to side and is easier to ride. She is also far thinner than T, leaving my legs to hang more naturally and taking some of the strain off my knees. Lucy is keen to stay up front and needs very little prodding to break into a gallop. For the first time since we last rode roped together, Ali and I ride up front. He sings songs about camels for a while, then stops in the middle of one. It is too hot to sing, he says. I offer him water. He declines. I make a point of always offering my bottle to the Bedu but they never take it. They each have a one-quart bottle of their own—the kind you see in army surplus stores. Ali proudly tells me that the Bedu need much less water than do we Canadians.

Right on schedule—we spot the bale of hay and the bag of oats that Manaa has dropped for the animals. It is 4:30 in the afternoon. The temperature—111 degrees. Bruce dismounts and produces his bottles for a refill from the *gerbers*. He is not faring well in the heat today, walking as one might after a couple of strong drinks. He speaks with a slight slur and takes more time than usual to answer when I ask after him. Musallim frowns at Bruce's need for more water, but bin Ashara approves and helps to untie a *gerber*. After taking a long drink Bruce wipes sweat from his face with his sleeve and talks: "Thank God we're camping...I can't ride any more...today...I'm too hot."

I begin to unsaddle Lucy when Ali tells me we are riding on to take advantage of the evening's 80-degree temperatures. The hay is tied to Sawad, the bull camel. We continue. This makes sense as we have several hours of light left and the temperature will only drop. Bruce re-mounts without complaint. One's perception of heat changes in the desert. Temperatures in the mid 80s once seemed stifling. Now, they seem cool in comparison.

We have already travelled 25 miles on the ground, taking us 19 miles closer to the coast. The sun is sinking, back and to our left, casting our shadows forward and giving depth to the dune's textures. Leigh is still up front with Jerry Purple Knees, and I am hoping that it will lift his spirits to be on a camel that stays with the pack. The branding has worked wonders with Mr. T. Perhaps the break from carrying my weight has also helped. Regardless, he is moving better proving the branding effectual, if strange to us as westerners. Musallim says Mr. T will recover well, but doesn't know how long it will take. He tells me not to worry.

After another four miles we stop again. It is 6:30. Bin Ashara leads us four hundred feet up a dune face. He explains that this location will be easier to defend than the open valley floor in case of attack. When I jump to the ground my legs collapse, dropping me to my hands and knees. I try to stand, but black out. Ninety-five degree heat isn't as refreshing as I'd hoped. The warmth has taken its toll. Back on my knees, my vision returns as my head pounds with each beat of my heart. Leigh offers some brotherly advice: "It's been over 113 degrees all day with no wind. We've only had only two quarts of water and that's nowhere near enough. Get some more to drink."

The three of us kneel over the *gerbers* and empty the dregs from two of them into our bottles. The water is dark and uninviting but taste is meaningless now. Although it is warm it feels wonderful in my mouth and throat. We drink two quarts each before we begin to feel better.

Bin Ashara calls me to help collect firewood. He points to a few twigs poking through the sand. Then, by demonstration, he shows that beneath the surface rests the hardy root system of the former bush. We dig out enough wood for tonight's tea and tomorrow's breakfast.

A plane passes overhead, the first since departing Salalah. We could easily be up there, beyond any thought of this struggle. We could easily be down here in Land Rovers or Hummers, as others have traversed sections of this desert. We chose to cross with camels. It is not possible to sense the rhythm and spirit of a land and its people through a window at fifty miles an hour. This journey is not about destination. Though at this moment I envy the people who are sitting comfortably in that plane sipping on cool drinks, I do not want to trade places. I will be back there soon enough.

٨ ذو القعدة ١٤١٩
February 25, 1999
Day 24 — 20 21' N 55 25' E

The morning is gone, and yesterday's heat lies again upon us. A bowl of *gerber* water is passed at lunch—we have already consumed today's two-quart allotment in this windless inferno. Every mouthful tastes of leather, with chunks of fat and hair and other unidentifiable pieces. The particulate matter collects at the bottom of the chocolate brown mixture. Bin Ashara works the bowl like a gold pan and sips the pungent broth.

Beetles of an impressive variety have taken up residence in our two bags of meat. We have almost finished one, leaving the meat-to-bug ratio at two to one. The beetles are easily mistaken for little bits of jerky. If we wait long enough after the bag is opened the beetles stir from their defensive coma and the dusty pile begins to team with activity. The chunks of fat become favourite burrows for beetle eggs. The highly caloric fat or *shaham* must be split apart before eating to prevent accidental larvae consumption. The smaller nuggets of meat are the best, as they are the best preserved and least likely to be harmful. The thicker bits might have been too slowly dried and may be the cause of my recent stomach and intestinal disorders.

The heat in the last days has sapped our energy. We are too lethargic to cook bread and we justify this laziness by the water we are conserving. Thus, the meat has become the main part of our daily meals. Musallim, a committed carnivore, is happy with this, as are Ali and bin Ashara. The Bedu appreciate food more in quantity than variety. Like Sherpas with *dhal bhat*, they are willing and happy to eat the same fare day after day—or maybe they just don't see the value in complaining.

Leigh tests the temperature and reports 126 degrees. We rig a camel blanket to create a patch of shade in which all six of us lie together like sardines. The camels feel the heat as well. Some have not moved from where we couched them to unload. Some huddle together, instinctively knowing the heat transferred between their bodies is less than that through the air. If it were not so hot, they would be off, hobbled and shuffling, in search of food. Lucy lies with her head on the sand looking exhausted. I get up and pull some hay from the supplies for her, but she is uninterested, a sign of her growing thirst. The effort has me sweating and light headed. The others have taken up my space in the shade and I try to edge my way back in. Sometime later Ali wakes us from a fitful rest. "*Irkab?*" he asks. *Ride?* Without a word, we saddle up slowly and move on. The heat is even too much for the camels. They are travelling only slightly faster than half their normal speed.

At first a welcome break from the discomfort of riding T, sitting astride Lucy is now quite painful. T's wide girth dispersed

78

79

"I knew instinctively it was the very hardness of life in the desert which drew me back there—it was the same pull which takes men back to polar ice, to high mountains, and to the sea." — W. Thesiger.

81

Even the desert blooms—the **zahar** flower heralds early summer.

80

Tireless camels—endles dunes.

82

Hamdulillah! Musallim smiles after rain.

83

Little insects challenge the desert's immensity.

84

A ten-year drought ends—rain pounds the thirsty sands.

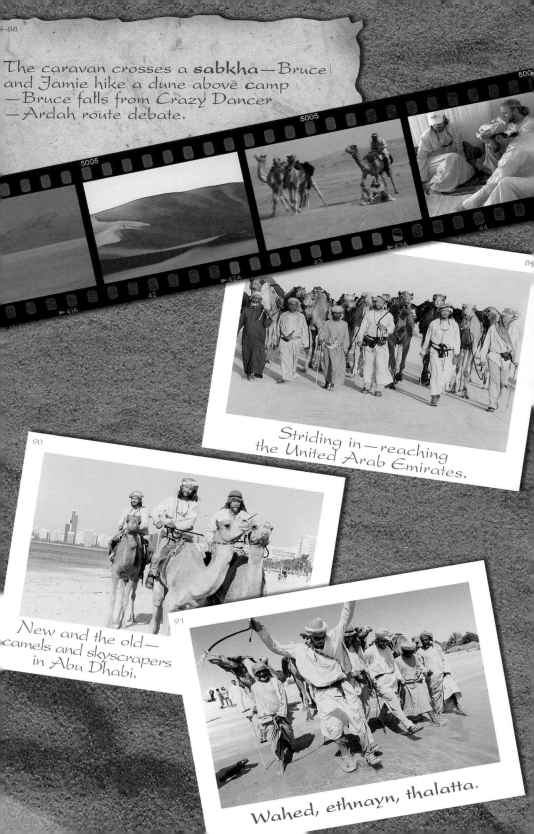

The caravan crosses a **sabkha**—Bruce
and Jamie hike a dune above camp
—Bruce falls from Crazy Dancer
—Ardah route debate.

Striding in—reaching
the United Arab Emirates.

New and the old—
camels and skyscrapers
in Abu Dhabi.

Wahed, ethnayn, thalatta.

Above all else.

Khunde, Nepal.
Barbara and Jamie wed.

Barbara and her husband,
Suhail bin Kanada.

95

Ali traveling fast.

Ali—a modern bin Kabina.

Ali rides across a **sabkha** flat.

98

Bin Kabina—Thesiger's inseparable companion.

99

Celebrating journey's end.
From one sea, to another.

100

Farewell to Mr. T

101

Endless hospitality
in Abu Dhabi.

102

Meeting His Highness,
Sheikh Zayed.

103

With Sir Wilfred
at Cou

5005

5005

104–107

The
expedition banner
A great explorer remembers:
—studying film footage
—Thesiger touches a picture of Labian
—Khobe, a future adventurer?

In caravan.

A welcome-home party.

One year later—Jamie reunites with Bedu team.

Taynoonah, pregnant.

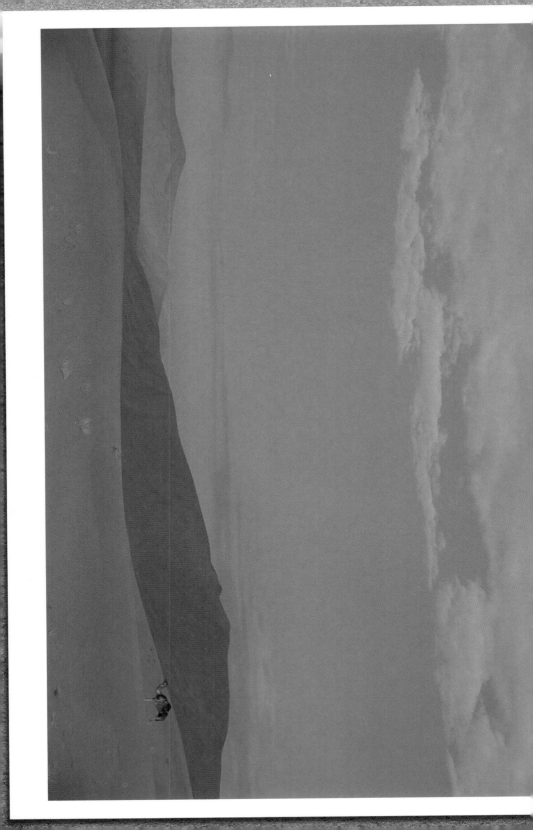

my weight over his back across my seat and thighs. Lucy, with her narrow back, focuses the weight of my torso and legs quite uncomfortably. It reminds me of a medieval torture I had seen in a London museum. Diagrams explained how a victim was seated on a triangular block shaped like the steep gable of a house. Weights were added to the feet of the sufferer, who was then slowly split in two from the groin.

In the heat and discomfort my head is getting heavy and hard to hold upright. Unlike the cold, there is no escape from this heat. On Everest, given proper clothes, calories and activity, cold *is* escapable. The heat here is as inescapable as a fever. Claustrophobic. We are riding through God's blast furnace, and it will either forge something new in our character or turn it to ashes. Is it any surprise that Jesus and Muhammad made dramatic personal discoveries in the desert? Imagine the power in the experience of being out here alone in this kiln, bereft of any resources. Christ's first miracle might not have been the conversion of water to wine at Cana. I think it was surviving the beginnings of his ministry out in the desert wilderness.

I filled a bottle with water at lunch and vowed I'd not drink any for at least three hours. Two hours are gone, but the water still taunts me as it sloshes about in my saddlebag. I search the dunes for any distraction. Their faces are smoothly sculptured, the colour of tanned skin. They flow gently into one another. Human shapes hide among the intertwining ridges. Muscled shoulders rise above the sensual curves of a delicate navel. The gentle shape of a female thigh rises to a hip and falls toward the waist with deep shadows to preserve modesty. A Siren arm of sand reaches out to me.

Musallim and Ali jump from their camels, snapping me back to reality. I join them, happy for the break and a chance to relieve myself—the first time since breakfast, thirteen hours ago. Three hours have also passed since my vow not to drink. The battle with thirst is won—momentarily. Ali drains the last drop from his bottle.

Musallim calls prayer. Ali walks away to join him, then turns back to me, eyeing my bottle. I unscrew the lid and before I take a drink I offer it to him, expecting and even hoping for the usual refusal. He takes it from me and drinks deeply. I am happy he now feels comfortable enough in our friendship to share my water, but wonder whether it isn't just a function of his terrible thirst. My delight turns to irritation as he gulps the precious water. The Bedu, finally, are thirsty. This is not unlike times on Everest when our Sherpa teammates began to tire. The Sherpas are legendary for their strength at altitude. Unfortunately this strength is often unfairly over-blown. A Sherpa friend of seven years talked to me of the pressure he felt to be "Sherpa" all the time. He felt as though he was on stage with climbers or trekkers. He admitted to faking being strong when he was actually tired. "Sometimes Sherpas becomes in trouble from climbing when they are sick and need rest. But everybody thinks Sherpas are always powerful and this is what we must be," he told me.

There is no doubt the Sherpa people are of a mettle unknown in most other cultures, but they are not the superhumans we posit them to be. They do tire, and when the Sherpas approach exhaustion, it is a bad sign for any expedition. The Bedu are of the same ilk. Ali is noticeably thirsty and by the way he now walks awkwardly off to pray, he too is suffering from the day's heat and the long ride. Differences between us are fading.

Tired camels are easy to control—they do not move from where they were couched. I lean against Lucy and watch the Bedu pray. The sun has set, leaving a burgundy slash across the sky. Humidity in the tropics, or the dust kicked up during a prairie harvest produce the same results, but not with this stunning magnitude. Silhouetted against the blood-draped horizon, our companions face into the remaining light to observe their early evening ritual. A dramatic picture, and the urge to film it is strong. I envy them this meditative moment and the peace that must come from such unshakable faith. The poetic meter of their prayers lends civility to what has been such a spiteful day. The air is cooling into the mid 90s.

The men rise against the light in unison. They pause with arms crossed and then vanish back into the pool of darkness in which they kneel. Lucy chews her cud and watches. In her wet eyes I can see the same scene reflected. I am tempted to grab my camera and film this, but refrain.

I have resolved at last what to film and what not to. At the journey's start, I filmed events and resented not being able to experience them directly. Conversely, when I didn't film I was free to enjoy the experience but missed getting some great footage. In the end, I was doing neither well. Now I am more discerning when selecting what to film and what to experience first hand. It will all be captured one way or the other. Right now, the camera stays where it is, and this moment is left for memory alone.

Prayers end. Leigh and Bruce ride up. We're thirsty and seize the chance to refill our water bottles. We have been consuming water at an alarming rate and have less than four gallons left. We are not sure when next we will see water and become quite alarmed. How could we have been so careless? Were we not rationing properly? With this realization, a leathery feeling takes over my throat, and my battle with thirst begins anew.

We ride on, passing the ghostly ruins of a small abandoned oil encampment, taking to the deep vehicle tracks that lead northward through the sand. Lucy is tired of me on her back and of pulling a fatigued Taynoonah, who keeps stopping by dropping to her knees. Twice, this has broken the tether, and Lucy voices her frustration with repeated bellows, punctuated by backward thrusts of her head to bite my knees. I shout and pull at Taynoonah to no avail, but at least it puts Lucy and me in the same camp.

Between the camel battles, I take in the sky. The moon is rising and beginning to outshine the stars that had been so vivid. We are a tight group in the dark. The relative coolness would normally re-energize the camels and riders alike, but not tonight. Ali sings again but his voice is weak and raspy. Long pauses separate the choruses. Musallim and bin Ashara join in to remind him of forgotten lyrics. The Canadians hum some of the tunes.

The last three days have been punishing for our group. We have doubled our planned consumption rates and still are losing strength and concentration. We will not be able to survive more than another day if we do not come upon the next well tomorrow. The map shows it twelve miles from here, but if it proves dry or too brackish, we'll be in terrible shape without re-supply. We have underestimated the dangers here. A fatal fall is an ever-present possibility in the mountains, but dehydration, though more subtle, is equally deadly.

The moon lights our path along the scars left by the oil rig service vehicles. The tire tracks cut into the sand from the north and east. In the right track, pools of salty slop float with iridescent circles. Much of this is hidden in the dark but because the road has been pressed a foot into the sand, we can follow it running blind.

The thought of a tall, cool glass of water grips my mind. A gust of wind pushes through our team. The ruts in the sand cut eastward and then disappear. The darkness is palpable. There are no features to guide us. The challenge now becomes navigation in this heavy darkness. We are left with the Bedus' keen sense of direction, the moon and, a vast map of stars. Even tested by the darkness, our friends keep us dead northward.

Purple Knees has done well for most of the day but suddenly stops, refusing to go on. Leigh takes to Mr. T who Musallim says is now fine. Attached to Leigh's saddle, Purple Knees is still reluctant to continue and pulls at every step.

The sudden smell of cigar smoke wafts through the air. The red glow of burning tobacco is seen as Leigh pulls on one of the three cigars he's brought.

Lucy protests by dropping to her knees again, fed up with hauling Taynoonah along. Musallim signals bin Ashara and we pull up on a dune face to camp. We quickly free the camels of their loads. Thirst preoccupies everyone. Ali collects wood, bin Ashara makes the fire, and Musallim assembles the ingredients for tea. Leigh, Bruce and I fill the water bottles and the teapot. Taking stock of the last of our *gerber* supplies, we discover three small goatskins remain almost full, with a total of five gallons—we have more water than we thought, but still a thin margin. This will be gone by morning.

The day ends with dried meat and a little of bin Ashara's coffee, a brew more to be chewed than sipped. Ali wants to use some flour to make *khobz*. Bin Ashara says no in the interest of conserving water. A search in the nearly empty supply bags yields a forgotten can of tuna from Mughshin. We each take turns digging meat out with our knives, followed by a sip of the packing oil. Ali again tries to make *khobz* but is stopped by Musallim. Sleep is more important than food just now. Besides, the bread would be too dry to eat. No amount of chewing and peristalsis could force that sawdust-like bread down my leathery throat.

Careful not to cut my tongue on the tin, I drink the last drops of tuna oil from the can and stroll away from the group to observe the herd. Few of the camels have moved from where they were couched. They are so exhausted and dehydrated that none of them have touched the food we picked up seven hours ago. Four of them lie on their sides, stretched out as if dead. Their only movement is the rise and fall of their rib cages as they breathe.

In the fifty years since Thesiger passed this way, the camels, as he warned, have lost much of their famous capacity to endure and work in the desert heat. Once, Thesiger travelled more than two weeks without water for his herd. Ours have been without water just four days. Before Thesiger's time, the Bedu had been known to ride up to fifty days between wells in the cooler winter months. In defence of the camels, Leigh adds that we are 55 pounds heavier than the average Bedu and that back in Thamarit, only a few weeks ago, it was a challenge for us to ride just a mile. We've been in the saddle for more than twelve hours today and covered 32 miles. This is our new distance record. Bin Ashara believes that there is a well nine miles away and the map confirms it. We plan to leave in the cool of the morning to reach the water where we will be able to drink our fill—and water our camels—if it is at all approachable. The water will encourage the camels to eat and thus regain their strength. Two days from now we hope to reach Butabol, where we will take a day of rest.

I scoop out a bed in the sand but cannot fall asleep, unable to stop thinking of another drink. My two water bottles are in my saddlebag under my head filled with tomorrow's ration and I have promised myself not to drink from them till the morning. But what damage could a little sip do? Just enough to wet my throat—no more than a mouthful. I break the promise and sneak a sip that becomes a large gulp. It does nothing to slake my thirst, or relieve the agonizing dry in my mouth.

At 11:30, I am still obsessed with thirst.

At 12:30, nothing has changed. Technically it's now "tomorrow." I allow myself another drink.

By 1:12, for the fifth time, I drink from the bottle, now almost empty. While training in Texas we drank over a gallon of water a day, even though we were outside less than eight hours and slept in air-conditioned rooms at night. Here it is much hotter and there is no escape, yet we have been surviving on two quarts. I finish off the first bottle, unconcerned about the bits of hair and fat that accompany the last filthy mouthful.

Gunfire! The camp stirs. It's the middle of the night. Musallim is already awake having fired the shot. When the ringing in my ears stops, I can hear two trucks racing along the valley floor a few hundred yards away. They, too, have heard the shot and turn toward us. Two shots are fired from the vehicles, signalling their friendly intention. When the trucks reach us, Manaa, Tuarish and Salim Ali jump out. Worried by the excessive heat and difficult terrain, they have come to check on us. We are moved by their concern and I am too thirsty to worry about this unplanned intrusion. Desert hospitality knows no restrictions in time or place. Well after three in the morning, we resurrect the fire and cook a meal with the new supplies of rice and water to feed our guests. Ali finally gets to make his *khobz*. I refill my bottle, so fortuitously relieved of the need to confess I'd emptied it.

Chapter Sixteen

٩ ذو القعدة ١٤١٩

February 26, 1999

Day 25 — 20 51' N 55 25' E

Sunrise. Our cooking pots stand in the sand before the camels. We fill them, tipping water from the barrels. The sound and smell excites them. Still hobbled, the camels jump awkwardly at the pots, jostling for access. Heads bob up and down, helping to pour water down each throat. Each camel shakes its head about, spraying water from floppy lips. The spray glints in the morning sun, pleasantly soaking us all.

Manaa declares that Jerry and Lucy are tired, no longer fit to ride. T is back on the injured list after his ride with Leigh last night. Manaa points to our new camels: Sawad, the arm-biting elephant-size beast, and Taynoonah, the berserk pack animal. I am not sure which I want to ride less. Taynoonah is the camel that kicked Manaa the very night she arrived in Thamarit. Since then she has barely been ridden, and even as a pack camel Taynoonah is hard to manage. Though the Bedu have ridden Sawad, his size intimidates. He weighs well over 200 pounds more than any of the other camels. Even the Bedu approach Sawad with extra caution.

"*Suhail, irkab Taynoonah. Abdullah irkab Sawad,*" Manaa directs.

Fear holds me in place till I see Leigh move toward Sawad. I gather my saddle blankets and other riding gear. Stalling for time, I first load T with a couple of light bedrolls, then couch him in the sand near Taynoonah. When I approach the new camel she starts

247

to gurgle and pump her belly. But forewarned is not necessarily forearmed: Taynoonah is especially cunning, and before I see it coming, she sprays me with the contents of her stomach. With a whip of her neck, through pressed lips, she launches a foul green stream with stunning speed and accuracy, blasting my face and shoulders. What an impressive bit of self-defence. The slimy vomit tastes of grass and bile and soaks my beard and hair. I take a few more blasts while saddling her, but, know enough now to keep my mouth closed.

In the wake of the camel shuffle, bin Ashara will now ride the unbroken pack camel bin Saybeen. He is the master, with a reputation for managing wild camels. When bin Ashara was a young man, he gained fame among the Bedu for breaking a certain bull camel. The bull had lived wild for several years, through repeated failed attempts by other Bedu to catch and break him. Bin Ashara took his turn tracking the rogue camel. After sneaking up on it, bin Ashara, as did Salim Ali in Thamarit, raced along side the fleeing animal and leaped onto its back, pulling on a handful of hair. The young bin Ashara managed to stay mounted until the maddened beast stopped bucking. He then triumphantly claimed the animal as his own and was crowned the region's most able rider. A poem commemorating the event was composed by bin Ashara's cousin, who witnessed the event.

Bin Ashara struggles anew to saddle bin Saybeen, who is bent on escape. The camel couched, bin Ashara ties her front legs together, then ties her head to her tail to stop her from jumping up. Looking much like an agitated pretzel, the camel tries to bite bin Ashara as he works. My battle with Taynoonah pales in comparison. He passes the girth line under bin Saybeen's belly. She bites at him and gets his arm, but does not break the skin. Calmly and without apparent anger, bin Ashara shovels two handfuls of sand into the camel's mouth when it tries to bite him again. Then, with the halter line, he ties her mouth shut. Bin Ashara is the one among us who has been the most loving with the camels. He is the one who speaks of them with the most reverence and respect. But bin Ashara also advocates maintaining order and safety, knowing that the camels will take advantage of any slack.

Leigh is ahead and is doing well with the large bull. Musallim waits for me and suggests we ride attached for the morning. He says Taynoonah is a dangerous camel—much more so than Mr. T. "*Khalee balak, khalee balak.* Be careful," he repeats, showing genuine concern for my safety. I heed his advice and tie a rein into Musallim's saddle before we begin to ride. Taynoonah bucks a little and resists my mounting by jumping up a few times, but once we are moving she calms down.

It's amazing what's been accomplished in the last month. Not long ago, even the thought of riding attached to another camel was nerve-wracking. Five weeks ago, who would have imagined we would ride more than ten hours in a day, travelling thirty miles, in control not of one, but two, and sometimes three camels?

Without warning, bin Saybeen races past us at a gallop, bouncing bin Ashara, who has lost control. The camel stops a hundred yards past us, where bin Ashara jumps to the ground, tightens the camel's girth, and remounts. Bin Saybeen twirls and jumps as she tries to throw him off. The crazed camel sprints back toward us, races by, then turns and races back with a leg action so erratic bin Ashara is in constant danger of being thrown off. He hangs on with great determination, pulling at the reins and swinging his camel stick in rhythm with the camel's bounds and leaps. I am not sure which concerns me more—camel or man. Bin Saybeen jerks to a stop and whips around in circles like a dog frantically chasing its tail, and then sprints off behind us, leaving clouds of dust suspended in the windless day.

Three hours into the ride the terrain is unchanged. Bin Ashara joins the group again, but bin Saybeen is still in a foul mood and has lost little energy since this morning. Bin Ashara rides with his knees tucked up under him, holding the rein with one hand, his camel stick with the other. That he can even stay mounted is itself an impressive display of balance and endurance. As bin Ashara passes, he yells at his camel. Ali laughs and explains that bin Ashara is swearing, but I cannot make out what he's saying. The Bedu are creative with their cursing and rarely rely upon simple words or phrases as westerners often do. I can only imagine bin Ashara's flying insults: "You will never drink sweet water again!" Or: "By God, you will be eaten at the end of this journey!"

The rest of us just watch in silence until Bruce speaks. "It's good things didn't evolve the other way around. We could have had camels strapped to our backs while *they* rode *us* across the desert."

Twelve miles on, we intersect a graded road, running east. The camels hesitate as they reach the unfamiliar surface, then step onto the well-used road where it turns north. The sound of engines is heard, large machinery—metal on metal—in the distance. At the crest of a dune, an oil camp comes into view. The compound is replete with refinery towers, a pump station, generators, and quarters for the workers. We ride past a large yellow sign declaring this place the Sahmah Flow Station. The dunes are flattened and pushed aside to accommodate the semi-permanent structures. Among the buildings grow mature green trees, watered by an intricate network of brown tubing that runs to the base of each trunk. Buildings, towers, and trees are all out of place and create a sudden and unwelcome sight, but at the same time a comforting one. This place isn't on our maps, nor have we had advance word of it from the Bedu. We did not expect this kind of break in the Quarter's emptiness. We have become accustomed to travelling for days in uninterrupted remoteness, save the odd old tire track. A moment ago there was nothing in any direction other than swells of sand rising and falling in and out of a cloudless sky. Now we ride past a sign posting the speed limit at 25 miles an hour. As we approach the compound, another sign advises that it is unsafe to pass. Four dogs leap up from the shade under a trailer and chase after us, barking.

A Bedu man, an employee of the Elf Petroleum Company, comes out to invite us into the mess hall. We are offered fruit, coffee, and bottles of cold water. I drink several quarts in a few minutes. With no bits of fat or hair or traces of salt, it is the best water we have had since the well of Mashadid. I use the toilet, sitting firmly on the seat, feeling happy not to squat. The face in the mirror is not pretty. The skin is greasy and covered by a thin mask of sand. The ratty beard is matted with sand, bits of rice and dried camel vomit. How foul we are.

Abdullah bin Hamood Al Rashdy is the production

supervisor of the Sahmah oil field. He politely informs us that the next shift is about to change and that we will need to leave to make room for the men. It was once customary to offer a nomad three days of shelter and food. The rules of desert survival need not apply here. Today's guest will not be tomorrow's host. There is no longer an endemic dependency on the kindness of strangers. Thesiger predicted that some of the nobility of the Bedu would be lost to this new way of life. In fact, Thesiger himself noted these changes on a return trip:

> When I went back to Oman and Abu Dhabi in 1977, for the first time since I had left there in 1950, I was disillusioned and resentful at the changes brought about by the discovery and production of oil throughout the region—the traditional Bedu way of life, which I had shared with the Rashid for five memorable years, had been irrevocably destroyed by the introduction of motor transport, helicopters and aeroplanes.

Is this what we are seeing here? Elsewhere we have witnessed indications that the traditional ways still survive. The Bedu we have met already have zealously extended invitations to stay with them, and I half hope to receive one from Abdullah. The offer never comes. At the start of this journey we chose not to stop when invited. Now that we aren't asked, I wish we were.

"Take all the water and the fruit you need," Abdullah offers, and we do. I drain the last pint from one of my water bottles and laugh as the brown fluid swirls away in the white sink. There are bits of goat fat, which need extra rinsing from my bottle and from the porcelain sink. I wash my face and hands thoroughly and fill both bottles with the water, which is stored in boxes stacked three high along the mess hall's walls. I grab an extra bottle of water for later and stuff two oranges into the pockets of my *dishdashah*. I have consumed a gallon and a half of water in the two hours we have been here, and finally need to relieve myself for the first time in nearly two days.

The heat outside is oppressive. In the short time we have been inside, I have become happily accustomed to the air conditioning. Stepping out into the desert is like opening an oven door to check on a baking pie. How quickly we have softened in the cradle of this unexpected comfort. In little more than two hours, it has begun to erode our toughness. I want to stay. We mount up and ride on instead. Bin Ashara and bin Saybeen resume their battle.

This luxurious little break in our journey leaves a sense of guilt. Have we cheapened the adventure? There is resentment for the water in my bottles, but I am not about to pour it out. The irony found in the very name of this desert is clear. The Empty Quarter is no longer empty.

I begin to rationalize. After all, who could come upon this place and not be seduced? No traveller in this desert, now or long ago, would pass a camp and not stop to receive the hospitality within, albeit that in the past the fare would have comprised leather bowls of camel's milk and scraps of goat meat, all served on the sand. Today we eat fruit and drink bottled water from glass decanters while we sit upright in chairs, out of the heat. Who could choose warm unpasteurized milk riddled with parasites over an icy bottle of Coke?

Back on our route, Musallim unties Taynoonah from his saddle. Immediately she slows and stops. I give her a tap with my *yad* and she starts to spin, kick, and buck, and then promptly sits down in the sand. I smack her rump, and Taynoonah's up and running. She stops, turns, runs, stops again, then drops in the sand. We are up again and this time she bucks in circles to the left, like a rodeo bull. The others have disappeared beyond a dune while Taynoonah and I continue our violent minuet. She pays no attention to my commands, and I cannot risk hitting her any harder with my *yad*. I'd hoped, the very night we'd met in Thamarit, that I would never have to ride her. Not only did she kick Manaa, but she is the same camel Salim Ali had chased down on foot. She probably remembers those incidents. Finally, Taynoonah notices her separation from the group and gallops to catch up, calming as we come near.

I still cannot get a sense of distance in the desert. There are too few features to offer any kind of relative measurement or provide any depth of field. To pass time, we place bets on distances, using anything that lies ahead, such as a scrub brush or a distinctive dune. The Bedu are most often the closest, though Leigh, who continues to develop his natural navigational skills, displays a knack as well. Surprisingly, all six of us have been way off on a couple of occasions. What someone thinks is a tree two miles away turns out to be a rock only a hundred yards ahead.

The day slips by in a blur of heat as I focus on Taynoonah. We cover 22 miles and make camp above a salt flat at 320 feet above sea level. Bin Ashara arrives an hour later, ending his daylong battle with bin Saybeen. The camel is still spirited, but controlled. The Bedu jump up to help unload the animal. Bin Ashara looks exhausted. He drops weakly by the fire for tea. He missed the *Salat al-Zuhr* (midday prayer) and the *Salat al-Maghrib* (evening prayer), occupied as he was with his mount. After tea, but before eating, he summons the energy to catch up. Every prayer session starts with washing, and bin Ashara "cleanses" himself with sand rather than water to preserve our rations. He rubs sand over his feet, then scrubs his hands. He symbolically washes his face, head and neck. It is all a gesture of respect before meeting with Allah. There is no official priesthood in Islam, and the direct relationship between the Bedu and God suits them well. Communication between the faithful and their God is personal and it occurs at regular intervals throughout every day.

Bin Ashara faces Mecca, an act which not only connects him with Allah, but symbolizes the unity of Muslims throughout the world. There is no wind. The only noise interrupting the prayers is the crackle of our fire. Each of the five daily *Salat* contains a prescribed number of *rakaa*. A *rakaa* constitutes one entire prostration cycle before Allah. Still standing, bin Ashara takes a deep breath and begins by raising his hands to his ears and says, "*Allahu akbar. Allahu akbar.*" *God is great.* His voice is raspy after shouting at Bin Saybeen all day, and softer than usual. His feet sink bare into the sand. Next to them is his head wrap. "*Allahu akbar,*" he says again. The tired Bedu places his right hand upon his left forearm over his navel and recites a prayer. "Glory to thee O God, Thy majesty. There is none to be served beside thee. Amen." Then, lowering his head, he places his palms on his knees and says again that God is great, adding, "Glory to my Lord the Great." Standing, he continues: "God accepts him who gives praise to Him. Oh, our Lord, Thine is the praise." Stiffly, bin Ashara drops to the ground to prostrate himself before Allah. Kneeling, he reaches forward and plants both of his palms in the sand, then leans forward to touch his forehead to the earth three times. In a whisper he says, "Glory to my Lord the most High." When he returns to his reverential position on his haunches, sand clings to his forehead, and one *rakaa* is now complete.

Bin Ashara stands to start the second *rakaa*, one of the total required for the day. It is finished in the same manner as the first. To complete this session, six more *rakaa* are executed, and he ends on his knees. "Peace be upon you, O Prophet, and the mercy of God and his blessings," he says. "Peace be upon us and the righteous servants of God. I bear witness that none is to be worshipped save God, and I bear witness that Muhammad is His servant and His Apostle."

Dark has descended. I can barely see bin Ashara as he turns his head first to the right then to the left, saying with each turn: "Peace be upon you and the mercy of God." The melodic prayers, the surrendering movements, the spectacular setting, are all quite beautiful. Bin Ashara rises and returns to the fire. No one pays him much attention but Bruce, who subtly offers him some painkillers, which he gladly takes.

Ali finds a yellow scorpion crawling among us at the fire. He smashes the little brute with a water bottle and throws it on the fire. Size does not matter when it comes to a scorpion, Ali tells me—every sting hurts. I examine the scorpion's tracks and they look quite familiar now. The prints in the sand match the mysterious tracks we see around our sleeping bags each morning.

The Bedu repeat bin Ashara's prayer from the night before. We pack up and walk a while to warm up the camels before we ride. The miles pass with few ways to measure them. Time bends in the shimmering heat and rolling sand. It fades in and then out and ultimately loses meaning. We simply ride. On and on.

The desert begins to reveal itself. What once seemed bleak and barren is no longer so. The sand passing beneath Taynoonah's feet relates a fascinating story of the wind in symbols more abstract than hieroglyphics, but no less telling. The prevailing winds explain their direction in the ground. Little arrows of fine sand gather on the leeward side of every object larger than the grains themselves. Pebbles, rocks, a twig, or an insect carcass—each leaves a trail of sand pointing along the wind's course. Even more fascinating is that the composition of the sand in the arrow depends directly on the size of the windbreaks, which sort the miniature geology of the various textures. The finer and lighter-coloured sand, with a texture similar to talcum powder, piles up behind the smallest. The grains sort themselves according to size behind increasingly larger barriers.

A gust of wind sweeps another layer along in the timeless eastward march of the peninsula's sands. The light grains of sand tumble faster and farther than the large grains, which roll reluctantly into the lee of dead saltbushes. The talcum-textured sand billows in the air and is lost in the azure sky. Another gust sweeps along the ground, and the scene is replaced once more while remaining the same.

Taynoonah's head floats above a flawless blanket of red and orange sand. It's astounding that only 11,000 years ago, lakes, visited by early humans, existed here and supported hippopotamus and water buffalo. The desert sands of the Middle East are a relatively recent fact of geological history. Arabia first entered a period of aridity some 23 million years ago when anti-cyclonic winds acted to bake and desiccate the land. Alternating wet and dry periods followed, further moulding and shaping the landscape. After the end of the last glacial epoch 10,000 years ago, a long dry period began. As the centuries of drought continued, plants died, leaving the ground to erode producing this sand, which by 5000 years ago covered the Empty Quarter. None of what can be seen now gives any indication of this diverse history.

My battles with Taynoonah yesterday have bruised my kidneys, and today they ache. In search of better support for my lower back, I follow the Bedu method and tuck my feet up under my seat. Our three Bedu friends use it often, but not constantly, as this position demands great flexibility and even greater balance, owing to its higher centre of gravity and decreased contact with the saddle. The position strains knees and pulls thigh muscles, but provides some relief to lower back all the way to the sacrum. The effort impresses the Bedu who shout their approval.

Having finally reached a truce with bin Saybeen, bin Ashara pulls up to demonstrate some other riding positions. Using his rifle, he shows the proper position to shoot while riding, with his feet tucked into the camel's hips for stability. By sliding back in the saddle to make room over the hump, he shows me how to ride with a passenger—healthy, sick, wounded. Or dead. Bin Ashara, in his role as our teacher of Bedu ways, makes special note of how to tie the passenger into the saddle's hump straps in case I need to speed away after a raid. Then he curls forward over the hump. This is the sleeping position. When bin Ashara starts to snore loudly, Ali, Musallim and I laugh. After a few seconds of "deep sleep" he awakens with a start and in one motion swings his rifle to his shoulder, scanning the horizon for raiders. Spotting me, he takes aim and fires a false round, mouthing a bang. I fall over Taynoonah's hump and bin Ashara shouts his victory. Everyone laughs together.

The animated demonstrations lift Musallim's sombre mood, but he quickly falls quiet again. He misses his family, he says. Musallim is a man of great contradictions. He is like the desert—one moment engaging and pleasant, the next aloof and sombre. Musallim will offer support and then chastise, help adjust a man's

256

dishdashah and then be indifferent to his thirst. Here is a man who shares poetry and criticism with equal ease. Musallim exemplifies what Thesiger discovered in the Bedu: "It is characteristic of the Bedu to do things by extremes, to be either wildly generous or unbelievably mean, very patient or almost hysterically excitable, to be incredibly brave or to panic for no apparent reason." We are all more judgmental than usual and vulnerable to mood swings in the 116-degree heat.

Leigh and Sawad suddenly jump from the line of our caravan and twirl about. The bull is not happy to be ridden today, and has been challenging Leigh throughout the morning. Sawad sits abruptly and attempts to roll over, an almost certain method of ridding himself of a rider, but this morning Leigh is unshakable.

When Leigh is back in the caravan line, Bin Ashara calls to him for directions based on his GPS. Here in the big dunes, the Bedu have less idea of where we are going. Unlike the terrain back in the Dhofar, these sands are less familiar to them. The Bedu have been embroiled in deep conversation all morning about the selling price for a camel Ali and his brother have been training. Enmeshed in the topic, they are now off track, and Leigh gladly re-orients them. Directional confusion should hardly be surprising here, with north and south being visually indistinguishable.

The rising dunes dictate our route. We have little choice but to wind our course between them, cutting past the rust-coloured fins of sand that grow from the gypsum floor into high ridges. The dune faces that fall from the crests are alluring, like mountain slopes of virgin snow. A lone tree grows well up on a leeward side—but where can it find the moisture and the nutrients to support life up there? Do its roots reach a hundred feet downward in the sand and then penetrate the ground for water? Or perhaps all we see of the tree is its top. Was it buried foot by foot till now, when only its very tip pokes out? There is struggle among the remaining limbs—like a child's arms flailing to keep above water.

Three feet of branches are still above the surface but for how long? This is one of the deaths that the desert issues—drawn out and agonizing. "Do you like that?" I ask, not needing any particular audience.

"Keif halak?" Ali asks. *How are you?*

"Ma aaref." I don't know.

"Eh el mushkilla." What's the problem?

"Mafi mushkilla, Ali. Ana asef." No problem, Ali. I'm sorry.

We ride on quietly, but I feel better only after a deep drink. The limited food and water in this heat is taking its toll. I've had nothing but five dates, two cups of *chi*, a cup of coffee, and one and a half pints of wretched water today. I am not thinking clearly. There is little physical effort to manage here, compared to climbing, since we ride all day. Physiologically, this crossing is more a challenge of adaptation than prowess. The psychology of this adventure, though, is more difficult than Everest.

For almost a mile we have been riding around the base of a particularly large dune, when suddenly the border patrol outpost of Butabol reveals itself. An Omani flag hangs limply from a pole in the calm. Not a breath of wind has blown since dawn. The temperature pushed 122 degrees today and is still above 115 even late in the afternoon.

We must present an odd sight to the pet dog now barking at our approach. A collection of green grass grows where wastewater runs out of a drain in the concrete wall surrounding the compound. A few trees host birds that watch our camels while we enter the courtyard. Barracks are built against two of the four walls inside, while the mess hall and wash hall complete the square. We will rest here tomorrow, then push on to Saudi Arabia's border patrol post at Ardah, 19 miles away. A dozen of the twenty men on duty welcome us with water, dates, and coffee. I drink three quarts of water and still feel thirsty. Remembering my outburst from earlier in the day, I add some re-hydration salts to two more quarts and drink them too.

We shower and settle into this island of comfort. Bin Ashara tells us he has received a message through the border police that Manaa is waiting for us in Ardah and that we should go there tomorrow, not the day after. Tired from the strain of these last days, no one wants to saddle up again tomorrow and leave this place, but bin Ashara insists that we follow Manaa's direction.

Unusual cloud cover this morning provides shade from the sun, casting lazy shadows on the sand. The uneven light gives more depth to the horizon as each chain of dunes basks in its differing degree of illumination. In the middle of the sky, beams of light cut through where the clouds allow, like a scene from a biblical movie, announcing an act of God. Quite out of place, a cool breeze tumbles across the plain as we embark at 7:30 in the morning.

There is no need for sunglasses or a head wrap, the sun softened as it is by the clouds. My washed hair floats in the breeze. With the right position in the saddle, the wind can be guided into the sleeves of my *dishdashah*, exposing my skin to welcome fresh air. The wind, entirely absent yesterday, is playful today. It races up a sandy slope, grabs swirls of light sand and dances with them up the face of a dune. Around and around they spin and twirl, like mobbing birds, while gravity looks on hopelessly. It is a subtle ballet, coloured in cinnamon and ginger. Staged timelessly. Choreographed with infinite skill.

We ride on and the wind has become more serious, blowing plumes of sand off the summits, darkening the sky. These are the largest dunes we have seen. Their ridges rise directly from the valley floor to some 400 feet above us. The ridge's knife-edges are sculpted by gusting wind, like the snow cornices on Everest. There is great pleasure in being able to look around so comfortably, as it seems Taynoonah and I have reached an understanding. She vomited on me again this morning, but we now ride along in harmony. I need very little effort to direct her. On the mountain, every step and every hand placement requires constant focus. For the moment, I am running on autopilot, free to look about.

A nondescript, man-sized concrete marker comes into view—the official boundary marker with Saudi Arabia, the very edge of Oman. The Bedu pay no attention to the survey post. For them it is quite meaningless in this orange sand. For the three of us, it means that riding camels into Saudi Arabia is not impossible after all. There is another post in the distance. We are in the neutral zone, a no-man's-land between two nations. I shout congratulations to Bruce and he waves back. We ride past the second marker and read the Arabic script on its brass plate. We are now in Saudi Arabia.

Today, Mr. T is roped to Crazy Dancer. Crazy and T have become friends and like being together. While the two camels enjoy their silent company, Bruce and I banter mindlessly about his university days. The subject turns to camels when I observe that Mr. T is by far the best looking camel of the entire herd. Bruce takes exception thinking Crazy deserves the honour but I press my argument comparing coat, colour and T's fabulous tail with its long knotless hair. Clearly, we will never agree about camels, and we continue joking with each other. Throughout the conversation, Bruce refers to Crazy Dancer as a female, when he clearly knows the camel is male. With this alarming gender-confusion, I suggest to Bruce he should drink up!

Suddenly our truck, with Tuarish and Salim Ali, races around the shoulder of another dune. The driver guns the vehicle toward us, then slides to a stop, unnerving the camels. Immediately, Musallim and Ali jump to the ground and trade places with the drivers. Ali complains of back pain. Musallim says he is fine, but tired. Salim Ali and Tuarish take to the camels with ease, and the truck drives off, taking the others the last few miles to Ardah.

We now turn on to a graded road and ride on among ever-grander dunes. A twisted and rusting oil drum sits half-swallowed in sand. The debris signals our approach to the settlement. Finally, from behind a dune, Ardah shimmers in the rising heat. While the settlement is only straight-line minutes away, a fenced military landing strip forces our route in a great circle and we arrive an hour later.

No one greets us. The place looks like a ghost town. A few trailers sit canted at odd angles—windows broken, open doors that bang in the gusting wind. The cab of an 18-wheeler squats down to its axles in the sand. The driver's side door is open and the interior coated with the talc-like dust. Its tires are flat, cracked from the sun. A few forlorn plastic bags flap in the wind, caught by a coil of barbed wire. Still no one appears.

The whole border post is contained in the space of a city block. Behind some newer trailers, a man-made pond excites the camels. The water smells foul and sulphurous, but looks inviting nonetheless. After a taste, bin Ashara declares it too saline, and we have to fight to keep the camels from drinking, for fear they'll take sick. A few men finally come to greet us and lead the way to better water in storage tanks. Like the surrounding equipment, the men are worn and tired-looking. Equipment, machinery, and people age here faster than elsewhere. This is a hard, corrosive place. Its dryness viciously desiccates, sucking the youth from everything. At the trailers, some young children appear. They, too, have faces that look beyond their years.

More men come to greet us. Among them are friends and extended family members of both bin Ashara and Musallim. We are taken to some mobile trailers where we are fed and will later sleep. Manaa rolls in with Chris Beal. They have spent the day driving north to scout our route. Chris is also here to ensure that the border crossing has gone properly. The wind has been building all day and now drives the sand across the ground. My kidney bruising is confirmed—there are traces of blood in my urine. We are thankful not to be sleeping out tonight. The trailer rocks slightly with every gust. Another long pull from my water bottle is in order, with worry for my kidneys. Bruce asks Manaa whether he had sent word for us to meet him here even though we'd planned a rest in Butabol. Interestingly, Manaa answers no. "Why would I?" he says. "Butabol is better for rest."

As we continue to talk, I can see, written in the furrows of their brows, the concern Manaa and Chris have for us. We decide to talk more in the morning, but agree we'll rest tomorrow in preparation for the hardest section of the journey, now just ahead. The dunes get bigger from here and the desert even less forgiving. We must gather all the strength we can in preparation for the massive dunes of the Uruq al Shaybah.

Chapter Seventeen

Day 28 — 21 13′ N 55 15′ E

A wind emboldened during the night now picks up billows of sand, limiting visibility to under a mile. We, the Bedu team, Manaa, Chris and a few local men gather around a fire in the shelter of a canvas tent to discuss the route north. Chris urges that we change our route and no longer go to Abu Dhabi via Liwa. Manaa concurs and suggests a new route to Abu Dhabi. Musallim, Ali, and bin Ashara sit, say nothing, and nod their assent between sips of coffee.

Bruce, Leigh, and I listen, eat some dates, drink our coffee, and ask about the proposed route change. "The dunes are very big to Liwa," Manaa says. "And the sand is soft." He explains this will slow our pace by half. When we first discussed it with him last month, Chris, who had driven part of the original route some time ago, had said it was tough but straightforward. Now he agrees with Manaa and adds that it may be impossible to navigate the Uruq al Shaybah. He tells us the only well in this 250-mile stretch might be too brackish for the camels. We're also told that, even if we do make it to Liwa and then the coast, it would take us more than thirty days. Not a problem—this is only a few more days than we'd planned. Manaa then adds that, due to the drought, worsening as we travel north and east, there is no grazing.

Worried we might miss the heart of the big dunes, we ask what they propose instead. Manaa suggests a more direct route through Umm a Zumul. "There is more hard sand this way, like in the Dhofar, and ten days to the UAE."

The conversation proceeds. The wind beyond the tent wall builds. The sand driving against the canvas makes it hard to hear. We ask questions about the two routes. Manaa and Chris answer. Pros and cons flow across the annex. We've heard all this before. In Mughshin we were told the soft sands ahead would slow us to 12 miles per day, down from the 25 we had been averaging from Shisur. The estimate was incorrect. Since Mughshin, we have been maintaining our 25-mile average. But do these explanations ever address the real issue? Regardless, it's clear which way Manaa and Chris want the team to go. But where do bin Ashara, Musallim, Ali, Bruce and Leigh want to go? Where do I want to go? Where *should* we go?

I sit back with a new cup of tea and watch the delicate film of blown sand floating on its surface. Though I have tried to resist, my prior expectations have clouded the reality of this adventure. Arrogantly, romantically perhaps, certainly naively, I came here in search of adventure too much on my terms. I should have come here searching for adventure more in terms of current Bedu reality. This is, after all, a place much farther removed from the mores of western culture than is the Khumbu, which has hosted climbers since the early years of the twentieth century. The three of us have been chasing our notion of adventure at the expense of reality. It seems now the only answer is to take the direct route proposed and reach the coast quickly. And safely.

Our Bedu team is uncharacteristically quiet as they listen to the discussion. Is there any interest in their hearts to see what's out there in the big dunes? They have taught us about camels and the desert. They have welcomed us into their culture, their homes, even, in part, into their families. They have given us the gift of an experience few outsiders could hope to share. Is asking our Bedu companions to go now into the big dunes too much? If we did ask, would they go willingly? Reluctantly? Or would they refuse entirely?

Manaa wraps up the conversation, telling us an 18-wheel tanker truck might be needed to carry enough water for the camels if we stick to the original route via Liwa. He adds that the decision is ours, that he'll back whatever decision we make. This gesture of support is surprising, as Manaa's tribe might want something else for us, and that would put irresistible pressure on him. As Thesiger says, "If a [Bedu] man distinguishes himself, he knows that his fame will be widespread; if he disgraces himself he knows that the story of his shame will inevitably be heard in every encampment." This stark alternative in mind, Leigh, Bruce, and I retreat to the trailer to talk.

Leigh feels certain that we should proceed straight to the coast although this is a substantial departure from our original plan that he was so adamant about adhering to in Mughshin. His concern for the Bedu and the camels and the team's success is well founded. I question his thoughts, as much as anything because I'm unsure of my own. But in the midst of the tension, this only offends him and the discussion becomes an argument. He shouts at me, thinking I'm accusing him of hiding behind excuses.

"Now you're making it like I'm using some kind of bleeding-heart camel concern as the reason I don't want to go into that desert!" Instead of backing off, I push Leigh for clarification. "Okay. Point A is—the camels are a concern. Point B is what?" I ask Leigh while Bruce sits silently.

"Point B is that the Bedu are a concern," Leigh returns.

"That they can't do it?"

"That they don't *want* to do it. That it's too dangerous."

Sadly, with the venom only brothers can spit, we continue to argue. We are getting nowhere. The arguments are meaningless anyway. Who knows what risk really awaits us en route to Liwa? Who knows whether we will travel twelve or twenty-five miles a day, whether the well water is too brackish, whether a tanker really is needed to supply water? Who knows whether the sands are really as soft as Manaa and Chris fear? We've placed our trust in Manaa so far, so why stop now? Regardless, the only fact remaining is that we indeed do know little of what really is out there. For this reason, if no other, I feel we should go on our camels and find out. Sir Edmund Hillary wrote: "What's the point of starting if you always know you're going to succeed?"

Wishing the Bedu were here to answer as well, I ask what is more important to the team as a whole— reaching the coast or the means by which we get there? The question evokes no answers. Getting a consensus from the team seems impossible without taking more time. I suggest we take a vote. Leigh is still firm on his stance for the direct route. "I vote we try and go to Liwa." I say, and add, remembering Manaa's precarious position, "We can always turn back and take the direct route if the risk is too great."

Leigh shakes his head. He can't empathize. Bruce runs his fingers through his hair, clasping them behind his head, feeling the stress of having to break the loggerhead. He pauses for a moment, then speaks. "My vote is to go north through the Rub al Khali, but miss the Uruq al Shaybah and complete the journey."

I bow to the decision. It is my task now to accept this outcome and rally behind the new plan. My tendency will be to retreat inward and let the divisiveness of the vote linger polluting the balance of our time together. This won't be easy.

The wind has not let up and makes opening the trailer door an effort. As we leave, a cloud of sand rushes in and settles on the cushions. We return to our Bedu team, announce our decision. They all nod, relieved. Manaa and Chris smile and start making plans for tomorrow's departure.

The die has been cast. Our new route will push through the balance of the Empty Quarter and cross the western edge of the quick sands, bending our path toward the coast to better our chances of reaching it. The sky is now dirty with sand. The sun is a muddy-red disk floating in the thickening air of a dead-dry earth. I take time to sit alone. I thought we could cast our votes and move on, but no one seems entirely content with the outcome.

Nothing is what it appears in the desert. Everything is in a state of constant change—exactly the opposite of what I had originally thought when we set out upon this journey.

The wind continues to blow. I visit the camel herd, giving some dates to Mr. T and the other camels. They seem at peace in the building storm. Camels are no strangers to the desert's changing moods, as we see in their evolutionary adaptations. In the driving sand, T keeps his nostrils closed, under the control of acutely toned muscles. Dense, fine hairs on the inside of his nostrils filter what sand penetrates, allowing him to breathe in the choking dust. Active tear ducts regularly rinse a camel's eyes. Remarkably, camels have two sets of eyelids. During a sandstorm an inner translucent eyelid closes to protect the camel's cornea while allowing reasonable vision. If this wind keeps up, T and the others will be making full use of their sophisticated adaptations.

١٣ ذو القعدة ١٤١٩
March 2, 1999
Day 29 — 21 30′ N 55 23′ E

The wind has let up a little this morning. When I mention this to Musallim, he laughs. This is only a lull, he explains. This particular wind is called the *eitnashar*, after the number twelve. It will blow a dozen days. Musallim grabs my arm and warns this is only day two. Leigh walks by. Sensing what we are talking about, he quips, "At least it's a tail wind!"

By noon, hours of riding later, the wind is blowing stronger than it did yesterday. The gusts are hitting us at 45 miles an hour—enough to make even walking a challenge. The sky is again dark. The sun is nearly gone, leaving just enough light to give the appearance of approaching dusk. Following the Bedu example, each of us has wrapped our *masar* about our face, covering our mouth, nose, and ears. Still, they fill with sand. My *dishdashah* flaps as the wind pushes at my back. The fine sand cuts through the fabric and clings to sweaty skin. We have experienced high winds before, but the raw power of this storm is an expression of the desert we have not yet seen. Our spirits lift with the enthralling novelty of it all. This is, after all, only the second day of the storm.

Three in the afternoon, the Bedu are riding about a hundred yards ahead, barely visible through blowing sand. The wind has only increased throughout the day. Leigh, trailing behind, has now disappeared. I shout to Bruce to see whether he has seen Leigh lately, but he is unable to hear over the wind. Up ahead, the Bedu stop in a sandy pass between two mountainous dunes. The risk of getting separated is too great to go on, if it's not already too late. In a storm like this, bin Ashara tells us to stay mounted and the camel, left to wander, will find its way back to the herd, guided by its acute sense of smell. Leigh catches up and we pile the gear in one spot under a blanket. Like drifting snow, sand covers anything unattended in minutes. I set my water bottle in the sand while I pack my saddle. When I return to it, I can find it only by the bump in the sand. My teeth are gritty but it is too windy to open a bottle. The thought of having to endure this storm for ten days looms like an impossible absurdity. But for now, the power of nature is thrilling. The demonstration somehow puts the trials of the last few days in a new perspective, and my spirits lighten.

I decide to hike up one of the dune ridges and ask Bruce if he wants to come. Together we trudge almost a mile to the summit. Our legs have atrophied during these weeks in the saddle. The deep sand reminds me of breaking trail through virgin snow. A blast of wind stings our ankles with driven sand. Dark plumes curl off the ridges and swirl into eddies. Wind and soft sand slow us, and it takes almost an hour to reach the top. On the summit we are actually above the blowing sand, and we sit to watch it ravage the valley floor. Like the storms that form in the valleys below Everest, clouds of sand rise, engulf us, then sink back below. Thin rays of sun penetrate the darkening sky, adding depth to the view. In every direction, dunes stretch out and vanish into the grey sky. A sudden blast hits our backs and dissolves the sand on which we sit, as if it were in an hourglass. We slide involuntarily off the eroding crest and get nature's message: It is time to go. Keeping an eye on the others so as not to get lost we pick the steepest face and race down.

Near the bottom, we think we hear a shot, a signal from the others. We hear another crack. But to our astonishment, it sounds like thunder. A few more sharp reports with the hint of lightning, and we're convinced. The wind, already howling, rises. The flying sand rises to vicious velocity, raking our exposed legs and arms. A drop of water hits my face, then more hit my feet. Little craters appear in the sand and disappear under the onslaught of the wind. A few drops are followed by a hundred, then thousands darken the thirsty sand to a deep rust. We are in the middle of southern Arabia in one of the longest dry periods on record, at the very moment the ten-year drought is broken. As the squall blows through, the huge raindrops are launched at us horizontally, scouring the air of dust and reaching us as a fine slurry of mud. I film Bruce as he walks past me, bent forward, trying to keep from being blown over. His front is soaked, his back still dry.

The Bedu and Leigh are huddled together and wrapped in blankets. The camels are sitting in the sand with their backs to the wind. I grab a blanket and sit by Leigh to bolster the sheltering circle. The squall line hits our little encampment with the wind gusting over sixty miles an hour, roaring past us with a familiar sound. Each of my attempts on Everest was affected at some point by howling jet stream winds raking the summit. This wind is familiar and oddly comforting.

Around us the sky is violent and angry. Through the mud on my goggles I can just see the dunes around us being ripped apart. If I could drink I would. But the biting wind has denied us water and food since morning. The rain pounds our backs. I am soaked, chilled, shivering. I put my head on my knees to hide from the tempest. When I close my eyes the sound of the wind and the chill at my back makes this place indistinguishable from a night spent on Everest's South Col, waiting for a chance at the summit.

Beyond the other physical challenges faced on Everest in 1997, I was tired of waiting out storm after storm. When the jet stream scoured the summit, we sat and waited. So shall we here. The wind's drone took away our psychological edge, just as weeks of inactivity took away our hard-won acclimatization to the altitude—and altitude is what it's all about on Everest. Any time spent above the 26,000-foot mark is unhealthy. At that altitude, the body does not simply atrophy but indeed begins to die. Even at Base Camp's 17,000 feet, climbers struggle constantly to keep up with attrition. We knew then that the longer we sat waiting out the wind, the less capable we would become of reaching the summit. At Base Camp, the energy and physical precision of well trained bodies faded, replaced by the last reserves, where we functioned not so much on physical strength as on what remained of our mental and emotional energy. The desert does the same. Its wind sucks our energy. No one moves. Life is reduced to naked simplicity. We sit in the sand. We survive.

If nothing else, climbing made us astute weather-watchers. We studied each nuance of sky, clouds, and wind. We began to sense, without being able to explain why, when a high wind was about to break, or cloud to yield clear sky. As our third week of waiting approached, there was something tangible in the flavour of the air, the whine of the wind, the appearance of the clouds that told us a change was coming. We immediately made ready to launch the summit teams against the Lhotse Face and Everest's South Ridge. Sure enough, the wind hesitated and started to sputter.

In the early afternoon of May 22nd, we were up on the South Col at Camp IV. There, to our chagrin, the winds were still blowing hard across that rocky saddle between Everest and Lhotse. Feeling uncertain of our forecasting intuitions, we were not optimistic about a safe summit attempt. We established our camp and crawled in our tents, brought in some snow and ice to melt on our stoves, had tea, filled our water bottles, and ate some boil-in-a-bag spaghetti. By six o'clock in the evening we were trying to rest in the howl of the wind and the rhythmic hammering of our tent fabric. Then, sharply at nine o'clock, the sound of the wind changed. As suddenly as it had hit the mountain, the wind's speed dropped by half. We unzipped the door of the tent, and looked out at the moon glowing softly through wisps of cloud and spindrift. The wind calmed to a light breeze on the Col, blowing at 40 or 45 miles an hour on the summit 3300 feet above.

We broke out of camp silently, almost reverently, so as not to disturb the wind. My body core was chilled a little, as now, and I shivered then as I do now in this rain. I had been dreaming of that moment for years. It was time to rise to the challenge. "Focus on the task. Let go!" I slipped into the rhythm of the climb. After two hours of ascending I was nicely warmed up, and my legs no longer burned as they had through most of the expedition. My lungs functioned with greater ease and no longer heaved heavily on my torn chest muscles. At our first rest break I turned my oxygen flow down to a litre per minute, a quarter of the normal rate, to conserve it for a possible emergency.

With Sherpas Gyalbu and Lhakpa, who had become my friends over the years, I moved upward, our headlamps carving illuminated arcs of ice and rock from the darkness. There, in a place as large as this desert, my world became the three-foot circle illuminated by my headlamp. But it held no terror. The surrounding cocoon of night gave comfort. The three of us were aware of the steep drop around us, but not distracted by it. We began to move well together, breaking trail out in front, ahead of the second part of our summit team. It was another indication of the kind of day I was having. Usually the Sherpas are well ahead. In pure strength and endurance, they put foreign climbers to shame. But on this day I was constantly bumping my head into Gyalbu's backpack when he took the lead. The rest breaks we took seemed unnecessary. Normally I couldn't wait for them to begin, and secretly hoped they wouldn't end. But on my summit day, I felt no interest in taking breaks and so we moved further and further ahead of our teammates.

Jason Edwards, our climbing leader, and his Sherpa partner were forced back below us. Jason was experiencing retinal hemorrhaging; patches of his sight were disappearing, and he could no longer climb safely. He made the smart but heartbreaking decision to descend and return to our top camp. Six of us remained—Alan Hobson, my business and long-time climbing partner, with Sherpas Kami and Tashi—and the three of us up front with ropes and other gear to fix the route.

The blowing snow swirled around us, forcing its way down the necks of our climbing suits, just as the sand does now in my *dishdashah*. In some places hard snow and ice made for fast progress. In others the snow gave way and we worked hard, up to our knees. We stepped up onto the Balcony—a bench-like feature often used by climbers to gauge their progress. We were ahead of schedule by an hour. Noon or 1:00 p.m. is often thought of as the "turnaround time" if the top has not already been reached. Late arrivals on the summit play a huge role in deaths on Everest, because late climbers are forced to descend in the dark. We were well within our time margins, but the weather was more important. Things are so unpredictable up there that turnaround could always happen much sooner.

On the Balcony we stopped to have a drink, a little to eat, and to wait for signs of the others. After twenty minutes' rest, our enthusiasm for the climb overtook us again. We were moving well and feeling strong. Waiting was only making our feet cold. Lhakpa guessed that the rest of the team would catch up with us while we were securing the route with rope higher on the mountain. I knew that Alan would be climbing safely with our two other Sherpas, so we continued, and soon the night's darkness began to give way to early morning twilight. With the first rays of sun, the Himalayas exploded in light. Clouds snaked along the valley floors. I could see the sun rising on my right, and to my left the moon was setting. In front of the sun, Everest's summit pyramid cast its shadow on monsoon clouds a hundred miles away. I imagined our party of three as minuscule dots on the trailing edge of the mountain silhouette.

Waiting to hit a wall of fatigue somewhere in this climb, I was constantly surprised by our strength and the speed of our progress. I was floating up through the heavy snow below the south summit, as if separate from myself, watching the day unfold. I had experienced transcendental moments like this while training in the Canadian Rockies, but it had never happened to me on Everest. We stopped below the south summit to wait again for our companions. I took the opportunity to film some of the astonishing grandeur unfolding as Everest's sister peak Makalu warmed in the sun. The cold began to penetrate our bodies in the rarefied air, so we cut short our stop.

We found ourselves atop Everest's South Summit hours ahead of schedule. For the first time, we could see the actual summit and the knife-edge ridge leading to the Hillary Step, a short but challenging bit of climbing. To the right, the ridge dropped 10,000 feet into Tibet, down the Kangshung face. To the left, it was a

7000-foot drop into Nepal. Sitting on the South Summit, we enjoyed a drink of water, and a lemon Pez candy. I took photos and scanned the ridge, following the route up to the summit.

From above, we saw flashes of lightning in the thunderheads soaring out of the dark valley to the right. Though the clouds were captivating, they signalled poor weather, so I noted their position below. Just yards away and almost entirely covered in snow lay the frozen body of the New Zealand guide, Rob Hall. He had died the year before, unable to retrace his way down in a storm. The three of us said a prayer for Rob and pushed a Tibetan prayer flag into the snow in his memory. The south summit of Everest makes a strange cemetery. Too dangerous to evacuate, the bodies of climbers who die at altitude are left where they lie. Finding Hall served as a sober reminder of the surrounding danger. We stepped off the South Summit with tremendous focus, fixed on our feet, bracing ourselves against the wind, and jamming our ice axes into the cornice. At one point, I punched the shaft of my axe clear through the crusty snow, leaving a hole that let me peer down to the Kangshung Glacier miles below.

We moved cautiously to the last real challenge between us and the summit—the forty-foot vertical cliff of rock and snow that is the Hillary Step. In early years, this short bit of technical climbing had frustrated expeditions. Above us we saw the evidence that the Hillary Step had not finished claiming climbers. The latest person to die hung there, entangled in the ropes left behind by the teams who had climbed here over the previous few years. This was the scene I had been reminded of by the dead limbs of the withered acacia near Thamarit.

Nearby, the American climber Pete Athans had stopped in his own summit journey long enough to free Bruce Harrod's body and commit it to the mountain. He searched the man, collecting his camera and ice axe to return to his family. The rope was cut. The fallen climber gone. It was impossible to process the moment, even less to comprehend these rough efforts to deal with the body in some dignity. The event would haunt me in the months to come, but the summit still beckoned. I shut out all the questions. Swung up and onto the summit pyramid, feeling disconnected from all that lay below.

Climbing along the last ridge on earth, Lhakpa, Gyalbu, and I pushed on toward the top. Having studied this place through photographs in any number of books written on the Everest quest, I was suddenly overtaken by a stunning sense of familiarity. Seven and a half hours from Camp IV, we could go up no further, and the distant Tibetan plateau stretched out before us. I stopped with the actual summit just beyond me and waved Lhakpa and Gyalbu through. A small gesture of thanks—I wanted them to be the first on top from our team, acknowledging that without them we would never have been there at all.

At 6:50 in the morning, Lhakpa and Gyalbu stood on the Summit, and I pulled out my cameras to photograph them. Lhakpa reached into his backpack and retrieved a Nepali flag to flap in the wind. With bare hands, Gyalbu scattered the rice that had been given him, blessed by the Dalai Lama. It was a special time for me to watch these two wonderful men have their moment on the summit together. Then at 7:10 on May 23, I took the final steps, as I'd visualized so many times since my boyhood traipsing around the Canadian Rockies. The dream that had been given shape when I was twelve years old came true for me at that moment, and I stood on the summit of the world.

It was minus 36 degrees Fahrenheit with a light wind. I pulled off my gloves, my face was warm, my hands were warm, and my feet were warm. I was breathing freely, feeling calm. We savoured the view and settled in to wait for Alan and our other Sherpa friends to join us. I walked off the top and down the northeast ridge to see if I could see the body of my friend Peter Kowalski, who had died near the summit only a few days before. I thought perhaps I could retrieve his camera for his family, but saw no trace of him.

After forty-five minutes on top, with still no sign of the others, Lhapka's oxygen mask began to sputter as it iced up. We had no desire to add more risk to the day and decided we could wait no longer. Lhakpa and Gyalbu drifted off the top while I lingered there alone. I stayed only five minutes but it was precious time. I wanted to stand on the summit in a moment where I could conjure up my teammates and all the friends and family who had made the climb possible. I believe in my heart that it was on their energy I floated up to the summit that wonderful morning.

I stood, transfixed by the view of the earth, and rocked up on my toes to be as high as I could possibly be, one foot in Nepal, one in Tibet. I could feel the mountain's mass beneath, and felt anchored to a place I had been a hundred times before in my imagination. I *knew* this place. I looked out and felt, as much as saw, the earth bending away from me in all directions. In my peripheral vision I could see the wonder of the earth's curvature. A wave of euphoria rolled through me as I realized that in this singular moment there was no more up, no more struggle. In the place of struggle came peace. A peace unlike any other I have known or could fathom. Bliss swept through me. It was clear to me that this had been a day for which I had been born, the greatest moment of my life. There was no sense of conquest, just gratitude. I spread my arms out, dropped my head back, and surrendered.

In my mind I step off the summit of Everest and return into the desert, which has become calm again. The rain has stopped and when I lift my head I see bin Ashara looking up into the sky, dancing and twirling his camel stick about his head, yelling, "*Hamdulillah! Hamdulillah!*" Quicker than it came, the storm has moved north, where the sky is still dark. To the south are rain clouds, but overhead the sky is light. Washed of any dull colour, the sand around us is now a rich red ochre. The air is clear of dust and smells fresh with humidity. My ears ring in the sudden tranquility.

"Thank God for this rain," Musallim says with a great smile. "I hope it will spread across the sands." He walks off and perches on a dune crest, happy now that the desert has been blessed with rain. We pick through the pile of gear and take stock. Nothing is missing, but everything is caked in wet sand. Musallim now herds in the camels—they are fine as well.

We bed down for the night under damp blankets. The rain returns at midnight, mercifully without wind. The canvas over-bags and camel blankets do little to keep out the water. I lie on my side, and little pools form under my shoulder and hip. My eyes are gritty. My hands are gritty, too, and of no use to clear my eyes. I try not to move about in my sleeping bag as the wet sand all over my body itches when I do. The pool of water around my left shoulder overflows into my armpit, but I understand how meaningless my discomfort is. This water will give life to the long-dormant seeds blown here by the wind years ago, now sleeping under the sand. In days ahead, thanks to this rain, the seeds will grow and the stalled cycle of life in the desert will roll on.

Everything is as it should be. I lie still in the wet and the cold, listening to the rain.

Chapter Eighteen

١٤ ذو القعدة ١٤١٩
March 3, 1999

Day 30 — 21 48′ N 55 29′ E

Yesterday's storm and the night's rain leave us waiting for the morning sun to warm the air and dry our camels' backs before we saddle up and ride on. Though we have changed our route, we have not escaped challenge. Along with the monstrous dune chains, we face a new and frightening obstacle. Our new route will take us into the Umm as Samim— "Mother of Poison." This is land underlain with dangerous quicksand often hard to spot till it's too late. Thesiger took a path to the west through the Uruq al Shaybah, the region with the biggest dunes in all the Empty Quarter, just to avoid this very quicksand. His route ended at the Liwa Oasis, a traditional stop for Bedu looking to water their camels, and a site never visited by Europeans until Thesiger. Manaa has assured us there is a path through the quicksand and, with enough water, we should be able to make it.

An hour's ride later we leave behind the hard-baked mud and sand of the welcoming flats, and take to much harsher terrain. According to Bedu reports confirmed by our map, the great dunes we now cross will fade into the quicksands within a day's ride northeast, where they have formed into a drainage basin some 190 miles wide. Traversing the basin is perilous, as the unstable ground can swallow whole camels and more. Through thousands of years, the coastal mountains near Masqat have poured their moisture into this depression through several major *wadis*. Repeated cycles of flood and drought have built a caustic concoction of encrusted mud and sand. Camouflaged by a dusting of sand, the crust looks safe, but ten inches below the surface lurks the engulfing muck.

Musallim tells stories of marauders who escaped pursuit via secret routes through the quicksands. One luckless party became lost. The men and camels all disappeared in the Umm as Samim, never to be seen again. Ali warns that, if we break through the surface, struggling will only speed our sinking.

We will cut a route through the edges of the Uruq al Shaybah where it intertwines with the fringes of the Umm as Samim.

The western reaches of the Umm as Samim stretch finger-like into the valleys between the dunes ahead. We stand at the edge of one of these fingers. It is 26 miles wide, its crust uneven and sharp. When the mineral-rich soup dries, it cracks, lifting and curling like prairie mud, only this is much harder. If we walk on this hard crust or *sabkha*, it will carve away the calluses on the camels' feet in just miles, laming them cruelly. So, we ride from one dune edge to the next, searching for solid, but soft ground and any tracks left by survey or other vehicles that have flattened the edges of the crust.

Midday brings us to the middle of the crossing. The shimmering crust mirrors the heat. There is not a breath of wind. Mirages distort our view in every direction. Summits of surrounding dunes float above what appear to be rippling watery pools of rising heat. We are squarely in the midst of what Thesiger called "a bitter desiccated land, which knows nothing of gentleness or ease." Now that I'm off my camel, I need to shoot some film of the team. Away from the track, jagged edges cut at my shoes and make walking awkward. From my hands and knees, I record the group along the quivering horizon. Salt stings my skin. Crystals disturbed by my footsteps drop and tinkle faintly, like falling glass. Stopping is impossible. The camels could not couch to rest; there is no smooth ground on which to sleep; there is no wood to burn. The place conjures up the same sense of vulnerability a mountaineer feels in the middle of a crevasse-ridden glacier. We will be able to relax only once we reach more sand.

Five hours after starting across, we reach the other side, without incident. We climb a steep sandy face, and camp in the saddle between two gigantic dunes, the largest we have seen. The camels unloaded, our conflict in Ardah behind us, Leigh, Bruce, and I take a hike up the western dune and are treated to a glorious vision. The mountainous sands of the Uruq al Shaybah roll on to the west, further than our imaginations can embrace. *Sabkha* flats extend to the east and widen into the basin of the Umm as Samim. To the south, dark rolling clouds threaten more foul weather. To the north are the faint beginnings of our descent to the Arabian Gulf. This new route offers a view into both the Uruq al Shaybah and the Umm as Samim, something our original route would not have granted us.

At the fire we drink tea. We chat and pick through the last of the dried meat before more rain drives us into our bedrolls.

١٥ ذو القعدة ١٤١٩

March 4, 1999
Day 31 — 22 08′ N 55 29′ E

We wake, eat a little, ride all day, eat again, and sleep. The simple rhythm of this unadorned life is appealing. Leigh has remembered today is my birthday and hands me a pair of socks to help protect my feet from the sun, knowing I've lost mine. At dinner, Ali splurges with our water ration to make *khobz*. He adds a little water to a pile of flour, which he has poured out on a pot lid, and then works dough into a large flatbread. He stirs the coals of the fire to flatten them, lays dough right on the coals for a moment, then flips it to the other side. Having sealed the moisture in the dough, Ali pushes away the coals and works the bread into the hot sand, covering it again with the coals before returning to his tea. With a handful of cool sand, he scrubs the sticky dough off his hands, periodically checking the bread.

After five minutes under the sand, the bread is pulled from the fire, and Ali breaks it into six pieces. Surveying each one, he gives me the largest section and wishes me a happy birthday. "*Wahed wa thalatheen. Enta shaybah,*" he says with a smile.

Thirty-one! You are an old man. Bin Ashara adds that, at my age, I should have children. Barbara will meet us in Abu Dhabi after the trip and we will start practising then, I assure him. He is happy with this answer, blows on his bread to rid it of sand and eats. The small fire only highlights our shaggy faces as we huddle nearby. There is no dimension to the figures, just flat faces against the darkness. Musallim breaks into a patriotic poem:

> God gives me my strength.
> He is my power.
> Our homeland is the most important thing
> And God will help me protect it.

He pulls a stick from the sand, adding it to the fire. The new light plays gently on the features of the bearded faces watching the blaze, intent on the poet. I film the scene. What is recorded might easily have taken place a thousand years ago—Bedu encircling hypnotic flames of a fire eating unleavened bread, sipping coffee, sharing stories in poetic form.

١٦ ذو القعدة ١٤١٩

March 5, 1999

Day 32 — 22 21' N 55 25' E

A day passes. Nearing its end, we ride through dunes larger than those we've seen. We come upon a Saudi border post, signalling our approach to the United Arab Emirates. Obscured by the blowing sand, the place could serve as a set for a post-apocalyptic movie. There is no stopping. Our faces are wrapped in cloth and our eyes are shielded with goggles. Several wretched dogs with ratty coats and thin bodies run after us barking, completing this scene of desolation. Are they trying to keep us at bay or begging us to take them out of here?

A wall-like *zibar* dune blocks our way. It seems too large to climb, its summit extending a mile before us, rising up 1300 feet. At the dune's base, bin Ashara does not hesitate. He leads us onto the dune following one winding ridge to the next. For an hour we climb, coming at last to a gully. Its headwall looks far too steep to ascend even on foot. Sand looms around us. Again without pausing, bin Ashara assaults the 40-degree face head-on. His camel cuts left and right to avoid the climb, but finally relents and pushes upward. Sand swirls about his camel's feet, sliding away, pouring down the slope. We follow. These wonderfully durable camels climb, and climb, and climb. The slope is so steep we are forced to lean forward over the humps to stop from sliding off their backs.

At the dune's top, all we can see is more dunes. The summit plateau is a mile across. It is so massive that hundreds of smaller dunes cover it, forming and reforming in the wind. The Bedu continue without stopping, seemingly uninterested in the vista. Down the other side, the camels step off the dune without hesitation. From their backs, eight feet off the ground, now leaning well back, the slope below appears almost vertical. Ali grabs the tail of his camel to prevent himself from sliding over the hump, down the neck and off down the slope.

Another *sabkha* flat stretches out between this dune and the next. We descend, cross the flat, climb another dune, descend again. The hours pass unmarked. There is only the present, no thought of future or past. I sway with Taynoonah's gait and feel at ease.

At the base of another dune we camp. All the loads are dropped. The satellite phone is set up. Leigh types out a report to students:

> Since the desert gale that pounded our camp with rain and sand on the night of the 2nd, we've been on a weather roller coaster. From utterly still moments at midday when the heat seemed to be boring right through us, to night storms bringing rain, to beautiful mild breezes just strong enough to cool the camels and the riders, we seem to have run the entire gamut of desert weather over the last few days. Currently we are hunkered down beside three small, 200-foot orange dunes while a strong north wind fuels a moderate sandstorm. Everyone is wearing goggles and trying to stay out of the

wind. When this storm first began, it looked like rain on the horizon. When I asked Ali whether *mattar* (rain) were on its way, he just shook his head and muttered *Raml. Sand.*

Over these past days we traversed the most awe-inspiring terrain to date. We have been treated to scenery so spectacular and intimidating that the photos I am sending can barely begin to present the scale of the geography here. The giant red and orange dunes tower above the salt planes. Riding through the passes between these goliaths, through small sand canyons or over ranges of smaller dunes, feels quite surreal. The sand is too perfect; our slow little band is an intrusion.

Happily, I can report that the crossing through the Umm as Samim is going smoothly and all riders and camels are present and accounted for. Everyone seems to be getting pretty tired as we have been on the road from Salalah for some thirty-two days now. But the Arabian Gulf finally seems more than just a faint hope, and if all goes well we may be there within ten days...

١٧ ذو القعدة ١٤١٩
March 6, 1999
Day 33 — 22 37' N 55 18' E

The wind has blown all night. Tired and less diligent after yesterday's long 31-mile ride, we did not consolidate our gear. Everything is now buried under sand and requires excavation. Musallim retrieves the precious *gerbers*. Leigh brushes off the computer case. Bruce is digging out a camel blanket when he feels a viciously sharp pain between his toes. Looking down, he sees a yellow scorpion escaping in the sand. We know that none of the scorpions in Arabia are lethal to an adult, but Leigh is concerned for Bruce, advising him to stay seated a while. His pain is obvious. Bruce is uncomplaining, but his arrested breathing betrays his discomfort. Leigh gets him some Ibuprofen. Bruce courageously ignores the pain, mounts up, and we ride.

Some hours later, I check with Bruce to see how he's feeling.

"One minute it feels frozen and the next minute it is burning hot," he says. "But mostly it feels like someone is cutting between my toes with a serrated knife."

At the end of the day, we find a large wind-carved swale in the sand, where we settle in to make camp. Despite Bruce's mild limp, he joins Leigh and me to hike up the nearest dune. We photograph the expedition banner on the windy summit, then return to camp for tea and dried meat. Bin Ashara hunches over the bag of camel jerky and pokes at the remnants. He picks up a piece between thumb and forefinger and taps it with his middle finger as a smoker taps a cigarette. Two beetles are dislodged and fall back to the pile of jerky. A few more taps to clear some sand and bin Ashara starts eating the jerky. We join him at the bag. The hard meat takes much chewing. At this point I am uncertain whether the effort might use up more calories than the meat provides.

Everything is now dusted with sand—everything we eat, everything we drink, everything we wear, and all our technical equipment. Our eyes give us the greatest trouble—fine wind-blown sand gets under our eyelids and scratches when we move or close our eyes. Our eyes constantly water but the tears cannot lift the grains of sand. This eye trouble, unlike most of the discomforts of the desert, is impossible to ignore. We wash our eyes nightly—sweet relief indeed—with a special moisturizing solution provided by Bausch and Lomb. Bruce is having particular trouble with one eye, so I apply some of the eye gel. It seems quick to relieve him.

Today, we have ridden 25 miles in eleven hours, and are now 19 miles closer to the coast. We are at an elevation of 219 feet, dropping more than a hundred feet in the last days, a sign of our progress to the Gulf. Eight p.m. We bed down at last.

Though Bruce has recovered from his scorpion wound, we are all looking more intently around our feet these evenings, scorpions being nocturnal. Having watched Bruce suffer from the yellow scorpion's sting, we are not as casual as we had been about the chance of being stung.

March 7, 1999 Saudi/UAE Border at Umm as Zumul
Day 34 — 22 43′ N 55 08′ E

Only days away from the coast. This morning, after riding for a few hours, we approach a nine-foot wire fence, held in place by concrete pylons set deep into the sand. This elaborate fence was built at great cost by the UAE government, not only to delineate their boundary, but also to keep Saudi camels out. The Emirates do not want the free-roaming Saudi camel stock to mix bloodlines with their animals. Here also is a two-lane gravel road running east-west, parallel with the fence, well worn by the patrol trucks that ply it daily, keeping an eye out for smugglers and other illegal passages over the borders. We take the road and head east up a hill toward the border patrol station at Umm as Zumul. Dust ahead signals an oncoming vehicle. It is Manaa. He races over the crests and brakes hard to stop in front of us.

From the driver's side window, Manaa shouts, "*Mafi sura. Mafi sura.*" We are not to take any pictures ahead. We are at the top of a hill, the border post just ahead. Its buildings are permanent concrete structures, surrounded by a high wall, complete with coils of barbed wire. In some shade next to the main gate, seven men sit playing cards and smoking a water pipe. Some are dressed in grey uniforms and others in green. Though we must be a strange sight, they only reluctantly break from their game to raise the red-and-white striped bar.

We have entered the United Arab Emirates, though no one truly knows where the border lies out here. Regardless of the fence, each state claims more territory than others will concede. Although we were in Saudi for a very short stretch of our route, it was critical to our journey that we get this permission. If Bruce had not succeeded in procuring this difficult permission, we would have been forced to skirt the Umm as Samim to the east and to detour hundreds of miles through Oman, adding weeks to our journey. More importantly, having access to the sands in Saudi has given us the special privilege of travelling amid the great dunes of the Rub al Khali, geographically the most wondrous part of the journey.

We spend the rest of the day watering the camels and processing paperwork and passports. The local security staff invite us to dinner. We sit with our hosts in a small courtyard inside the walls. The grounds are pleasant, with grass, trees, and songs of birds. We learn that the large buildings around us are not actually part of the border post, but a high-security penitentiary. This explains the different uniforms, as some are guards. All keep their hair and beards trimmed short to military standards. Not unlike Alcatraz, the former penitentiary in San Francisco Bay, those who escape here would face an ocean of superheated sand beyond these walls.

What the inmates eat is unknown, but we are well fed on rice and goat, hommous and pita. The questions asked us are mostly social. "What is it like to ride a camel for such a great distance?" and "Why are you doing this crossing?" Our answers are basic. No one is certain if they are able to empathize with our desire to test our mettle against so formidable a place. Certainly, this must be something of a hardship post for them. We try to explain that we are also very interested in learning about Arab culture. "Why? Are you a spy?" There is no need to answer through the laughter. Near the end of the gathering Bruce and I both think we can hear the faint yells of men somewhere in the bowels of this austere compound.

١٩ ذو القعدة ١٤١٩
March 8, 1999 Ramlat ar Rabbad
Day 35 — 22 49' N 54 53' E

Using the satellite phone, Bruce contacts the Canadian Embassy in Abu Dhabi to advise them of our approach. Through Ambassador Stuart McDowall, Bruce learns that the President of the United Arab Emirates, Sheikh Zayed bin Sultan al Nahyan, has requested our presence at his palace to celebrate our journey. Sheikh Zayed has been the president of the UAE since the country was first formed in 1971, but was the leader of Abu Dhabi as early as 1966. Abu Dhabi is one of the seven sheikhdoms or emirates comprising the union. The British had governed here until the 1960s in what they called the Trucial States wanting to maintain their dominant presence in the Gulf. They left just before the full scope of the area's oil reserves became known, and Zayed rallied the other six emirates to form a stronger whole. He became President, and has remained so for five consecutive terms.

His Highness is expecting us on the 13th of March. We have no idea how this date was chosen, but we still face 190 miles to go in five days. Close to 40 miles per day could prove impossible. Once the Bedu hear of this request, they leap into action, convinced we can do it. Thrilled with the idea of meeting this famous leader and certain he will bestow magnificent gifts upon them, the Bedu are loath to keep him waiting.

The day's travel is taxing for everyone. Endless dunes and dead-end *sabkha* flats limit us to just 17 miles of northerly progress after a ride of 30. The day passes in concentration on navigation and attention to the camels.

٢٠ ذو القعدة ١٤١٩
March 9, 1999 Ramlet al Hamra
Day 36 — 23 19' N 54 52' E

Heavy clouds sit with us this morning—indication, perhaps, of our nearness to the coast. Clouds keep the temperature from rising above a hundred degrees. Bin Ashara says we should ride thirty-four miles today. We laugh at the thought. Thirty-two miles is our one-day record so far, and that almost disabled the camels and us. I doubt we could do that again without medication. Bruce felt comfortable in the saddle after he took painkillers for the scorpion sting. Any more saddle soreness and I'd seriously contemplate getting stung by a scorpion to justify taking a dose. Leigh and I discuss the "best" place for a sting.

The team stops for prayers at one o'clock, our first break since leaving camp six hours ago. We don't want to keep the President waiting—our break is only thirty minutes, just enough time for tea and some meat. There are only two edible pieces of jerky that I can find, but bin Ashara continues to uncover gems among the beetles and sand.

The last of the clouds that have kept the day mercifully cool burn off at sunset. This has been a long day and shows no sign of ending. Riding ahead, Ali is swallowed up in the dusk. I decide a scorpion bite is not a necessary condition for gaining access to the analgesics in the first aid kit.

By the light of the stars we eventually make camp, then bend our stiff limbs to sit around the fire. We'd thought it impossible, but we've ridden 40 miles today, and are now 34 miles closer to the coastline at Abu Dhabi.

٢١ ذو القعدة ١٤١٩

March 10, 1999

Day 37 — 23 45′ N 54 43′ E

Though yesterday felt achingly long, the camels are still strong, having eaten well at the border a few days ago. The bellies on Taynoonah and Mr. T remain at a healthy circumference. Their digestive tracts, like the rest of the herd, are extremely active and have covered the ground in droppings through the night. At each pile of manure, numerous black, thumb-sized beetles labour. Their presence out here is a testimony to the persistence of life. These beetles join their cousins the ticks, in astonishing fecundity. Brought on wing and guided by the promising smell, the beetles are tireless in their work. They use their legs, equipped with scoops and carving edges, to chop and cut at the piles. A few hang back from the work, scavenging at the edges waiting for an errant morsel to happen their way, but most dive headlong at the treasure, until eventually each piece is processed, and the desert is pristine once again.

Each dung beetle endeavours to collect its share of the manure and shape it into progressively larger balls. There is history in their work this morning. Leigh and I saw ancient Egyptian art in Cairo featuring these industrious creatures. Some of them are content with a grape-sized prize, while others work until a ball the size of a plum is fashioned. A few are greedy enough to amass a tennis ball-sized cache of nutrients. Paying little attention to its colleagues, a dung beetle will suddenly flip onto its front legs, and kick its spiked hind legs up against the sphere. A couple of heaves to overcome inertia, and the ball rolls a little and stops. Happy with the progress, the beetle takes a break, then climbs on top of its creation to survey the route ahead before returning to the ground to push again. Suddenly another ball rolls down a little slope with its owner attached and smashes into the hungry worker. After the collision, the beetles take a moment to gather themselves. Without apology, the reckless driver shakes its legs free of the errant ball, takes its position again, and starts pushing back up from where it came.

Uninjured, the beetle shakes loose of its trophy and starts digging. Sand flies furiously as it is removed from the slight embankment, thrown over a shoulder. An opening takes shape. Soon the beetle crawls in, kicking the excavated sand out with mighty thrusts of its hind legs.

Once satisfied with its new abode, the beetle pulls and pushes his dung cache into the hole and disappears after it, blocking the exit from within. Beneath the surface, away from the heat and other beetles that might steal its booty, the little creature is now secure and perhaps leaning back against a wall admiring its handiwork. We will ride under the sun on empty stomachs, while our industrious dung beetle dines on the spoils of its labour. In a matter of hours the presence of our camels will be detectible only by their footprints. Beneath the sand's surface the feast goes on.

I steer Taynoonah clear of the dung to avoid disturbing the beetles, and move on with the others. The miles pass. The dunes begin changing from the sharp peaked red and orange mammoth *barchan* dunes we have been traversing to rounded golden rollers. The dunes are becoming smaller as we continue north. There is no apparent pattern or rhythm to their shapes. Much of the sand we have travelled through rolls like ocean waves under the prevailing winds. But these lesser dunes are more susceptible to the wind's momentary contradictions, gusting this way and that, leaving dune sculptures that twist and curl. None is more than 30 feet high but each pitches us at a different angle as we ride up one side and down the other. The camels lurch and rock, lean and tilt as they negotiate the terrain.

The new dunes challenge both riding and navigation skills. There is no self-evident line to take. At the top of each rise we scout ahead, see nothing but more sand, then disappear below our line of sight again. Taynoonah labours up one dune, reaching its summit before T, and immediately starts down the other side. T cannot keep up and the rope joining them finally snaps. Again and again until it snaps. Suddenly free, T turns back on his own and disappears down the bowl. Worried he might bolt, I jump to the ground and sprint with Taynoonah to gather him. He has gone straight for the shrubs he has seen growing in the bottom of the swales, and I catch him tearing into a sedge bush. We reconnect and continue. A sign of a gentler coastal climate, the basins between the dunes shelter more and more vegetation, while a few *ghaf* trees add splashes of green to the washes of ochre and yellow. The riding is exhilarating.

With more miles, the smaller dunes begin to take on a more organized form. At the crest of one I am certain the smell of the ocean is carried on the breeze, but there are no glimmerings of water on the horizon. In the next valley, a fenced and graded road runs east to west across our path. Ahead of us, Ali is waiting at a gate in one of the two chain-link fences that parallel the road on either side. We take up the gravel route, heading west for a few miles before it bends north. Between the road and both fences grow two lines of tiny trees.

The crest of another rise reveals the fenced road stretching five miles ahead. These barriers of barbed wire were built to prevent roaming camels from eating the rows of stunted trees. Each tree is fed water through plastic tubing that stretches the length of the road, part of Sheikh Zayed's ambitious plan to "beautify" the desert with oil revenues.

Beauty is important to Zayed, whose ambition since taking power has been to render the desert easier to live in than when he was a boy. Zayed himself was born eighty years ago in the fishing village of mud huts that was Abu Dhabi at the time. The village remained largely unchanged, dependent on pearl exports, until that market collapsed in the 1930s. The British presence in the Middle East, bolstered by the Allied victory of 1918, brought with it some development as the region was carved into a series of protectorates. It was not until the fifties, when the world entered its current petroleum boom, that the Emirates began to flourish. Modern cities grew in Abu Dhabi and Dubai, and skyscrapers now rise from the desert at the ocean's edge. With his characteristic generosity, Zayed has always focused on sharing the nation's wealth with his people by improving their lives, through modern infrastructure, education, medical care, and rational leadership. He is well respected abroad and revered at home. And he definitely loves trees. But his efforts to grow them out here seem wasted. By the look of this road, little traffic passes by. Taynoonah keeps eyeing the green sprigs, and if left alone she'd eat a few miles' worth of them.

In a great cloud of dust, Manaa races over a crest toward us. He has spent the day scouting a route and has found a shortcut. He is excited about the time we will save. Ali, Musallim and bin Ashara talk endlessly about the meeting with Zayed—how honoured they are to meet this man. The talk focuses on the gifts the President will offer. I'm thinking an official letter of congratulations, complete with presidential seal, to match the one Canada's Prime Minister gave me after climbing Everest. The Bedu are thinking something else. They're sure gold will be involved, perhaps a new Land Rover for each of us, or a grant of farmland near Abu Dhabi.

At another gate, we leave the road and camp in the sand. With the shortcut, we face another sixty miles in two days to make the coast and our meeting with the President—now seemingly more important to Ali, Musallim and bin Ashara than reaching the coast. Bruce and I place a ration of ibuprofen in our saddlebags, just in case tomorrow's shortcut doesn't work out, knowing the

Bedu will want to ride on regardless. My wife Barbara is on a plane somewhere between England and Abu Dhabi when we fall asleep. She is coming to Arabia to visit the land and see us reach the coast.

٢٢ ذو القعدة ١٤١٩
March 11, 1999
Day 38 — 24 19' N 54 43' E

Even bin Ashara agrees there is no edible meat among the beetles, after a few minutes of examination. He shakes the sand and bugs from the bag and shrugs his shoulders. We each eat a handful of dates, the last of our food, pour the remaining quarts of turgid water from the *gerbers* into our bottles and mount up. Manaa races off in the Land Rover to make sure of our route into town.

Two hours into the day's ride, it's time for the analgesics. On our empty stomachs the drug digs in quickly. Though my saddle fails to become the leather sofa I had envisioned, the edge is taken off the pain. Bruce and Leigh partake as well. Six hours later we take a second dose; a few hours later Manaa returns with Salim Ali and Tuarish. The sun sets. Tired after a long day, Musallim, bin Ashara, and Ali jump from their camels and into the trucks. Salim Ali and Tuarish take their camels, tie them together and ask for ours as well. Manaa wants us to take a break and ride with him. We explain that we want to continue, though the offer is tempting. Salim Ali and Tuarish mount up and take off. Bruce, Leigh and I make chase. The camels are gaining energy in the cooling air, as are we. Pulling up in his truck beside us, Manaa tries again. "Please Salah, and Suhail rest!" We shake our heads. "Abdullah," he says as he drops back to Leigh. "Stop this camel and have rest."

"*Mafi mushkilla, Manaa,*" Leigh replies.

"No one will know," he pleads. But we will know, we tell them.

"You Canadians make me very angry."

"Angry or hungry?" Leigh asks, breaking us into laughter.

"I am not sure what word. *Hungry* or *angry*? I think you make angry with me!" Manaa shouts through his own laughter and drives off. Past the dust, I can see him waving his long finger in the back window.

The trucks gone, we are alone again. These are some of our last hours in the desert. A wind blows sand and paper wrappers among the camel's legs. A water jug is caught among a few rocks and a dead shrub. It has lain under the baking sun long enough to look as if it has been burned in a fire. Plastic bags, faded and translucent, rustle in the wind.

Tonight sometime we will camp at the edge of the city. I am suddenly unready for the journey to end. Not long ago, when hunger and thirst and saddle pain drove away any pleasure, I longed for today to come. Here it is, and now I wish it weren't.

Another gust moves the sand which collects in mounds around the rocks. With another breeze camel dung rolls along the sand, and a plastic bag darts like a rabbit. Fifty years ago there might have been local hares here trying to dodge our caravan's shots as we kept an eye for meat to supplement our otherwise tedious meals of dates and rice. Tonight, food will be brought to us from town.

Salt rides the air in every breath we take. Darkness envelops the group. Tuarish convinces his camel to run, challenging the rest of us to follow. With a tap Taynoonah is at a gallop, as are Sawad and Crazy Dancer. The riders sing. Though we cannot see it, we know, moment by moment, we are getting closer and closer to the coast.

Nearly sixteen hours after departing this morning, we connect to an asphalt road that crests the last dune of the desert. We have travelled fifty-two miles today. The lights of Abu Dhabi blot out the stars. The noise of this modern city is jarring, the reek of exhaust obnoxious. A caravan of vehicles arrives, members of the local Bedu community who have come to greet and feast us. Car radios blare through sunroofs with Egyptian hits. Cell phones ring. Horns honk. People yell. It's too much, too fast. A fire is lit in the sand beside the road and plates of food prepared in town are set out on carpets.

Musallim, Ali and bin Ashara are swallowed up in handshakes and nose kisses. Next to us, the local men and boys are extremely clean and extraordinarily well dressed in fine *dishdashahs*. "*Suhail*," Ali shouts. "*Wayn Barbara?*" *Where is Barbara?* Ali knows about Barbara's arrival and wants, along with the others to meet her. Ali has been asking about her daily for more than a week. Manaa puts his cell phone to my ear. As it rings, he explains that Barbara is at a hotel in Abu Dhabi waiting for me to call. The phone is answered. I ask for her room and am connected.

"Hello." Barbara's voice.

"*Hamdulillah, Barbarella, Salaam Alaykum,*" I say.

A local man offers to drive me to her and then bring us back to the celebration. In an instant, we are in the car, racing under streetlights and neon amid heavy traffic. Thirty minutes and I walk through the hotel lobby, unconcerned with the strange stares. My own odour fills the elevator.

Barbara and I have been united like this before. She was in Kathmandu the day I summited Everest in 1997. She had been leading trekking groups into Base Camp for the last month for our sponsors, Colliers and Lotus, and was planning her next trip to India. The day I reached the top I spoke with her by radio from Camp Four and asked her to marry me. I was unsure at the time whether the pause that followed was a delay in the signal or her indecision, so I jokingly threatened to jump if she said no. "Yes!" she screamed through tears and agreed to meet me in the Sherpa village of Kunde in a week for the wedding I'd already planned.

When I later left Base Camp, Barbara was somewhere in the valley below, a few days' hiking away. During the walk down I searched for her around every corner, across every field. I had given up looking when I dropped down on a steep trail into a gully where a rapid brook tumbled over worn rocks. The banks of the gully gave root to a forest of rhododendrons. The flowers high on the branches had dropped their petals. A carpet of fuchsia covered the path and the tree roots. Shafts of light cut through the branches leaving circles of bright colour on the carpeted floor. Up along the path a woman in a long red dress strode toward me, tanned, moving fast, fit from weeks of hiking in the Himalayas.

She floated into my arms. We were married 48 hours later, on the first of June in a day-long Tibetan ceremony, among the Sherpa people who had adopted us into their village.

Two and a half years later, an elevator door opens here in Abu Dhabi. I knock on her door and Barbara floats back into my arms. While she packs her gear, I eagerly eat the leftovers of her food from room service. After the drive we're back with the group. Barbara meets the team, who seem genuinely happy to see her. They shake her hand, welcome her to the fire and produce food that has been saved for us. Bin Ashara and Bruce show Barbara how to eat with her right hand and pull out chunks of tongue, heart and other bits for her.

Before bed, Barbara meets Taynoonah and Mr. T. We curl up together next to the camels under the filthy blankets. I smell dreadful, but Barbara lets me hold her tightly just the same. Most of the guests drive back to their homes in town. We are left in the silence to which we have become accustomed. I point out to Barbara the comforting noise of the camels chewing their cud, and we look to the southern sky to enjoy the remaining stars. My mind races with the end-of-journey paradoxes. I am thrilled to see my wife again, and glad, too, that the journey is almost complete. But I am saddened to be at the adventure's end. Despite the arguments, disappointments, hardships, and pain, I don't want it to be over. This is an awkward time, suspended somehow between two worlds. I feel as if I belong to neither.

I have cursed this journey at times, especially when we changed our route in Ardah, and then even wished briefly for it to end. Now my wish is granted, I want to be back among the remote dunes under the vast sky with the team and the camels, listening for more of the desert's secrets.

Barbara helps saddle up T and Taynoonah, then leaves with Manaa. A debate breaks out about what highway to take into Abu Dhabi. I get away to shoot some footage and be with my camels. Our route clearly decided or not, the Bedu mount up and head down the hill on the asphalt road toward downtown. I saw the busy-ness of this burgeoning city last night and am fearful of how the camels will react. *Inshallah*—everything will be fine. We ride out of camp. I look back to see the edge of the desert before it slips from view—but it is already gone.

Not expecting to see water for a while, we're surprised when we come upon a flooded *sabkha* flat that taunts us with its sparkling contents in the new light. It has been thirty-nine days since we left the ocean in Salalah. Several police cars come to escort us in. Members of the local media materialize, three or four cameras hanging awkwardly from their necks. Friends from the Canadian Embassy arrive as well, and Barbara is now driving with them. Teachers from local schools, who followed our journey on the internet, come with signs of congratulations. Locals drive by and honk their horns, some to cheer us on, others angered at being delayed.

Television, radio and newspaper reporters hang from car windows and ask endless questions. "How do you feel to be at the end?" and "What was the hardest part of the journey?" I pretend it's too noisy to answer. Throughout all of this unfamiliarity, the camels remain remarkably calm. Hours of riding in the chaotic traffic lead us over a bridge to the Island of Abu Dhabi. There, off to the left, is the water of the Arabian Gulf. We cannot reach it, blocked as we are by a concrete divider running the length of this treed boulevard. Grass grows thickly as do flowers that fill gardens. For what seems an hour we are tempted by the ocean, unable to reach it. The reporters are relentless, stopping to photograph us as we pass by, jumping back in their jeeps to race ahead and repeat the process.

A break comes in the wall, the traffic is stopped and we ride across to the beach, jumping from our camels for the last time. Holding hands, we stand in a line with our camels staring over our shoulders. At the water's edge we count to three.

"*Wahed, ethnayn, thalatta.*" And we all step in.

Hamdulillah—we've made it. Everyone claps and cheers around us. We all share hugs. Leigh grabs Ali and tosses him in deeper, only to grab him again, realizing he can't swim. Tears also come with the sense of triumph and relief. I dive in and pull myself downward into the cooler water. It is quiet and comforting, like the inner desert. I swim deeper until the sand is washed from my skin and clothes. Short of breath, I turn and swim toward the light. My tears mix with the warm water of the Gulf.

Chapter Nineteen

Our final days in Arabia pass in a blur of dinners with dignitaries, celebrations with the local Bedu community, media interviews, and our memorable meeting with the President of the United Arab Emirates, Sheikh Zayed bin Sultan al Nahyan. For all of us, this is a great honour. That His Highness has asked to meet us astonishes both our companions and our Embassy staff.

Murals on large buildings bear the President's likeness. Every office we enter displays his photograph, as do most houses. His smiling, grandfatherly face hangs from taxicab rear view mirrors and is stickered on every window and license plate. One of the President's protocol officers, Mohammed Al Hossani, personally drives us from one meeting to the next. On one trip, Mohammed's son sits in the back seat with me. Every time we pass a picture of the President the four year-old boy points it out and sings, "Papa Zayed, Papa Zayed." Invariably his father breaks from conversation with me and joins in.

Officials from our Embassy report the President has been following our journey and is excited to meet us. This is unprecedented, according to our Ambassador, who himself has been trying to get audience with the President and has not even had his calls returned of late. Now the President's office is calling him! Thesiger met with Zayed after his second crossing of the Empty Quarter. The two men became friends and remain so to this day. This was before Zayed's astonishing rise to power, and the

Bedu and Thesiger spoke highly of him then. "I had been looking forward to meeting him," Thesiger wrote, "for he had a great reputation among the Bedu. They liked him for his easy informal ways and his friendliness, and they respected his force of character, his shrewdness, and his physical strength. They said admiringly, 'Zayed is a Bedu. He knows about the camels, can ride like one of us, shoots, and knows how to fight'."

The day following our arrival, we meet the President. Smelling clean, soaked in *oad*, the Bedu are very excited. They have used trailers to transport the camels closer to the Palace. From our hotel we drive to our camels, mount up, and ride ceremonially with the Royal Camel Guard, who escort us to the grounds of the Al Wathba Palace, the President's official summer residence. Our camels look exhausted and weak compared with the great animals of the Guard. They stand a foot taller than our camels, uniform in appearance, with perfect tanned coats trimmed in all the right spots. They are disciplined, ridden with expertise by men who seem bewildered by but interested in our ragtag team. As motley as we might look, we feel desert-tested and desert-proven. Our Bedu companions ride with pride, as do we, amid this impressive group.

We enter the palace grounds and ride for several hundred yards on an interlocking brick road lined with tall palms and an endless bed of flowers. Below the palace we couch our camels on a sandy curb and wait. Word arrives that the President is coming and wants not only to speak with us, but to inspect our mounts. Frantically, the camels are lined up side-by-side and readied for review. We then stand on parade with them and wait. And wait. And wait.

For the Bedu, the anticipation is unbearable. Bruce and I joke with them that we'll tell the President they are wearing so much perfume because they've forgotten to wash. They panic, pleading with us not do this. I say I want to give the President a big hug when I meet him, and bin Ashara threatens me with a curse if I do. We are told emphatically that these kinds of jokes are wrong, and are then instructed to shake the president's hand gently due to his arthritis. I grab their hands to practice and squeeze. "*La, la, la, la!*" they shout. "*Suhail, mafi zein,*" they say—*No good*—and walk off to check their saddles again only to come back a moment later, begging us to be serious.

After another hour a few black Mercedes arrive. A dozen men in fatigues with sub-machine guns jump out, scan the crowd and secure the area. More cars arrive with another dozen guards and military personnel, who then take up watch at various points around us. They keep turning to their shoulders to speak into microphones and push earpieces in deeper to receive orders. Still more cars arrive and the crowd falls silent. Two of the President's sons step out. More men arrive in *dishdashahs* and sport jackets with compact machine guns. Then a car arrives which everyone swarms around. When the rear door opens, out step two well-polished black boots, not the sandals everyone else is wearing.

His Highness Sheikh Zayed emerges from the swarming group and stands before us. He is stocky and wears large dark sunglasses. His face is handsome, bearded. The rich fabric of his clothes hangs from rounded shoulders. He looks us over, then speaks.

"Where are the Canadians? I can only see Bedu!"

Everyone laughs and I feel a little more at ease. We line up to meet him and, through an interpreter, exchange pleasantries. Leigh announces that his name is Abdullah bin Kanada al Musahali el Kathiri and the President laughs again. I do as I've been told and shake the President's hand softly. He returns my weak grip as Thesiger did, with power and a long, hard squeeze. There is no arthritis in that handshake. The President's hands are heavy and strong, not what I'd expect from a head of state. But Zayed is no ordinary leader. He grew up in the desert and knows its hard ways. As a young man he was accomplished with a rifle on the back of a camel, and was involved in a number of battles.

Musallim is the last of our group to meet the President, and he reads one of his poems. The group applauds. Photos are taken. The President leaves and the meeting is over—or so we presume. Through the protocol officer, we are told the President has invited us to his Palace for coffee. Stunned by this rare invitation, we are driven to the palace entry and park in the shade of a marble roof. We walk through a hallway lined with guards to a large sitting room filled with a hundred people or more. The polished marble floor is layered in carpets. The walls are lined with ornately carved wood couches, deeply cushioned. One side of the room is open, with large windows between thick pillars offering a view of Abu Dhabi and the ocean beyond. A warm breeze blows through the hall. Seated, waiting for us, his back to the windows, is the President. To his left, a couch sits open for us. The people lining the room sit quietly. I later learn they are ministers, military leaders and other officials of state, waiting for our arrival and departure, stalled in their daily work with the leader.

Through an interpreter, the team, along with Manaa, describes our journey to the President. We talk about how hot it has been, and the quality of water at the wells. The President asks about the strength of our camels and about our riding ability. He wants to know what we think of the desert's beauty, and whether we've found the journey too hard. While we speak, we are offered coffee and bowls of *halwa*, a sweet treat made with pistachios. Unthinking, I dig my fingers into the food, still feeling some of my hunger from the long trip. Seeing this, our Ambassador shoots me an embarrassed scowl and signals to the spoons laid beside the bowl. He then proceeded to show me properly how to take a small portion of the jelly mixture and eat it politely with the utensil. Seeing this, Zayed laughs and says, "This man has not lived in the desert." The *sheikh* then digs his own fingers into the *halwa* and tells us to forget about the spoons and eat like the Bedu we have become.

Over more coffee His Highness becomes pensive and tells stories of the challenges he has faced leading his people. He mentions that a good friend many years ago said that camels would grow flat backs before Zayed could unite the Emirates into one country. "I have not seen that man in thirty years," he says loudly for all the room to hear. "But camels still have humps!" When vehicles were introduced into the region, he says, the Bedu complained that their camel herds were losing value. "'God will not desert you,' I told them," he said with a shake of his finger overhead. He tells us about his supporting the construction of camel racetracks and developing a racing circuit with prize money.

This has created a demand for well-bred camels and made the traditional skills of the Bedu valuable again.

His Highness goes on to share his concern that his people might forget their heritage and take for granted the luxuries they now have. People must suffer through hardship to fully develop character, he tells us. "I am proud of the comfort enjoyed here, but worry people might forget the struggle that preceded it, and thus not truly appreciate what they have."

Our Ambassador signals that it's time to go. When we stand to say goodbye, Sheikh Zayed thanks us for undertaking the journey, as it will serve as a reminder to people across Arabia of their desert roots. The honour is ours, we assure him, and depart. Though our meeting was originally scheduled at just twenty minutes, we have been with the President two and a half hours. We later learn he was annoyed by our early departure, wanting us to stay for dinner and meet more of his sons. Our protocol officer, Mohammed, later comments on the historic length of our visit, saying his staff has not for years seen the President so energetic and enthusiastic.

During the meeting, Manaa made a gift of our camels to Sheikh Zayed, and now it is time for us to bid them goodbye. Bruce and I, with Barbara, go to visit the animals one last time. The camels sit chewing their cuds. I click my tongue to make the sound I made everyday during the trip when I approached them in the morning. From different places in the herd, Taynoonah and T lift their heads and tune their ears to the sound. Bruce and I busy ourselves packing up the saddles to take home. I grab some dates from the truck and sit a moment with Taynoonah. I feed her and rub her head with a *thank you* for her carrying me across the desert. Then I sit with T a while and scratch his nose, recalling our first encounter, when I tossed dates at his feet, too leery to get any closer. I open my hand with the dates and his dexterous lips take them gently.

I am taken aback by my sadness, by the catch in my throat as I rub his face and say goodbye to my handsome friend. I have depended on these two to carry me and my gear. When the trip got tough, I took considerable comfort from our relationship. Our camel companions are the real heroes of our crossing. I very much wish I had the means to tell them.

We race back to the hotel for one last feast with our Bedu companions in their presidential suite, which occupies much of the hotel's top floor. Days ago when checking in, the Bedu refused to take individual rooms, preferring to be together. The furniture in their suite has been pushed aside, and we eat a marvelous room-service meal together on the floor, clustered around the food, much as we did in the desert. The beds in the rooms have also been pushed aside, sheets and pillows placed on the floor. While Leigh, Bruce and I take willingly to the soft mattresses in our private rooms, the Bedu sleep together around an imagined fire. All have been to the barber for haircuts and beard trims. They look younger to us, eyes brightened by the rest, food, and water. I am already beginning to miss the life we have led with them.

We ask the Bedu what they will do now. Musallim is going back to Salalah, bin Ashara to his camel camp in Wadi Qitbit, and Ali back to Thamarit where he has camels to train for an upcoming race. All are keen to return to their families and share the stories of adventure, but no one has any intention of going soon. They say they are guests of the President and until he asks them to leave they will stay. "Maybe we go in one month, maybe we go in one day. It is in the hands of God," they say.

We finish our meal and begin our goodbyes. I can find no words to describe what I am feeling. We have shared our fears and triumphs, our struggles and moments of joy. We have yelled at each other and laughed together. We have slept like brothers in the sand by a fire and huddled tightly against the wind and rain. We have ridden silently for hours only a yard apart and sung songs together to our camels. Fittingly, just as we so unceremoniously left the fires at night in the desert, we simply brush noses, shake hands and leave. Ali runs to me and gives me a hug. In my hand he places his freshly filled bottle of *oad* and wraps my fingers around it. *"Maa salama, Suhail,"* he says. *"Maa salama sadig,"* I answer. And so ends our time among the Bedu of the Bait Kathir.

At the plane's door I stop to breathe in the place once more, but don't look back. In the air I can detect the fragrance of the desert beyond the city. This smell will be my last memory. I know it will be months before I can process this time in Arabia, so I take another breath and step in.

We have organized a layover in London. Between flights, we race in a cab along the familiar route to Meadow Hill. The ride is a blur of spring colour, too much to absorb after the desert. We were here just three months ago, but it seems so much longer—I feel much older. Sir Wilfred stands in his wool suit awaiting our arrival, and when the cab stops he charges out to greet us with a hearty *"Salaam alaykum."* *"Alaykum as salaam,"* we respond after a hesitation, caught off guard by the old adventurer's Arabic.

"Kayf halak?" he demands.

"Hamdulillah!" we answer in unison.

Thesiger invites us to the garden to share the news. Crowding around him, we play sections of the footage we have shot and show him photos we have taken. He asks about the Bedu and the strength of our camels and the water's quality at the wells. He is fascinated with the images and studies them closely, recognizing the saddles we used as identical to his. The time passes easily and much too quickly.

We try to explain how we feel our trip pales in comparison to what he accomplished, but he will have nothing of it. "Indeed, to the contrary. Think of what you have achieved," he says. "I knew it would not be easy, and I suspected you would meet many difficulties." We sit listening to him, wanting to believe what we are being told. "It is probably the last time it will be done. Ten years from now, no Bedu will want to do it." His comments are generous and I feel honoured he would view our journey in such a fashion.

Sir Wilfred picks up a photo of Leigh and Labian on the beach in Salalah. With his fingers he gently strokes the picture of the camel's head. With sadness in his voice he says, "You're making me feel terribly homesick." I realize we are the first people in the years since he left Arabia with whom Sir Wilfred could truly share his desert experience. We are, in a small way, tangible links with his beloved desert, the men he so admires, and the camels he depended upon and even loved.

"May I see another bit with the camels?" he asks, pointing to the video camera Leigh holds. On a screen smaller than a man's wallet, Sir Wilfred watches more of our caravan of camels striding gracefully through the red sands. He leans forward to the camera's little screen so as to miss nothing, and watches us talking about a campfire. He nods in recognition when the group starts singing at the fire. When the tape is done he leans back and looks at us with tears pooling in his eyes. "For a moment, I was right there with you," he says, a lump gathering in his throat. "In fifty years I have never seen anything so fine." We have offered him a renewed connection to "the happiest five years" of his life, as he describes his time in Arabia.

It is time for Sir Wilfred's medicine, and for us to catch a plane home. We sit with him, back inside, and wait for our cab. He rests in a large leather chair, fiddling with his well worn Ethiopian walking stick, when he starts to speak in Arabic. *"Daem Allah di kollo, beniadem ya doom."* *God endures, mankind does not.* "I don't know why that popped into my head. It was a riding song that bin Kabina used to sing at night when we went to sleep. You have reminded me of it."

The cab arrives and we say goodbye. "Go in peace," he tells me, shaking my hand energetically. As we drive away, he stands waving. The last of the great adventurers.

Epilogue

On returning to Canada, our team folded. Bruce returned to river guiding and started planning his text trip. Leigh called on his newfound courage and quit his law firm to begin another adventure, deep in the corporate world of alternative energy sources. I returned to our sponsors, delivered new slide presentations, and started writing this book. We all began visiting some of the 45,000 schoolchildren who followed our journey.

Then I went back.

The Boeing's tires screeched as it touched down at Salalah International. The airport smells flooding in the opened door marked my last purely "western" moment on this spring 2000 return. Outside the aircraft, amid the clamor of tarmac and terminal, through the smells of aviation fuel and tire rubber, came the soft, earthen, unmistakable aromas of the two great boundaries of Bedu life—ocean and desert.

It's all gone now, Thesiger seemed to have been telling us. But when I returned to Arabia the year following our adventure, it was all still there.

"It," for Sir Wilfred Thesiger, was the Bedu way of life, the lifeways and wisdom of the desert, ways which had brought Sir Wilfred and his Bedu companions across the Empty Quarter and these strong, proud tribal people through more centuries of living than European civilization can count.

After a year's absence, I was drawn forward into some wonderful moments of friends re-met, hands shaken, noses kissed and stories re-told for the first time in a year. I was awash in warm welcomes, great feasts, and generous greetings.

Thamarit has changed only a little, but the change is important to my friend Manaa. Now a year out of the desert and fully returned to his professional life supervising construction, Manaa has a block of newly completed condominiums to show me. Bright, decidedly contemporary, they could be planted anywhere money and market would permit. Manaa, cell phone ever in hand, has new projects to undertake. Our time together is peppered with calls made and answered, all about this or that facet of a project in progress. But when a matter of importance arises, Manaa knows, and those who work with Manaa know: The elders must be consulted.

Ali rubs noses with me. The feeling is simultaneously alien, long ago, yet somehow yesterday-familiar. The clasped handshakes are western, perhaps universal—the nose-kissing is unmistakably Arab. We perform both rituals. Neither takes precedence, neither seems to outweigh the other in significance, but here a greeting between two friends would be incomplete without both. Ali talks about the camels he and Tuarish are training, Musallim recites a poem, and bin Ashara shares stories of a lost camel he's been tracking.

I later share the news that my wife Barbara is pregnant. Our Bedu friends are delighted. Now, they say, we'll be *family*, and nothing to the Bedu is more a vital part of living than family. I now know the companion for my next adventure will be Barbara herself, as we bring a new life into the world—a baby boy we'll name Khobe. I don't know yet whether fatherhood is more like a desert or more like a mountain, but Barbara promises it's bound to be some of each and much, much more. The congratulatory emotions expressed by the Bedu are fuller, even in some way more heartfelt, than those I receive at home in Canada. In the desert, *individuals* do not survive—*families* do, and the Bedu grasp more fully than anyone I know the importance of family.

Taynoonah's pregnant too! Traditionally, Bedu camels are precious working partners, as much depended upon as any human. Camels were our lifeline across the desert, and I am eager for news of them. Word comes that the Bedu woman who originally sold us bin Saybeen used the proceeds to buy another camel, sold that, and subsequently traded her way to a handy profit. I learn why...Once in a lifetime, so far as it's possible, each faithful Muslim, man or woman, must make a pilgrimage to Mecca. Fifty years ago, perhaps even twenty, before the onset of the great drought that has stricken this region, the woman would likely have ridden that camel to complete her pilgrimage. Instead, she has traded and sold, traded and sold, not to acquire the most reliable camel, but to buy a plane ticket to Mecca, far up the peninsula. Her pilgrimage of weeks has become, by shrewd barter and commerce, hours.

This would sadden Thesiger, who sees the Bedus' movement from desert to coast, from nomadic to sedentary lifestyle, as the loss of a culture. Sir Wilfred is distressed at the Bedus' abandonment of the camel, except for wagered racing. There is a sadness, too, in the imposition of western material culture on this and other parts of the world. This imposition produces some bizarre juxtapositions...a shop in Kathmandu sells multi-flavoured bubblegum...on a Tokyo street, a *geisha* glides past a clerk in heels who's spent a month's salary on a gold lamé bag bearing the licensed likeness of Mickey Mouse...the aching slowness of communication via camel caravan, versus the cellphone in Manaa's hand.

I have learned this: *Material culture is not culture.* Material culture is only part, and not the sole defining part, of a culture. We tend in the west to define ourselves materially. Once, we may have defined ourselves by our labour; functionally, our labour was who we were. Now, clearly, our function is not so much to labour as to consume. 7-Eleven and Wal-Mart loom in our lives as large as water and the camel ever did in Bedu life. We preach to other cultures the gospel of consumerism—buy, consume, buy more. The loss is theirs. And ours.

The greater loss will come if we, because we define ourselves materially, continue to define other peoples the same way. I mistakenly did this initially with the Bedu. When I watched the man trying to fasten his *khanjar* belt about his thick waist, I was convinced Thesiger was right in claiming all that was great in the Bedu has vanished. Now, I depart from that view. Not all is lost. Much has changed for the Bedu, but the changes operate more at the cultural surface than at the core of who they are. The Bedu have phones and Land Rovers and condos. The camels and related skills have faded, but we mustn't conclude that Bedu culture is gone. A culture as old and as tested as the Bedus' cannot be pushed aside by two generations of change, however extensive.

Bedu culture, I warrant, is still alive and well and proud of its ancient roots. Manaa has his cellphone, but uses it to ask his elders' guidance. Ali shakes my hand, but adds his nose kiss. And a Bedu woman sells her camel to buy a plane ticket—so she can answer the sacred Quranic imperative of pilgrimage, an imperative a full millennium older than my own small life.

Another small life—our son's—awaits. Khobe will bear a name evocative of the desert, because Barbara and I intend, through the adventure of parenthood, to bring to him a full measure of the warmth and loving care still to be found in the Bedu who trekked with us across time and the Empty Quarter.

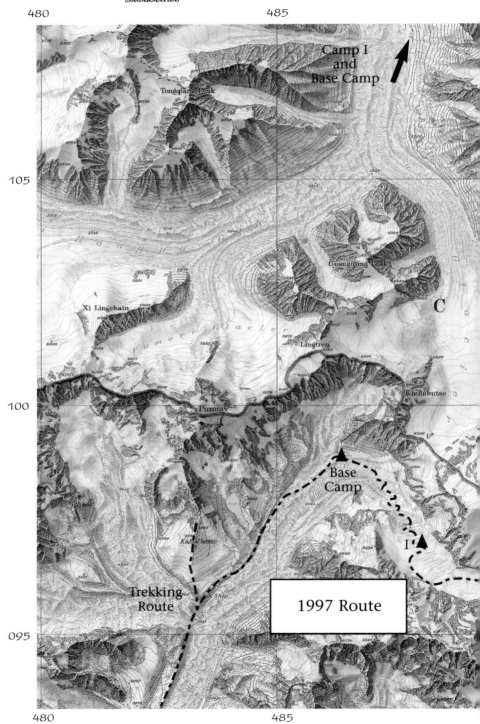

Camp I
and
Base Camp

Tongqiang Peak

Guangming Peak

Xi Lingehain

C

Pumori Glacier

Langtren

Khumbutse

Pumori

La

Base
Camp

I

Kala Pattar

Trekking
Route

1997 Route

Shop

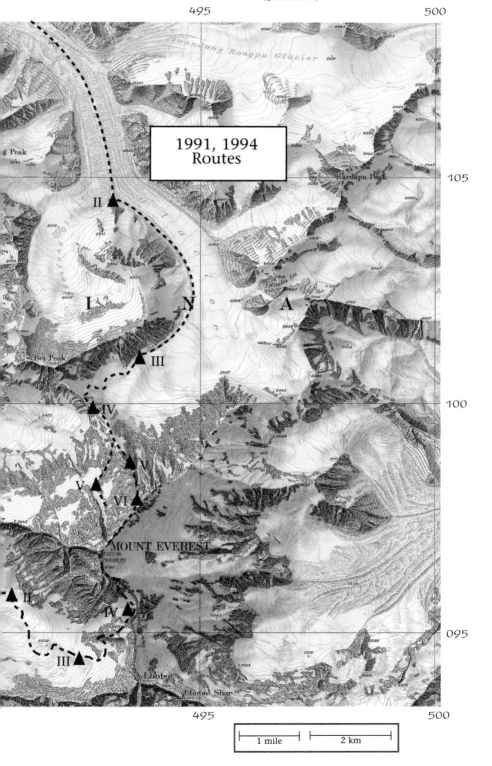

1991, 1994
Routes

Glossary

Term or Phrase	Definition
abal	A bush from which a dye is made, used for camouflage in the desert.
abayah	Traditional costume of Arab women, a long, loosely shaped dress.
ACE	"After Common Era." Year 1 or later in the western calendar. Functionally the same as "A.D."
Al Kathir	From the region now called **Yemen**, the people ancestral to the modern **Bedu**. Claimed by Thesiger and others to be the descendants of Shem, son of Noah.
Allah	God. Formed from the Arabic *al-Ilah*, "the God," creator of the universe and all humankind. Paraphrased from the **Quran**: both a transcendent and eminent perspective; on the one hand there is nothing like Him, and on the other hand He is closer to humans than the jugular veins on their necks. (42:11).
Ashara	The numeral ten. Here capitalized since, as used in the text, it is the name of an individual.
astrolabe	Navigational instrument, forerunner of the sextant.
barchan	Crescent-shaped dunes whose "horns" point downwind. Barchan typically form in locales where the wind nearly always blows from a single, constant direction.
BCE	"Before Common Era." In the western calendar, prior to the birth of Christ. Functionally identical with "B.C."

Bedu /Bedouin	These are the people known in older western books and film as the *Bedouin*. Bedu is preferred as the name people of this ethnicity use for themselves; *Bedouin* is in fact an awkwardly doubled anglicized plural.
Bismilla	*Praise be to God!*
col	High mountain pass.
crampon	Pronged claw-like apparatus attached to climber's boot, enabling purchase on ice.
crevasse	Crevice or chasm in glacial ice.
cwm	Pronounced "coom," this Welsh-derived name refers to a cirque, a bowl-shaped glacial mountain valley.
Dhofar	A region of **Oman**, whose principal claim to western fame is as the origin of **frankincense.**
dishdashah	Traditional costume of **Muslim** men.
dromedary	Arabian camel of one hump, distinguished from the two-humped bactrian camel of Asia.
Dubai	One of the **United Arab Emirates.** In 1971, on British withdrawal, Dubai came together with other emirates to form the **UAE.**
Eid el Fitr	Celebration of the end of the fast of **Ramadan.** The feast of **Eid el Fitr** traditionally lasts three days and is associated with forgiveness.
Everest	The world's highest mountain at 29,035 feet (sometimes disputed), this Himalayan giant

was first climbed in 1953 by Sir Edmund Hillary and Tenzing Norgay. Some 600-plus climbers have summited since, and more than 150 have perished in the attempt.

frankincense   Scent made from the **olibanum** tree.

gadha   Shrub (*Arthrocnemom fruticosum*) with fleshy fruiting spikes, a favoured food of camels. Native to the Arabian peninsula.

gahwa   Coffee. (Literally: "strong.")

gerber   Goatskin bag used for carrying water. Typically contains about 4-5 gallons.

ghaf   A large mimosa-like tree (*Prosophis spicigara*) with flowering branches and trailing fronds.

habob   Wind.

hadut   The cedar arch forming the main frame of the Bedu camel saddle

haluva   Paste made of pistachios and used variously as an appetizer, condiment or snack. Sometimes known in the west as *halvah*.

Hamdulillah!   Literally: *Praise be to God!* Not unlike the Christian's *Hallelujah!*

Hijra   Migration. Associated more particularly with Muhammad's flight from **Mecca**, 622 AD, marking the first year of the **Muslim** lunar calendar.

Hillary, Sir Edmund 1920-   With Tenzing Norgay, climbed Mt. Everest in 1953.

Hyalomma dromedarii   Scientific name for the major species of tick infecting Arabian camels.

Inshallah!	God willing!
Islam	The religion founded by Muhammad (570—632 ACE). **Islam** literally means "submission to God." English speakers often confuse **Islam** and **Muslim**, and may benefit from the reminder that **Islam** is the name of the faith, and **Muslim** the noun or adjective applying to the person who practises **Islam**.
Jabal Dhofar	Mountains in the **Dhofar** region of **Oman**.
Jabalies	People of the **Jabal Dhofar**.
K2	Himalayan mountain, elevation 28,250 feet, considered a more "technical" climb than **Everest**.
karabiner	A spring-loaded closeable metal ring, often D-shaped, allowing climbers to link their harnesses to ropes, or to route a rope in a particular direction without tying or restricting it.
khamr	Intoxicant. Literally: "to cover." **Islam** forbids intoxicants.
khanjar	Ceremonial knife carried by Arab men.
khar	Saddlebags.
Khareef	Monsoon occurring in the **Dhofar** region, unique in **Oman**.
khobz	Bread.
Khumbu Icefall	On **Everest's** north side, an especially steep portion of glacier, featuring massive chunks of ice sliding downslope.
kohl	Made from animal fat and ashes, originally applied under the eyes to reduce sun reflection, later as a cosmetic.

Koran	Common older spelling of **Quran**.
Lawrence, T.(Thomas).E.(Edward) 1888-1935	The subject of the film *Lawrence of Arabia*, T.E. Lawrence is the most iconic western figure associated with the Arab east. During World War I, Lawrence, then a British Army officer, organized bands of native tribesmen to serve as guerilla warriors for the British cause.
Lhotse	A companion mountain to **Everest**, elevation 27,890 feet.
masar	Traditional **Bedu** headwrap.
Masqat / Muscat	Formerly part of the British protectorate of **Muscat** and **Oman**, Masqat is the major port of the modern nation of **Oman**.
Mecca	The holiest city of **Islam**, home of **Muhammad** for much of his life, and the site of the Kaaba, a cube-shaped building within the Mosque of Haram. After his conquest of **Mecca**, **Muhammad** cast out religious idols from the Kaaba. In the daily ritual of prayer, **Muslims** around the world face the Kaaba, a gesture of their unity.
moazzin	Man who calls **Muslims** to prayer.
Muslim	Literally: "one who submits." The adjective or noun applied to those who practise **Islam**.
Namche Bazaar	Village in Nepal through which many **Everest** expeditions pass.
Nuptse	A companion mountain to **Everest**, elevation 25,850 feet.
olibanum	Sap extracted from the incense tree (*Boswellia carterii*), from which **frankincense** is made.

Oman	Formerly a British protectorate, **Oman** was until 1975 known as the "hermit of the middle east," for following a highly isolationist policy. Now an oil-rich nation.
oryx	A species of ungulate found in Arabia, driven near extinction by over-hunting.
Pez	A candy in the shape of tiny, coloured bricks, sacred to the author and other North American children, manufactured for several delicious decades by Pez Candy, Inc. of P.O. Box 541, Orange, Connecticut, USA 06477-4021.
Qara Mountains	A mountain range in the **Dhofar** region of **Oman**.
Quran	From the Arabic *Quraa*, "to read." **Quran** thus essentially means "the reading," not unlike the Christian expression "the Word." The central sacred text of **Islam**, comprising the collected oral revelations received by **Muhammad** over twenty-three years beginning in 610 ACE, written in Arabic. Sometimes rendered **Koran** in western texts.
rakaa	One cycle of prostration within a **Muslim** prayer.
Ramadan	One of the Five Pillars of Wisdom central to **Islam**, observing the month-long fast of **Ramadan**—during which the faithful must abstain sundown to sunset from food, drink, and sexual relations—is a vital part of **Muslim** religious practice.
Rashid	A **Bedu** tribe. Members of the Rashid were of invaluable service to Thesiger during his explorations.

Rub al Khali	The Empty Quarter.
sabkha	Hard crust of mud, such as often found in association with quicksand.
Salaam alaykum!	*Peace be with you!* A common **Bedu** greeting.
salat	Prayer.
Salat al-Maghrib	Evening prayer
Salat al-Subh	Morning prayer
Salat al-Zuhr	Midday prayer.
saltbush	A low shrub with small leaves and grey flowers, *Atriplex* spp. Native to every salt desert in the world, a plant furnishing fodder, but extended use will dehydrate animals.
Sawm	One of the Pillars of **Islam**, the practice of fasting during **Ramadan**.
shamal	A north wind.
shaybah	Old man, elder.
shaye	Tea, generally from India. Sometimes, in English, spelled *chi*.
sheikh	A somewhat amorphous term, sometimes mistakenly translated as 'chief.' In Arabic cultures, a tribal group likely has several sheikhs, who may variously lead a nation, a tribe, a band, an extended family grouping, or may serve as religious leaders. The role of sheikh is determined not entirely by inheritance, but also importantly by one's dedication to the principle of listening to elders.
shokran	*Thank you.*

soof	Wool or sheepskin saddle-blanket.
suq	Marketplace.
tamar	Dates.
tarthuth	Herb (genus *Cynomorium*). A stem bearing a small red flower at its top, mushroom-like in appearance. The plant identified as "juniper" in the Bible.
Thesiger, Sir Wilfred 1910-	First westerner to cross the difficult eastern sands of the Empty
UAE	**United Arab Emirates.**
Umm as Samim	Literally: "Mother of Poison." Refers geographically, to the quicksand in the **UAE** traversed by our group
United Arab Emirates	A nation on the Arabian Gulf, formed in 1971 as a federation of several Arab sheikhdoms.
Uruq al Shaybah	Literally: "Chain of old men." The largest dunes in the Empty Quarter, located on the borders of **Oman**, Saudi Arabia, and the UAE
VHF	"Very High Frequency." The range of frequencies of radios carried on our expedition.
wadi	Dry riverbed.
wali	Mayor or other senior elder of a village or settlement.
wasir	Sarong-like garment worn by **Omani** men under the **dishdashah**.
wasm	A brand upon livestock; the practice of branding.

Western Cwm	A high glacial valley below **Everest**'s south face, named cwm ("koom") by George Mallory, adopting the term for valley derived from his native Welsh.
yad	Stick used by camel herders.
Yemen	A nation on the Gulf of Aden, south and west of **Oman**, bordered by **Oman** and Saudi Arabia. The place of origin of the Al Kathir, ancestors of the **Bedu** people.
Zakat	Almsgiving.

Selected Bibliography

INTERNET SOURCES

Adventurers—The Empty Quarter

Calgary Board of Education, 1999, "The Empty Quarter."
Address: http://www.alwaysadventure.net/
[Accessed: 8 May 2000.] Quoted at pp. 36, 44, 100, 179, 191, 202, 281.

Wynn, Jeff, 1999, "The Empty Quarter Expeditions."
Address: http://www.wynn.org/EmptyQuarter/ [Accessed: 8 August 2000.]

Sir Edmund Hillary
Encyclopedia Britannica, 1999, "Sir Edmund Percival Hillary."
Address: http://www.britannica.com/seo/s/sir-edmund-percival-hillary/
[Accessed: 19 September 2000.]

George, Don, 1998, "A man to match his Mountain," *Salon.*
Address: http://www.salon.com/bc/1998/12/cov_01bc.html
[Accessed: 19 September 2000.]

T.E Lawrence
Wilson, Jeremy, 2000, "The Lawrence of Arabia Factfile.
Address: http://www.castlehillpress.co.uk/index2.htm
[Accessed: 19 September 2000.]

Sir Wilfred Thesiger
Drabelle, Dennis, October 1998, "The Frontier Comes for the Explorer."
Outside Magazine. Address:
http://www.outsidemag.com/magazine/1098/9810frontier.html
[Accessed: 29 June 2000.]

Culture
Government of Dubai, Department of Tourism and Commerce Marketing,
"Dubai Information: Focus on Dubai."
Address: http://dubaitourism.co.ae/dtcm/html/information/focus.htm
[Accessed: 29 June 2000.]

Encyclopedia Britannica, 2000, "Dress."
Address: http://www.britanica.com/bcom/eb/article/printable/
9/0,5722,108949,00.html   [Accessed: 14 July 2000.]

Saudi Embassy, 1996, "Blending Tradition and Progress in the Desert."
Address: http://www.saudiembassy.net/publications/magazine-winter-96/
blending.html [Accessed: 19 July 2000.]

Arab Net, 1996, "Saudi Arabia culture, Gahwa—an age old custom."
Address: http://arab.net/saudi/culture/sa_gahwa.html [Accessed: 19 July 2000.]

History
Jordan Astronomical Society, 2000, "Arabic Star Names."
Address: http://www.jas.org.jo/star.html [Accessed: 19 September 2000.]

Project Astro Utah, 2000, "Orion: Your Personal Guide to the Stars."
Address: http://www.clarkfoundation.org/astro-utah/vondel/slimone.html
[Accessed: 19 September 2000.]

The Free Arab Voice, "Mathematics and Astronomy."
Address: http://www.fav.net/arabCivilMain.htm [Accessed: 5 September 2000.]

Paul Lunde, Zayn Bilkadi, 1997, "Arabs and Astronomy."
Address: http://users.erols.com/gmqm/arabastro.html
[Accessed: 5 September 2000.]

Muller, Walter W., 1997 "Outline of the History of Ancient Southern Arabia."
Address: http://www.gpc.org.ye/Ancient1.htm [Accessed: 10 March 2000.]

NASA's Obsevatorium, "Remote sensing to the Rescue"
Address:http://www.bonus.com/contour/ubar/http@@/observe.ivv.nasa.gov/nasa
/exhibits/u.../ubar_3.htm [Accessed: 1 June 2000.]

Haynes, Ed, 1997, "Oman."
Address: http://haynese.winthrop.edu/mlas/oman.html
[Accessed: 5 June 2000.]

Environment
Nature Exporer.com, 2 August 2000, "Life in the Desert."
Address: http://www.natureexplorer.com/LD/LD1?LD0107.html
[Accessed: 2 August 2000.]

UAE interact, 2000, "Natural Emirates: Geology and Fossils."
Address: http://www.uaeinteract.com/uaefrm.html [Accessed: 29 June 2000.]

The Kingdom of Saudi Arabia, 2000, "Agriculture and Water Resources."
Address: http://saudiembassy.net/profile/ag/ag_water.html
[Accessed: 13 March 2000.]

Baldwin, Rob, "The Sultanate of Oman."
Address: http://www.arabian wildlife.com/past_arw/vol2.2/oma.htm
[Accessed: 21 July 2000.]

Eriksen, Hanne, Jens, "Desert Birds: Birding in the Sultanate of Oman."
Address: http://www.osme.org/osmeweb/dsrtbrds.html
[Accessed: 17 May 2000.]

Parasitic Plant Connection, 1998, "Cynomoriaceae."
Address: http://www.science.siu.edu/parasitic-plants/Cynomoriaceae/
[Accessed: 27 July 2000.]

Duke, Jim, 1998, "Biblical Botany."
Address: http://www.ars-grin.gov/duke/syllabus/module12.htm
[Accessed: 24 July 2000.]

UAE Ministry of Agriculture and Fisheries, "Water Scarcity is Uprooting Farmers."
Address: http://rkw.hct.ac.ae/ilc/ex/dhaidqr.htm [Accessed: 24 July 2000.]

Amin, Noah, "Improving Desert Environment through Water Reuse. Evolution of Improving Sanitary Drainage in Combating Pollution." *Water Magazine.*
Address: http://www.watermagazine.com/jc/Desert.htm
[Accessed: 24 July 2000.]

Wynn, Jeffrey C., and Eugene M. Shoemaker, 1998, "The Day the Sands Caught Fire." *Scientific American.*
Address: http://www.sciam.com/1998/1198issue/1198wynn.html
[Accessed: 2 August 2000.]

Walker, Alta S., 2000, "Aeolian Landforms. Global Atmospheric Circulation."
Address: http://www.brrg.esci.keele.ac.uk/Teaching/npm_general_resources
/geospace/aeolian/aeolian.html [Accessed: 2 August 2000.]

Camels

Graham, Dale, 1996, "Information about Camels."
Address: http://www.llamaweb.com/Camel/Info.html
[Accessed: 3 March 2000.]

CAMELL Expedition, 1999, "Anatomy and Physiology Training
and Husbandry Productivity."
Address: http://www.atlas.co.uk/camell/cinfman.html
[Accessed: 28 March 2000.]

Flake, Carol, 1996, "Sport of Sheikhs: Camel as Champion."
Address: http://www.travelcorner.com/Camel/Camel5.htm
[Accessed: 20 March 2000.]

Islam

Masih, Abd-ul, 1998, "Christians Common Questions About Islam."
Address: http://arabicbible.com/christian/q_about_islam_practices.htm
[Accessed: 16 March 2000.]

BOOKS

Amundsen, Roald. *The South Pole: An Account of the Norwegian Antarctic Expedition in the "Fram,"1910-1912*. London: John Murray, 1912. Quoted at p. 27.

Anani, Ahmad and Ken Whittingham. *The Early History of The Gulf Arabs*. Singapore: Longman Singapore Publishers Ltd., 1986.

Asher, Michael. *Thesiger*. London: Viking, 1994.

Bailey, Clinton. *Bedouin Poetry from Sinai and the Negev. Mirror of a Culture*. Oxford: Clarendon Press, 1991.

Clarke, Peter. *The World's Religions: Islam*. London: Routledge, 1988.

Cole, Donald. *Nomads of the Nomads: The Al-Murrah Bedouin of the Empty Quarter*. Chicago: Aldine Publishing Company, 1975.

Cragg, Kenneth and R. Marston Speight. *Islam From Within: Anthology of a Religion*. Belmont: Wadsworth, Inc., 1980.

Encyclopaedia of Islam CD-ROM Edition, 1999, Koninklijke Brill NV, Leiden, The Netherlands.

Fabre, Jean Henri Casimir. *The Sacred Beetle and Others*. Toronto: McClelland, Goodchild & Stewart, 1918.

Gauthier-Pilters, Hilde and Anne Innis Dagg. *The Camel: Its Evolution, Ecology, Behavior, and Relationship to Man*. Chicago: The University of Chicago Press, 1981.

Groom, Nigel. *Frankincense and Myrrh*. London: Longman Group Limited, 1981.

Hawley, Donald. *Oman & its Renaissance*. London: Stacey International, 1977.

Haykal, Muhammad Husayn. *The Life of Muhammad*. Indianapolis: North American Trust Publications, 1976.

Hellyer, Peter, Simon Aspinall, Lucy Munro and Marijcke Jongbloed. *United Arab Emirates Yearbook 1998*. Abu Dhabi: Trident Press, 1998.

Hornbein, thomas F. Everest: The West Ridge. Seattle: Mountaineers, 1998. (Quoting George Leigh Mallory). Quoted at p. 26.

Huntford, Roland. *Shackelton*. New York: Atheneum, 1986.

Kelly, Kathleen and R.T. Schnadelback. *Landscaping the Saudi Arabian Desert*. Philadelphia: The Delancey Press, 1976.

Keohane, Alan: The Bedouin: Nomads of the Desert. Trafalgar Square Books, 1999. Quoted at p. 81.

Netton, Ian. *A Popular Dictionary of Islam*. Atlantic Highlands: Humanities Press International Inc., 1992.

Peck, Malcolm. *The United Arab Emirates: A Venture in Unity*. Boulder: Westview Press, 1986.

Pye, Kenneth and Haim Tsoar. *Aeolian Sand and Sand Dunes*. London: Unwin Hyman, 1990.

The Holy Qur'an. Translation, Text and Commentary by Abdullah Yusuf Ali. Elmhurst: Tahrike Tarsile Qur'an, Inc. 1998]

Sherif, Faruq. *A Guide to the Contents of the Qur'an*. London: Ithaca Press, 1985.

Thesiger, Wilfred. *Arabian Sands*. London: Longman Group Limited, 1959. Quoted at pp. 21, 26, 37, 46, 60, 62, 79, 83, 103, 106, 116, 130, 135, 139, 144, 155, 158, 191, 203, 212, 215, 228, 251, 298.

Thesiger, Wilfred. *Desert, Marsh and Mountain: The World of a Nomad*. London: William Collins Sons and Co. Ltd., 1979.

Waddy, Charis. *The Muslim Mind*. London: Longman Group Limited, 1976. Quoted at p. 37.

Wolfe, Michael. *The Hadj: An American's Pilgrimage to Mecca*. New York: Grove Press, 1993.

ARTICLES

Gerson, Ran. 1982. "The Middle East: Landforms of a Planetary Desert through Environmental Changes," In *The Geological Story of the World's deserts*. (T.L. Smiley, Ed.). *Striae*, Vol. 17, pp. 52-75.

Khalaf, Sulayman. 1999. "Camel Racing in the Gulf: Notes on the Evolution of a Traditional Cultural Sport," *Anthropos* Vol. 94, pp. 85-106.

Karim, Goolam, Mohamed. Winter 1989-90. "The Symbolism of Prayer in Islam," *Dialogue and Alliance* Vol. 3(4), pp. 32-40.

Neilson, Kjeld. June 1991. "Ancient Aromas Good & Bad," *Bible Review*, pp. 26-33.

Photo Credits

Jamie Clarke, Insert#1-3,5,7,10,11,16-26,30-34,36-40,46-60,62-68,70-73,
76,77,81,82,84,88,95-97,101,102,105,108,110,112.

Leigh Clarke, Insert#4,6,8,12-15,42-45,61,75,80,83,85-87,106.

©Gulf News, Dubai, Insert# 9,35,69,79,89-91,94,99.

Graphic Design by Metrographics,
Photos by Bruce Kirkby, Insert# 27.

Artwork by Courtney Duggan,
Photo by Gary Groeneveld, Insert# 28.

Gary Groeneveld, Insert# 29.

Bruce Kirkby, Insert# 41,74,104.

©Wilfred Thesiger/Pitt Rivers Museum,
Oxford University
Permission granted by Curtis Brown Group Ltd., Insert# 78,98.

Lhakpa Tshering Sherpa, Insert# 92.

Jeff Rhoads, Insert# 93.

Barbara Clarke, Insert# 100.

Dixie Dean, Insert# 103.

Elliott Fong Wallace, Radiologists, Insert# 107.

Ian Clarke, Insert# 109.

Ali Salim, Insert# 111.

Chapter headings photography: by Chris Davis.
Chapter Two heading photograph: by Dominique Keller.

Page 4 background photograph by Bruce Kirkby.
Page 5 background photograph by Jamie Clarke.

Also by Jamie Clarke:

The Power of Passion
Jamie's first book (co-authored with Alan Hobson) is the story of
their first two attempts to climb Mt. Everest in 1991 and 1994.

Above All Else
One of three documentaries by Jamie Clarke, *Above All Else*
chronicles Jamie's summit bids, culminating in his 1997
success.

Visit Jamie's website:
www.jamieclarke.com

Jamie is available for speaking presentations.
Contact Jamie's agent:
www.jamieclarke.com
phone (403) 230-2760, ext. 222
fax (403) 230-2773

Azimuth Inc.
A Jamie Clarke Company
201, 18ᵗʰAvenue NE
Calgary, Alberta, Canada T2E 1N3
www.jamieclarke.com